EDUCATION, DEMOCRACY AND DEVELOPMENT
does education contribute to
democratisation in developing countries?

EDUCATION, DEMOCRACY AND DEVELOPMENT
does education contribute to democratisation in developing countries?

CLIVE HARBER & VUSI MNCUBE

SYMPOSIUM
BOOKS

Symposium Books Ltd
PO Box 204, Didcot, Oxford OX11 9ZQ, United Kingdom
www.symposium-books.co.uk

Published in the United Kingdom, 2012

ISBN 978-1-873927-71-7

Printed and bound in the United Kingdom by
Hobbs the Printers, Southampton
www.hobbs.uk.com

Contents

Preface

If you were to glance at a political map of the world 30 years ago where authoritarian and totalitarian regimes were coloured blue, and democratic and semi-democratic ones were coloured red, then most of Africa, South America, Asia, and the Middle East would be coloured blue. The same map 30 years later would look strikingly different, with large parts of the 'developing' world now coloured red rather than blue, but the Middle East would have remained stubbornly blue. In recent years, however, the 'Arab Spring' has also witnessed a wave of democratic protest and reform across the Middle East. As will be discussed in chapter 1, such changes in the politics of developing countries are far from perfect or complete, but there is no doubt about the general direction in which change has occurred.

Much writing on education is concerned with access to education, or the quality of education in relation to educational outputs, such as literacy and numeracy or examination scores. There is also a strong focus on the role of education in relation to economic development. However, we have long been interested in the potential role of education in facilitating, supporting, and sustaining democracy – or not. As far as anybody is aware, human beings do not have any genes determining whether they are democrats or autocrats, therefore democratic or authoritarian values and behaviours must be learned. There are many such agencies of such learning – the family, the media, and religious groups – but we have been particularly interested in the school as a source of political learning. As this book shows, we are not alone in this interest as there has been a long-standing concern with the relationships between education and democracy amongst philosophers, social scientists and educationalists. However, in this book we have chosen to explore not just the relationships between education and democracy, but to focus in particular on how these relationships manifest themselves in so-called 'developing' countries.

While the first four chapters of the book take a broad geographical perspective on education and democratic political development, chapter 5 is a detailed discussion of one particular country – South Africa. South Africa, which was ranked 123rd on the United Nations Development Programme's (UNDP) Human Development Index (out of 187 countries) in 2011 (UNDP, 2011), provides a useful case study of educational and political change in one country because of its authoritarian apartheid past, the role of education in the struggle against apartheid, and the overt attempt to use education as a tool of democratisation in the post-apartheid era. Both authors are familiar with South Africa, one being a South African citizen, and feel that education there is a microcosm of many of the tensions and contradictions inherent in the relationships between education, democracy and development that are described and analysed in more general terms in the rest of the book.

Finally, we would like to thank the Leverhulme Trust for their support in providing an Emeritus Fellowship to Clive Harber which greatly facilitated the sustained academic collaboration that led to the writing of the book. Thanks also to Noriko Sakade for her help in reviewing education policy statements on Ministry of Education websites for inclusion in chapter 3.

CHAPTER 1

Politics, Democracy and Political Development

Politics and Democracy

Disagreement is a marked and inevitable feature of all human groupings. This is true whether it is a family, a group of friends, an institution, a state, or an international organisation. Disagreement occurs because people have different attitudes and values, both because they are diverse as individuals and because they differ according to social identities based on factors such as culture, social and economic status, gender, region, and religion. There is therefore a need to manage and resolve disagreement and conflict (not necessarily the same as violent conflict) through a decision-making process which provides the rules by which we live. Some have the authority or recognised legitimacy to make decisions on behalf of others, while others can influence decisions through the possession of power of some sort – the ability to influence the action of others through the use of persuasive or coercive means at their disposal, such as access to the media, economic power or the threat of force. This, then, is the essence of politics and it is an unavoidable feature of life whether within the family, an institution like a school or university, or at the macro level of the nation state or internationally between nation states.

At the levels of state and society the bases of potential disagreement are many – ideology, economic interests based on occupational position, ethnicity, gender, religion, the protection and furtherance of particular pursuits, and so on. Pick up a newspaper on any day and it is relatively easy to find numerous examples of social and political disagreement and conflict. The demands of the groups that represent these divisions are fed into the political system via bodies such as pressure groups (e.g. trade unions or business groups), or in a more aggregated way through political parties. The decision-making bodies are usually some form of executive (e.g. a cabinet or president) who proposes policy, some sort of legislature who discusses and modifies policy and passes laws, a civil service or state bureaucracy that advises on and oversees policy, and a judiciary and police system that implements and enforces laws.

However, political systems differ in the way that these processes take place, primarily in the extent to which citizens of the country can actually influence political processes and outcomes. Here there is an important distinction to be made between authoritarianism on the one hand, and democracy on the other, a distinction which also has significant implications for education, as will be argued and explained throughout this book. Authoritarianism is a type of political system where the government is not representative of the people, and where the final power to remove a government is not in the hands of citizens as voters as there are no genuinely free and fair elections. There is no free political choice and the government is not accountable to the people for its actions. As the government is not accountable, it is free to do as it wishes and there are therefore no guaranteed human rights. Citizens have little say in how the country is run and rule is by edict and dictat. Single party and military regimes fall into this category. The surrounding political culture in which such regimes exist is not characterised by full information, regular discussion, and encouragement of a range of viewpoints. Diversity, critical thought, and participation are not encouraged or are suppressed. The leaders know they have the right answers and the role of the people is to obey and do what they are told. Those who do not obey are punished accordingly. Communication is top-down and hierarchical. The ideal citizen is one who is submissive, behaves according to the wishes of the regime, respects authority, and doesn't ask questions. In its most extreme form, it has been described as totalitarian as the state attempts to control all aspects of life, including the economy, the media, religion, schooling and family life, as well as government policy and political activity. Nazi Germany, the Soviet Union and Communist China, particularly under Mao Tse Tung, have been used as examples of states that have been described as totalitarian. State sponsored violence exercised by the police, secret police and army is a feature of both authoritarian and totalitarian regimes where it is used to suppress criticism and opposition and punish those responsible.

The concept of democracy, on the other hand, derives from the Greek words *demos* (the people) and *kratos* (rule), so rule by the people as opposed to a monarch, dictator or unelected elite. There are many different definitions of democracy (Davies, 1999) but the following captures its salient features:

> Democracy embodies the ideal that decisions affecting an association as a whole would be taken by all its members and that they would each have equal rights to take part in such decisions. Democracy entails the twin principles of popular control over collective decision-making and equality of rights in the exercise of that control. (Beetham & Boyle, 1995, p. 1)

However, what most definitions seem to have in common is a concern with:

- Rights: a set of entitlements which are protected and common to all individuals
- Participation: the free involvement of individuals in the decision-making process
- Equity: fair and equal treatment of individuals and groups
- Informed Choice: the tools to make decisions which are based on relevant information and reason.
  (Davies et al, 2002, pp. 4-9)

Democracy is exercised through democratic institutions and processes, such as regular free and fair elections, a free media, the rule of laws that are equally applicable to everyone, freedom of association, and the freedom of speech, but it is not possible in the absence of individual democrats. Democracy is only sustainable in a supportive political culture where a sufficient proportion of the population have a high commitment to democratic values, skills and, particularly, behaviours. A useful distinction here, which also has important implications for the role of education in sustaining and consolidating democracy, is between thinner or shallower democracies that, while still functioning as democracies, operate in a minimal manner primarily at the level of the state, and thicker or deeper democracy that permeates both the state and the wider society. Carr and Hartnett (1996, chap. 2) distinguish between what they term 'classical' democracy, which had its origins in ancient Greece, and 'contemporary' forms of democracy. They argue that in modern times the former has been rejected as utopian. Studies of the actual workings of democracies in mass industrialised societies suggest that, rather than a more participant understanding of 'rule by the people', what occurs in practice is more minimal. People have a right to choose between rival political elites at regular elections much as consumers choose between products in the market place. The role of citizens is therefore more limited than in classical democracy and high levels of passivity and political apathy are actually important to maintain stability and guard against system overload. A core principle of this form of 'contemporary democracy' is that it provides a means of selecting political leaders which curtails an excess or abuse of power through certain empirical conditions, including regular elections, universal suffrage, rival political parties, a representative system of government, a free press, and an independent judiciary. It is assumed that people have no obligation to participate in decision-making and most ordinary people have no desire to do so. A rigid distinction is therefore made between an active elite political leadership and the passive majority of ordinary citizens. Democracy flourishes, according to this model, in an individualistic society with a competitive market economy and with minimal state intervention. This does not require conscious or explicit education for democracy as active citizens are not desirable.

A core principle of classical democracy, on the other hand, is that individuals are able to participate in the life of their society, including decision-making. In such a society citizens enjoy equal opportunities for self-development, self-fulfilment and self-determination. This requires a society in which there is a knowledgeable and informed citizenry capable of participating in democratic political debate on equal terms. The fuller or 'classical' model, however, requires a commitment to develop a democratic society, as well as political system. Fuller versions of democracy require much greater levels of democracy and equality in our daily interactions, relationships and behaviours in the workplace, and in social and domestic activities. This requires a conscious attempt to remove prejudice and discrimination on the basis of, for example, race, class, gender, sexual orientation, religion, disability and age. A citizen in such a democracy would celebrate social and political diversity, work for and practice mutual respect between individuals and groups, regard all people as having equal social and political rights as human beings, respect evidence in forming their own opinions and respect the opinions of others based on evidence, be open to changing one's mind in the light of new evidence, and possess a critical and analytical stance towards information. The democratic citizen would possess a proclivity to reason, open-mindedness and fairness and the practice of cooperation, bargaining, compromise and accommodation.

The British statesman and former Prime Minister Winston Churchill once put it that democracy was the worse form of government – apart from all the others. Here he was acknowledging that democracy in practice is often far from perfect in living up to its own ideals but, however flawed and imperfect in reality, it still remains preferable to any authoritarian alternatives. In the next two sections, we turn to the idea of development and examine how debates about development have gradually incorporated democracy as *the* goal of political development, before going on to discuss why this has been the case.

The Idea of Development

Concern with the idea that societies and states 'develop' over time, usually with the assumption that development means that matters are improving in some way, goes back at least as far as Aristotle, and has occurred in many different cultures (Fagerlind & Saha,1989, chap. 1). Post-Second World War discussions of development were originally primarily concerned with economic development – the growth of wealth and output as measured by indicators of national wealth, such as the gross national product. The main division was therefore initially between the industrialised countries of the Northern hemisphere and the poorer, more agriculturally based countries of the Southern hemisphere. Over time attempts to measure development have become increasingly more diverse and sophisticated with a whole range of different social indicators, such as health, education, gender, well-being, and environmental protection, being added.

While attempts to classify states as 'developed' or developing' are fraught with difficulty and controversy, perhaps the most authoritative international statement on issues surrounding human development is the annual publication of the United Nations Development Programme (UNDP) entitled the *Human Development Report* (*HDR*). This ranks all the countries of the world from 1 to 169 according to a wide range of variables, but special emphasis is laid on what they term the 'Human Development Index'. This is a composite index of what they consider to be the three key indicators of human development. These are life expectancy at birth, years of schooling, and gross national income per capita. (It is worth briefly noting here that it is thus assumed that enrolment in formal education is always, necessarily and inherently good for individuals and society – something that will be challenged in this book.) However, the twentieth report (UNDP, 2010) also includes a wide range of other indices of development, and in the most recent report, for example, three new indices were included – the Inequality adjusted Human Development Index, the Gender Inequality Index, and the Multi-dimensional Poverty Index. Indeed, the New Economics Foundation has constructed what it terms the 'Happy Planet Index' where countries are ranked by life satisfaction, life expectancy, and ecological footprint. On this index, Costa Rica (48th in the UNDP's Human Development Index) comes top.[1] Bhutan even has its own Gross Happiness Index which presents an alternative model of human development rooted in Buddhist philosophy (Kendall, 2009, p. 419).

Nevertheless, classification of countries as 'developed', 'less developed' or 'developing', and as being situated in the 'North' or 'South', remains difficult and by no means clear cut. This is partly because ranking and categorising is inevitably to some extent subjective – change the indicator(s) regarded as important and you change the ranking. It is also problematic because significant change can occur quite rapidly so that some countries, such as Singapore or Brunei, originally regarded as 'developing', have now 'developed', while some 'developed' countries (Japan, New Zealand and Australia, for example), are located geographically in the South. Moreover:

> All of these binary labels, in fact, assume and fix the focus of
> developmentalist debates on states at a time when divisions
> between rich and poor, 'North' and 'South' are as great or
> greater within countries as across them, thus concealing the
> issue of how inequality and poverty affect 'Northern'
> geographical spaces as well as 'Southern', and how people,

groups, and development-like resources flow within and across state boundaries. (Kendall, 2009, p. 421)

While recognising these difficulties, we are nevertheless primarily concerned in this book with countries below the top fifty in the UNDP's Human Development Index, i.e. generally not those countries that are ranked as 'Very High Human Development', but mainly with those countries classified as 'Medium' and 'Low Human Development', and in the lower reaches of the 'High Human Development' category (UNDP, 2010, pp. 148-151). This corresponds closely with, for example, Smith's classification of about 100 states in Africa, Asia, The Middle East, Latin America, and the Caribbean with a combined population of over 4.8 billion, accounting for 75% of the world's total, and nearly 58% of the world's land area (Smith, 2009, p. 1).

Most recently of all, and of direct significance to the subject of this book, has been the design and inclusion of political indicators of development. In the 2010 Human Development Report, for example, the quantified indicators of 'empowerment' were political freedom and democracy, human rights violations, press freedom, journalists imprisoned, corruption victims, democratic decentralisation, and political engagement (UNDP, 2010, pp. 164-167). As this suggests, the UNDP now has an explicit model of political development where the goal for all countries is the attainment, sustainability and consolidation of democracy. Strongly influenced by the ideas of Amartya Sen on human capabilities (who writes the introduction to the twentieth edition and is further discussed later in this chapter), the 2010 report continues its long-term explicit support for democracy:

> The 1990 HDR began with a clear definition of human development as a process of 'enlarging people's choices', emphasising the freedom to be healthy, to be educated and to enjoy a decent standard of living. But it also stressed that human development and well-being went far beyond these dimensions to encompass a much broader range of capabilities, including political freedom, human rights and, echoing Adam Smith, 'the ability to go about without shame'. (UNDP, 2010, p. 2)

It notes with approval that the proportion of formal democracies has increased from fewer than a third of all countries in 1970, to half in the mid-1990s, to three fifths in 2008, and that many hybrid forms have also emerged. Overall, it argues that:

> While real change and healthy political functioning have varied, and many formal democracies are flawed and fragile, policy-making is much better informed by the views and concerns of citizens. Local democratic processes are

deepening. Political struggles have led to substantial change in many countries, greatly expanding the representation of marginalized people, including women, the poor, indigenous groups, refugees and sexual minorities. (UNDP, 2010, p. 6)

Others such as Smith, while acknowledging a broad trend more in the direction of democracy, are somewhat less optimistic about the extent to which a process of democratisation has genuinely and consistently taken place in developing countries. He also notes that the Arab Middle East has a huge democratic deficit with no states being rated as 'free' by Freedom House in 2006 (though this situation began to change in 2011). He notes that all but four countries rated as 'not free' in 2006 were developing countries (Smith, 2009, p. 14). Nevertheless, Smith does also recognise that, despite the problems often actually experienced in establishing and maintaining democracies in developing countries, democracy ought to be the goal of political development because of its potential to provide a government regarded as legitimate by a population. However, this definition of political development *as* democratisation has not always been so clear and unambiguous – or sometimes even present – in academic and theoretical debates about the nature of political development.

Political Development Theory

Democracy has had an ambivalent relationship with modern political development theory. The chapter on political development in a key textbook on education and development published as the Cold War was coming to an end, with the approaching collapse of communism, only very briefly refers to democracy in passing, and the word isn't in the index at the end of the book (Fagerlind & Saha, 1989). The most influential post-war academic writers on political development were a group of American political scientists associated with the Social Science Research Council's (SSRC) Committee on Comparative Politics, who published a series of books from the late 1950s to the early 1970s (Higgot,1983, p. 17). O'Brien (1972) shows how the early writers showed a strong commitment to representative democracy as a political goal. A key figure in this emphasis on democracy was the American political scientist Gabriel Almond. While genuinely democratic processes cannot be achieved overnight or in the immediate future, 'in the new and modernising nations of Asia, Africa and Latin America, the processes of enlightenment and democratisation will have their inevitable way' (Almond, 1970, p. 232). A corollary of this aim of democratic political development was the emphasis given to the importance of political culture and political socialisation. Political culture is the pattern of values and attitudes about politics held by a population which influences the ways in which a society's political institutions operate.

Political socialisation is the process by which these values and attitudes are learned from various agencies, such as the family, the mass media and the school. For writers such as Almond, therefore, the key issues were the nature of the political culture that would be supportive of democracy, and how and where those values might be learned.

However, O'Brien (1972) argues that in the second half of the 1960s, in the light of a pattern of civil wars and military *coups d'état* in post-colonial countries, the earlier optimistic emphasis on democracy gave way to a new, more pessimistic emphasis on the importance of stability and order. From the perspective of the United States of America embroiled in an escalating war in Vietnam, order and stability appeared preferable to the disorder and instability in which their communist arch-enemy could thrive. Better a pro-American authoritarian regime than the risk of an unstable democratic one. The final book in the series of books was entitled *Crises and Sequences in Political Development* (Binder et al, 1971) and effectively represented the collective thinking of the SSRC. Political development was seen as a political system's capacity to cope with five crises: legitimacy, identity, participation, penetration, and distribution. Governmental capacity referred explicitly to governing elites and crises were therefore seen from the perspective of threats to the position of those elites and the necessity of elites for the maintenance of order. As one commentator has noted, 'The interest in order of those at the top is given a logical precedence over the interest in social justice at the bottom' (Sandbrook, 1976, pp. 180-181).

Even the book in the series explicitly concerned with education and political development (Coleman, 1965) avoided the question about the direction of political development by defining a 'modern' state as neither democratic nor non-democratic. For Coleman, a modern state is a participatory state but this can either be participation in the coerced, centrally directed and monolithic fashion of an authoritarian state, or equally by free and voluntary association in a democratic state. The contribution of education to political development in this case would be the mass inculcation of bureaucratic skills:

> Formal education has a cardinal role to play in producing the
> bureaucratic, managerial, technical and professional cadres
> required for modernisation. Moreover, literacy helps a
> government with penetration i.e. the population will be
> sufficiently literate to understand what the government wants
> them to do. (1965, p. 17)

Since the early 1970s and particularly since 1989 however, the emphasis in debates about political development has returned strongly to democracy and democratisation. Huntingdon (1991) has termed this the 'third wave' of democratisation, which began with the overthrow of the Portuguese dictatorship in 1974 and accelerated with the collapse of

Soviet communism and the Warsaw Pact in 1989. The end of Soviet communism not only removed one, authoritarian, model of development but also meant that Western governments were less likely to support dictatorships simply because they were pro-Western and anti-communist. Western aid increasingly came with pro-democracy terms and conditions attached. Moreover, there was rising dissatisfaction inside developing countries, both with the failure of elites to provide human rights and freedoms, and to deliver social and economic progress. For example, in relation to the growth of interest in democracy inside sub-Saharan Africa, it has been argued (Harber, 2002) that military and one party regimes exacerbated poverty and failed to deliver economic growth and social welfare and justice for a number of reasons.

First, authoritarian rule is not marked by openness, transparency and accountability. It therefore creates an ideal context for corruption. Second, authoritarian rule has been marked by violence caused by civil unrest, violent repression, and wars against neighbours. Third, wars and the existence of military governments resulted in levels of military expenditure which were far too high, essentially unproductive, and dangerous in that in Africa the military has often been used against the civilian population, as much as being there to protect it. Fourth, authoritarian governments thrived on, and deliberately created, an atmosphere of repression, censorship, intimidation and intolerance. This stifles debate and the internal search for creative solutions to developmental problems, including the issue of poverty reduction. Fifth, under authoritarian systems the needs and interests of the poor can too easily be ignored by unelected and unresponsive elites more concerned with self-enrichment. In relation to the political empowerment of poor people, the UNDP, for example, has argued that:

> People must organise for collective action to influence the circumstances and decisions affecting their lives. To advance their interests, their voices must be heard in the corridors of power ... Ending human poverty requires a democratic space in which people can articulate demands, act collectively and fight for a more equitable distribution of power ... Government that acts in the interest of poor people is easier to achieve in democratic political systems where the poor represent a significant electoral bloc. (UNDP, 1997, pp. 94, 103, 105)

Sixth, an important aspect of this is rural poverty. This is particularly significant because the majority of the African population live in rural areas. Post-colonial political elites have been essentially urban elites unresponsive to rural needs because the undemocratic nature of their rule has made it unnecessary to answer to a rural electorate. Indeed, independence frequently led to a worsening of conditions for farmers, as shown by the changes in prices paid to farmers, rural revenues, or the distribution of public expenditure.

But does the introduction of democracy then improve the prospects for social and economic development? Leftwich (1996, 1998) uses the term 'developmental states' to describe those states where genuine economic and other forms of human development has and is taking place. These historically, however, have been both democratic (or semi-democratic) and authoritarian, and the contribution of democracy to other aspects of human development remains a contentious issue. Thus, since Lipset's research (1959) showing a relationship between democracy and higher levels of economic growth, there has been continuing debate about the actual nature of the causal relationship. Does a higher level of economic development cause or facilitate democracy, or is it the other way around, i.e. that democracy leads to better economic growth? Or are both true? Ersson and Lane (1996) did find an empirical relationship between democracy and human development as measured by the Human Development Index and the Physical Quality of Life Index, but not with economic growth or degree of income equality – and the direction of causality was not clear. They concluded that, at the very least, democracy was not an obstacle to economic growth or fair income distribution. Helliwell (1994), in a study of 125 countries between 1960 and 1985, found that while the first relationship (that democracy is associated with countries with higher levels of economic development) held true, the second (that democracy actually contributes to economic development) did not.

It is also important to note that there are some important examples of countries which cast doubt on any straightforward relationship between democracy and economic and other forms of development. India was 119th out of 169 on the United Nations Human Development Index in 2010 despite being a functioning democracy since 1947. China currently presents an example of increased economic liberalism and very rapid economic growth, but in the continuing context of an authoritarian, one party state. Perhaps the most definite comment that can be made is that, as the examples of North Korea and Zimbabwe suggest, authoritarianism is certainly no guarantee of social and economic development. Moreover, a comparison of 135 countries over a 40 year period showed that rapid development is as likely under democracy as under a dictatorship and, echoing Ersson and Lane (1996) above, that there was:

> not a shred of evidence that democracy needs to be sacrificed on the altar of development. The few countries that developed spectacularly during the past fifty years were as likely to achieve that feat under democracy as dictatorship. (Przeworski et al, 2000, p. 271)

However, another important question is, can democracy be successfully introduced into developing countries anyway? In Africa, and as a result of such internal and external factors as discussed already in this chapter, since the end of the Cold War, some form of pluralism has been introduced or reintroduced into over 30 out of the 53 countries in Africa (Gyimah-Boadi, 2004, p. 5). However, while there has been genuine progress in terms of more free elections, more political choice, greater constitutionalism, a more active civil society, and greater freedom of the media in a number of countries, some countries remain authoritarian. In others, actual regime transitions to democracy in Africa have been only patchy, resulting in talk of 'partial reform syndrome' and 'semi-democracies'. There are still issues of patrimonialism, clientelism, and associated official corruption and economic mismanagement, even in countries that have moved in a democratic direction, and 'prospects of consolidation remain weak in all but a handful of countries' (Gyimah-Boadi, 2004, p. 10). In a table going up to 2002, Gyimah-Boadi ranks two countries in Africa as consistent democracies, eight as recent democracies, ten as semi-democracies and twenty-one as autocracies (pp. 16-17). In 2009, the Mo Ibrahim Foundation even failed to award its annual prize of £3 million for good governance in Africa which is given to democratically elected leaders who have left office in the previous three years. This was because they couldn't find anyone to award it to (Tran, 2009). Indeed, Leftwich (1996, p. 18) argues generally in relation to developing countries that unless there are conducive existing state politics in the countries into which democracy is introduced, then it will fail and can actually have anti-developmental consequences. If politics in such countries are, and continue to be, predatory, patrimonial, and cronyist, then democratisation will not, and cannot, take place. In 'fragile' states, for example, where corruption, violence and lack of transparency and trust are normal then state, institution and human capacity building will need to precede, or at least accompany, any attempt at democratisation (Davies, 2011).

Interestingly, for this book's focus on the role of education, Leftwich returns to modernisation theory to argue that unless certain socio-economic and political preconditions exist which are associated with development towards a 'modern' society, such as an ethic of science and rationality, industrialisation, urbanisation, bureaucratisation, differentiation and specialisation of social structures, the principles of individualism, and political stability, then democracy will not take root and succeed (1996, pp. 6-11). Without an existing, relatively modern social and economic infrastructure and accompanying values and behaviours, then attempts at political democratisation will fail as they will not have the required social foundations to build on. He argues:

> And the history of developing societies in the last 30 years
> suggests that it would be foolhardy to ignore some of the

insights of that large body of theoretical and empirical
scholarship on modernisation ... For whatever its many
limitations, modernisation theory in general terms assumed
the intimacy of politics with other social and economic
processes, especially in the course of change, not its extrusion
from them. (1996, p. 21)

While political modernisation theorists were primarily concerned with
what constituted the modern polity, the work of Alex Inkeles (1969a, b;
Inkeles & Smith, 1974) focused much more on individual modernity,
what a modern individual might look like, and which socialisation
agencies most contribute to individual modernity. For him, a modern
citizen is one who takes an active interest in public affairs, is informed
about important events and participates in civic affairs. Most
importantly, the citizen must understand the ways in which bureaucratic
rules and impersonal judgement replace treatment based mainly on
personal qualities, on family ties, or friendship and connections, for the
modern polity is 'suffused with bureaucratic rationality' (1969a, p. 1122),
whether this citizen lives in a democratic or authoritarian state. In his
empirical work, he found education to have the strongest relationship of
all variables to the possession of modern (i.e. bureaucratic) attitudes,
values and behaviour. This is partly because the pupil at school learns
new skills, such as reading, writing and arithmetic, so that he or she will
be able to 'read directions and instructions and to follow events in the
newspaper' but also because of the bureaucratic nature of the hidden
curriculum:

School starts and stops at fixed times each day. Within the
school day there generally is a regular sequence for ordering
activities: singing, reading, writing, drawing, all have their
scheduled and usually invariant times. Teachers generally
work according to this plan ... Thus, principles directly
embedded in the daily routine of the school teach the value of
planning ahead and the importance of maintaining a regular
schedule. (Inkeles & Smith, 1974, p. 141)

Indeed, Kendall (2009) argues that this near-hegemonic, bureaucratic
model of formal, Western-style and state-provided schooling defines and
constitutes 'education' for development in the twenty-first century – as
sanctioned at the global Education for All conferences at Jomtien in
Thailand in 1990 and Dakar in Senegal in 2000, and as inscribed in the
UN's Millenium Development Goals. The essential features of this taken
for granted model of modern education are that children learn primarily
from adults about high stakes academic subjects, on a fixed schedule, in
an indoor setting, that includes particular features (desks, chairs,
chalkboards, written teaching and learning materials). Moreover, there is
an imagined linear development model from informal, family-provided

education, concerning daily tasks and survival skills, to 'modern' schooling systems:

> The international development model of education posits that mass, state-sponsored schooling is: (1) central to the creation of a 'modern' nation-state; (2) central to the development of 'modern' workers and families; and, thus (3) central to a state's 'modern' economic growth and international acceptance. The general conceptualisation of education and development has received critical attention since its inception, but has yet to be significantly challenged. (Kendall, 2009, p. 422)

As will be discussed in more detail in chapter 4, the true extent to which schools in developing countries can actually perform this role of modernising bureaucratic socialisation is open to some question, considering that they themselves are not completely sealed off from the surrounding society, and inevitably also reflect both its 'traditional' and 'modern' norms and behaviours in their daily practices. However, if formal education potentially contributes to democracy mainly indirectly through providing the basic, modern bureaucratic and organisational skills, attitudes and behaviours upon which more explicitly democratic values might then be built, then its role is necessary but not sufficient and, as we shall see in this book, many have argued for a more explicitly democratic role for education. On to a modern, efficient bureaucratic institutional base must be added knowledge and experience of explicitly democratic values and practices in order to contribute to a democratic political culture, as well as a bureaucratic, modern one for, as Diamond has argued:

> Prominent theories of democracy, both classical and modern, have asserted that democracy requires a distinctive set of political values and orientations from its citizens: moderation, tolerance, civility, efficacy, knowledge, participation. (1993, p. 1)

The renewed interest in democracy and democratisation as political development in the 1990s, following the collapse of communism, brought with it both a renewed interest in the role of political culture and development in political science, and a greater appreciation of a 'developmental' theory of democracy, where democracy everywhere is seen as work in progress, developing at different rates, in different ways and forms, in different countries (Diamond, 1999). Diamond argues that until the early 1990s, political scientists interested in democratic theorising were more concerned with the elite political culture needed to establish democracy than the mass political culture necessary to sustain it. He notes (1993, p. 7) that perhaps it is no coincidence that the importance of a mass democratic political culture was more evident in the writing of those concerned with programmes of civic education and mobilisation in developing countries and, in support of the importance of political culture in a democracy, cites John Stuart Mill's observation that:

> The people for whom the form of government is intended must be willing to accept it; or at least not so unwilling as to oppose an insurmountable obstacle to its establishment. They must be willing and able to do what is necessary to keep it standing. And they must be willing and able to do what it requires of them to enable it to fulfil its purposes. The word 'do' is to be understood as including forbearance as well as acts. (1993, p. 12)

Early on in the development of a literature on political culture, Inkeles (1961) contrasted the components of an ideal type authoritarian political culture with democratic political culture. The former included faith in powerful leaders, hatred of outsiders and perceived deviates, a sense of powerlessness and ineffectiveness, extreme cynicism, suspicion and distrust of others, and dogmatism. The converse, a democratic political culture, would embody flexibility, trust, efficacy, a critical open-mindedness, tolerance of other viewpoints and mutual respect for the persons holding them, a belief in the equality of people as human beings, and a respect for evidence in forming opinions. And, as Inkeles put it, an attitude towards authority which is neither blindly submissive, nor hostilely rejecting, but rather responsible, even though always watchful. These facets of a more democratic culture have important implications for the structure, processes, and relationships of education that will be further discussed in the remaining chapters of the book when exploring whether education does or can contribute to a more democratic political culture, as well a bureaucratic, ordered and modern one.

Democracy *as* Development

> A tyrannical regime might deprive the people of their freedom, but in return they are offered an easy life. A democratic regime might fail to beat poverty but the people enjoy freedom and dignity. (Al Aswany, 2011, writing on Egypt at the time of the popular uprisings in early 2011)

Perhaps to stress the role of democracy in causing or facilitating economic growth and other aspects of human development is to miss the key point – that democracy is *in itself* an important form of development. In *Development as Freedom* (1999) the economist and Nobel Prize winner, Amartya Sen, argued that democracy *is* development for two reasons:

(1) *The evaluative reason*: assessment of progress has to be
done primarily in terms of whether the freedoms that people
have are enhanced;
(2) *The effectiveness reason*: achievement of development is
thoroughly dependent on the free agency of people. (p. 4)

Sen is arguing both that the achievement of democratic government and
human rights in a country is a form of development in its own right, but
that it is also necessary for, and certainly not a barrier to, the effective
achievement of other forms of development, such as poverty reduction,
economic growth, and social provision. As Sen puts it:

the general enhancement of political and civil freedoms is
central to the process of development itself. The relevant
freedoms include the liberty of acting as citizens who matter
and whose voices count, rather than living as well-fed, well-
clothed and well-entertained vassals. The instrumental role of
democracy and human rights, important as it undoubtedly is,
has to be distinguished from its constitutive importance.
(1999, p. 288)

We have dealt with this effectiveness or instrumental argument in some
detail already, though Sen adds the argument that historically
democracies have been more effective at avoiding or dealing with serious
crises, such as famines, than other forms of political system (1999,
chap. 7). Here we shall primarily be concerned with his first, evaluative
argument for democracy as a form of development in itself.

Sen's theory is that the purpose of development is to improve
human lives by expanding the range of things that a person can be and
do, such as being healthy and well nourished, knowledgeable and an
active citizen. So, development is about removing obstacles to what a
person values and can do in life, obstacles such as illiteracy, bad health,
lack of access to resources or lack of civil and political freedoms. In Sen's
words, it is about increasing human capabilities and removing barriers to
these capabilities. Crucial to Sen's theory is the notion of freedom – from
social and political oppression, and from severe inequality of
opportunity that restricts human participation, and freedom to exercise
autonomy in making decisions about one's life. Human development is
about enlarging active agency and genuine choice for people from all
sectors of society. Sen is therefore a strong supporter of the promotion of
human rights and democratic forms of government as providing the only
suitable context for the development of capabilities and democracy is
therefore a form of development in its own right regardless of any
possible social and economic benefits or spin-offs (e.g. 1999, pp. 15-17).
This freedom to make choices and to function in a capable way based on
what is valued in a democratic setting *is* development.

What are these capabilities? Sen himself has always argued against providing a list, stressing the need for public participation and dialogue in deciding what are valued capabilities in different situations and contexts. Sen argues for a deliberative model of democracy with the process of decision-making – who makes the choice – being as important as the outcome itself:

> a dialogical democratic process encouraging open and public debate, discussion and dispute around proposals for development or development priorities in order to arrive at a collective and reasoned determination of what are the best policies and capabilities. Those affected by any policy or practice should be the ones to decide on what will count as valuable capabilities. (Walker & Unterhalter, 2007, p. 12)

Sen himself has a strong general faith in education and schooling in developing whatever capabilities are decided on (for example, Sen, 1999, pp. 284, 296; Walker & Unterhalter, 2007, p. 14), though some educationalists, including the present authors, would question the extent to which many formal education systems actually educate for capabilities, given that many education systems and schools historically and currently do not necessarily provide empowering democratic values, skills and knowledge (Harber, 2004, 2009). However, the question of how people can, and sometimes do, obtain or learn the political capabilities that empower them to function more effectively in a democratic state and society, and therefore have the 'voice' to be able to participate in deliberative democracy, certainly has important implications for formal education. This raises the key issue of how education is, and should be, structured and organised, particularly in terms of the distribution of decision-making power, in order to help to produce citizens who are fully capable of functioning in a democratic state. This will be the main concern of the rest of this book and in the next chapter we begin by exploring both the historical and theoretical, as well as the empirical relationships, between education and democracy.

Conclusion

Politics is an integral dimension of human behaviour. However, the way in which politics can take place varies from context to context and in this chapter we have focused in particular on the differences between democratic and authoritarian politics. We have seen how politics has increasingly entered into debates about the nature and direction of development, with an emerging consensus that democracy should be the goal of political development, even if it is not practiced universally and has not always been easy to obtain when attempts have been made to institutionalise it in a country where existing preconditions are not promising. Empirical evidence about the relationship between democracy and economic and other forms of social and economic development – and the nature of any causal links – is ambivalent except in the sense that, while democracy may or may not be of benefit, it is certainly not a barrier to other forms of development. But perhaps the most persuasive argument in favour of democracy as the goal for development is the moral argument that democracy is an important form of development in itself, regardless of other social and economic benefits.

Note

[1] http://www.happyplanetindex.org

CHAPTER 2

Education, Democracy and Political Development

Education and Politics

Concern with the relationship between education and politics goes back at least 2500 years. In *The Politics* Aristotle wrote:

> But of all the safeguards that we hear spoken of as helping to maintain constitutional continuity the most important, but most neglected today, is education, that is educating citizens for the way of living that belongs to the constitution in each case. It is useless to have the most beneficial rules of society fully agreed upon by all who are members of the politeia, if individuals are not going to be trained and have their habits formed for that politeia, that is to live democratically if the laws of the society are democratic, oligarchically if they are oligarchic. (Aristotle, 1962, pp. 215-216)

Education is inherently political, as it involves values in relation to fundamental goals and purposes such as 'What kind of individual and society are we trying to shape?' These questions cannot be answered in a factual or technical way because they are questions of opinion and ideology – hence they are political. Education is as inherently about the transmission of political ideas, values and behaviours, as it is about the transmission of information and understanding. Not surprisingly, therefore, the relationship between education and politics has long been a concern of philosophers.

Jaros (1973, pp. 9-12) provides a succinct account of classical thought on this relationship, which was mainly concerned with how education could be used for purposes of social control to maintain the status quo and stability and to prevent disorder. For Plato, for example, the one best state was the earthly reflection of the divine Idea or Form which, once achieved, must remain as it is. The way that change was to be avoided was to use education for social control, to teach citizens to accept their proper roles in society. The citizens of the Republic are to be indoctrinated so as to limit their aspirations to their current place in society, otherwise instability and disorder would ensue. Much of *The Republic* is taken up with prescribing the proper training patterns for the different social classes that make up the proposed ideal state. Confucius also saw a key role for education in social and political control. He disliked the use of force and coercion in political control, and instead preferred the family to teach children to respect and honour their parents, so that this will later be transferred or generalised to wider political authority. St. Thomas More in *Utopia* wrote of the need to socialise children into supporting the state when they are still young and pliant as these values, if rooted early, will contribute later to the defence and maintenance of the state. Later, Rousseau in *The Social Contract* argued that it is important that the young are affectively socialised. The citizens were to be trained to conform as it is necessary for them to be taught what it is that they really will. Jaros points out that Rousseau was one of the most enthusiastic advocates of political indoctrination, writing in *Considerations on the Government of Poland* that 'it is education that must give souls a national formation, and direct their opinions and tastes in such a way that they will be patriotic by inclination, by passion, by necessity' (cited in Jaros, 1973, p. 12).

These writers, then, were concerned not with education for democracy, but with education for political socialisation and political indoctrination. We can define political indoctrination as an attempt to intentionally inculcate values and beliefs as facts or truths. The process may involve deliberately falsifying or ignoring evidence, as well as presenting it in a biased way. Historically, this process has been associated with totalitarian states such as Nazi Germany and Soviet Russia where individuals have little access to alternative viewpoints. Political socialisation is the learning of preferences and predispositions towards political values and attitudes, though often in contexts where other viewpoints are available. It is just that some ideas and values are taken more seriously than others. The ethos of schools in a particular country, for example, might sometimes provide cooperative experiences for children or even teach about the benefits of cooperation. Nevertheless, at the same time, an overwhelmingly daily emphasis and priority is given to examinations, class rankings, prizes, and competitive sports. Children experience and learn that competition is far more important in life than cooperation. This is an example of what the Italian writer Antonio Gramsci (1977) described as 'hegemonic' ideas, that is the dominant ideas in a society that support the ruling group and which are given far greater credence than other ideas in the media and in the education systems, and indeed become taken as granted and seen as natural and inevitable.

Both indoctrination and socialisation assume a 'correct' answer to social and political questions that young people must learn to accept as correct and the only right answer – the answer provided by those with power and authority. The following are two examples, one from a novel based on experience in Afghanistan just after the Taliban were removed from power in 2001, and the second from an autobiography of a woman brought up as the daughter of revolutionaries in South America where she describes her experience of school in Bolivia in the 1980s:

> When the schools open this spring there will hardly be any textbooks. Books printed by the Mujahideen government and the Taliban are useless. This is how first-year schoolchildren learn the alphabet: J is for Jihad, our aim in life, I is for Israel, or enemy, K is for Kalashnikov, we will overcome, M is for Mujahideen, our heroes, T is for Taliban ... War was the central theme in maths books too. Schoolboys – because the Taliban printed books solely for boys – did not calculate in apples and cakes but in bullets and Kalashnikovs. Something like this: Little Omar has a Kalashnikov with three magazines. There are twenty bullets in each magazine. He uses two thirds of the bullets and kills sixty infidels. How many infidels does he kill with each bullet? Books from the Communist period cannot be used either. Their arithmetic problems dealt with land redistribution and egalitarian ideals. Red banners and happy collective farmers would guide children towards Communism. (Seierstad, 2004, pp. 62-63)

> There were Indians on our school grounds. Construction workers who toiled twelve hours a day building the new gymnasium with no breaks, no bathroom access, no water, for slave wages. They were visible from our classroom window, and the teachers referred to them by pointing their lips towards the outside, 'In today's speech lesson', Senorita Karina would say, 'we will learn to speak in a quiet, articulate voice, unlike those illiterate, uneducated Indians out there who yell, swear and have no use for proper Spanish grammar'. Our science teacher called them dirty Indians, though I knew it was they who'd taught the Europeans about washing. She informed us that the answer to the 'Indian problem' in Bolivia was mass sterilization. In Catholicism class, the Indians were accused of practicing black magic, casting spells and giving people the evil eye. My heart was sick by the end of the day. (Aguirre, 2011, p. 85)

Schools can, and do, attempt to socialise or indoctrinate a whole series of messages about, for example, nationalism and national identity, attitudes towards other nations, gender, race and ethnicity, religion, economic systems, equality and inequality, war and peace, political participation and leadership. They can do this through the selection of subjects taught on the curriculum, through the content and interpretation of each subject, through the values in textbooks, through the talk and behaviour of teachers, through teaching methods, through the organisational structure and processes of the school, through the symbols displayed in the school (flags, posters, pictures), through the content of assemblies, and the nature of extra-curricular activities (for numerous further detailed examples of how political socialisation takes place in schools in developing countries, see Dawson et al,1977; Fagerlind & Saha, 1989, chap. 5; Harber, 1989, 2004; Bush & Saltarelli, 2000; Bray & Lee, 2001).

An important dimension of this is the difference between the political socialisation of the elite few in private schools and the experience of the many. Some have linked the increasing prevalence of private education in developing countries to the growing global influence of neo-liberal economic policies under the auspices of the World Bank with its reduced emphasis on the state and an increased emphasis on the private sector in education (Mehrotra & Panchamukhi, 2006). While there has been a concomitant increased academic interest in private education in developing countries in recent years, both in terms of making up shortfalls in state provision and as a genuine alternative to state provision for the poor (see, for example, Day Ashley & Caddell, 2006; Srivastava & Walford, 2007), here the main concern is with more elite forms of private education. In Britain, traditionally these are the famous 'public' (i.e. expensive and private) schools such as Eton, Harrow and Winchester, and their products always have been and continue to be disproportionately represented in political elites in, for example, politics, the media and the military. The confidence, experience and expectations of leadership and social connections provided by private schools is in marked contrast to socialisation for more limited and routine expectations of citizenship found in many state schools (Harber, 2004, pp. 34-35, 2009, p. 99). One particularly notable example is Kamuzu Academy in Malawi which became known as the 'Eton in the bush' and was set up by the then President Hastings Banda deliberately for the purpose of elite recruitment and is now an expensive private school in an otherwise very poor country (Carroll, 2002). In a study of Cameroon, Congo and Kenya, Boyle (1999) argues that African political elites utilised the growth of expensive private schools after the introduction of structural adjustment programmes in the 1980s to help retain the privileged positions of their families. Indeed, he argues that:

> The early Twenty First Century will find in most African cities
> a network of well-equipped and staffed pre-primary and
> primary schools to fill the educational needs of local elites.
> Not only will this situation mimic the colonial antecedent in
> which expatriate children and the children of a few privileged
> indigenous citizens took classes from European teachers, the

curriculum these children followed then and now derives its substance from the educational trends current in Europe and North America. Over the past decade, African elites have recreated pockets of a colonial educational past.
(Boyle, 1999, p. 177)

Likewise in Nigeria, expensive private schools have enabled the rich to purchase educational advantage (Rose & Adelabu, 2007). In India, a higher proportion of upper caste children are enrolled in fee-paying private schools and the same schools are not a factor in the improvement of gender and other forms of social equity (Mehrotra & Panchamukhi, 2006).What these fees buy for more affluent groups in many developing countries is better school facilities, a more personalised approach to learning, and better teachers, and the result is both better academic achievement and, importantly, better social and organisational skills (Kitaev, 2007, p. 102). In Nepal, the difference in academic results is stark: in 2005, 29% of 171,440 government school students passed the School Leaving Certificate, while 80% of the 44,863 private schools' entrants passed (Caddell, 2006, p. 463). Caddell argues that elite schools in Kathmandu tend to emphasise the cosmopolitan school environment – their international staff, the choice of non-Nepalese curricula and examinations, and the range of international colleges and universities that their graduates have attended. Principals emphasise how attending their institution allows young people to become doctors or engineers, and enables them to move away from their village.

However, private schools can also be socially and politically divisive in another way when, as in India, there are caste-specific, language-specific, and religion-specific schools. Religious schools also, for example, exist in Thailand, Indonesia, and Malaysia (Kitaev, 2007, pp. 96, 101). Davies (2008, chap. 3) argues in some detail, using evidence from both developed and developing countries, that such segregation is bad for society and can contribute to the development of violent forms of political extremism. She concludes:

> Schools segregated by faith or ethnicity do not help social
> cohesion. At best they do little or no harm to integration; at
> worst they are incubators for unitary views, stereotypes of the
> 'other' and a dishonest pretence at equity. (2008, p. 97)

Nevertheless, it is also important to note that not all private schooling in developing countries serves only the rich and children of the elite (Tooley, 2009), and that, because of their freedom state control, internationally private schools have also often been the site of more progressive and democratic forms of education (e.g. Entwistle, 1971, pp. 52-54; Gribble, 1998; Carnie, 2003).

What is of particular interest for the purposes of this book is the authority structure of formal education for the many – what political model of decision-making does schooling currently socialise most young people into? Who has power and authority in schools and classrooms? In a previous book, one of the present authors wrote that:

> In terms of schooling, the dominant or hegemonic model globally, with exceptions that will be discussed later in the book, is authoritarian rather than democratic. Education for and in democracy, human rights and critical awareness is not a primary characteristic of the majority of schooling. While the degree of harshness and despotism within authoritarian schools varies from context to context and from institution to institution, in the majority of schools power over what is taught and learned, how it is taught and learned, where it is taught and learned, when it is taught and learned and what the general learning environment is like is not in the hands of pupils. It is predominantly government officials, headteachers and teachers who decide, not learners. Most schools are essentially authoritarian institutions, however benevolent or benign that authoritarianism is and whatever beneficial aspects of learning are imparted. (Harber, 2004, p. 24)

A review of literature on schooling in the same book which included Africa, Asia, the Middle East, South and Central America, and the Caribbean, provided considerable evidence in support of this argument. In many such countries an additional factor was the colonial history of education. By the 1930s, colonialism had exercised its sway over 84.6% of the land surface of the globe (Loomba, 1998, p. 15). When formal education was eventually provided, missionary schools and those of the colonial state were used to control local populations by teaching the superiority of the culture of the colonising power and by supplying the subordinate personnel necessary for the effective functioning of the colonial administration (Altbach & Kelly, 1978). In a study of the ex-British colony of Trinidad and Tobago, for example, the author argues that:

> Schooling was intended to inculcate into the colonised a worldview of voluntary subservience to the ruling groups, and a willingness to continue to occupy positions on the lowest rungs of the occupational and social ladder. A number of effective strategies were used in the process, but the most significant among these was the instructional programmes and teaching methodologies used in colonial schools ... Values, attitudes and behaviour were highlighted such as the habits of obedience, order, punctuality and honesty.
> (London, 2002, p. 57)

Some of the characteristics of colonial schooling in Trinidad and Tobago outlined by London include: mindlessness, verbatim repetition, character development, mastery of rules as a pre-requisite for application, use of abstract illustrations, monotonous drill, inculcation of specified norms for cleanliness and neatness, and harsh discipline. He concludes by arguing that schooling is one of the places where colonial forms and practices have persisted and remained essentially the same throughout the post-colonial period.

A similar authoritarian stress on conformity and obedience existed, for example, in British India (Alexander, 2001, p. 92), Francophone Africa (Moumouni, 1968) and Portuguese Mozambique (Azevedo, 1980; Searle, 1981; Barnes, 1982). In a study of contemporary schooling in India, Mali, Lebanon, Liberia, Mozambique, Pakistan, Mongolia, Ethiopia, and Peru, for the Department for International Development (DfID) and Save the Children, the authors emphasise the continuation of models of classroom discipline and teaching methodology first instigated under colonialism (Molteno et al, 2000, p. 13).

In Africa, many post-colonial governments did not hesitate to use schooling for political control purposes of their own (Harber, 1989), while in Indonesia, 'the development of mass education at the start of the 1960s was motivated by a concern to promulgate an authoritarian political ideology and to instil an unquestioning acceptance of authority' (Watkins,1999, p. 4). Post-colonial governments in Malaysia have used schooling for political and ethnic control (Watson, 1982), and in India the Hindu Nationalist government of the early 2000s changed the curriculum and school textbooks to reflect their ideology (Behal, 2002a). In chapter 4, which discusses the obstacles to more democratic forms of education, we consider further evidence of the existing authoritarian nature of schooling in developing countries, with its roots both in the history of education in the colonial powers and in colonialism, as a continuing obstacle to greater education for democracy.

Education and Democracy

Unlike political indoctrination and socialisation, a genuine education for democracy is not a form of social and political control. It does not aim for the inculcation of a right answer or a particular viewpoint. It is an attempt to create critical awareness of political phenomenon by open, balanced discussion of a range of evidence and opinions. It encourages individuals to make up their own minds about issues after considering the arguments and evidence. Education for democracy is not neutral – no education is neutral – but it does not, either deliberately or by default, transmit one-sided views of substantive values (e.g. in relation to controversial issues, such as privatisation, the environment, nuclear weapons, or abortion) as 'true'. Its values are procedural and concerned with how issues are discussed and how people relate to each other, and it operates the democratic citizenship values set out in chapter 1.

As with education for social control, there also is a history of philosophical and theoretical concern with education for democracy. John Stuart Mill in *Representative Government*, for example, argued not only for securing ever more representative government, but also that 'universal teaching must precede universal enfranchisement'. He felt that a certain basic education was necessary to make the informed political choices required in a democracy. So, for Mill, education has an explicitly political and democratic purpose (Kingdom, 1976). Carr and Hartnett further argue that because individual autonomy lies at the heart of liberal democratic societies, it is not surprising that rational autonomy has been a key theme of writing on democracy and education. This emphasis on rational autonomy reflects the view that the freedom of individuals is always a matter of developing their capacity (or to use Sen's word 'capabilities') to think, act and choose on the basis of their own rational reflections. They cite Mill from his famous essay *On Liberty*:

> the free development of individuality is one of the leading essentials of well-being. It is ... the proper condition of the human being ... to use and interpret experience in his own way ... To conform to custom, merely as custom, does not educate or develop in him any of the qualities which are the instinctive endowment of a human being. The human facilities or perception, judgement, discriminate feeling, mental activity and even moral preference, are exercised only in making a choice. (Cited in Carr & Hartnett, 1996, pp. 47-48)

However, perhaps the theorist that contributed most to ideas concerning education for democracy was John Dewey. Opposing theorists of limited, elite-run contemporary democracy as discussed above, Dewey argued that in a democracy ordinary people need the information and understanding on which to base their political judgements and choices in actively participating:

> all those who are affected by social institutions must have a share in producing them and managing them. The two facts that each one is influenced in ... what he becomes by the institutions under which he lives, and therefore he shall have in a democracy a voice in shaping them, are the passive and active side of the same fact. (Cited in Carr & Hartnett, 1996, p. 60)

Moreover, Dewey saw democracy as more than just a set of institutional arrangements and structures at the level of the state. For him, democracy was also a mode of 'associational living', that is democratic values and behaviours must also permeate society and the relationships of daily life.

He argued that schooling did not prepare young people to live in democratic states and societies, but rather existed to fit people into existing roles and social arrangements. Teaching methods in schools were authoritarian and bred democratically undesirable social attitudes, such as obedience and self-interest. Genuine education cannot take place by directing or controlling what pupils think. If education is to help to form democratic citizens then this must take place in an educational environment where the skills, values and behaviours of democracy can be learned through participation in cooperative deliberation, shared enquiry and collective decision-making. In order to educate for democracy, education itself must be democratically organised and possess a culture of democratic relationships, and thus be a microcosm of a wider democratic state and society. Dewey was, though, very well aware that formal education was inextricably linked to existing power structures and entrenched interests and would be very difficult to transform in line with democratic principles (Carr & Hartnett, 1996, pp. 54-64).

During the 1960s and 1970s, which was a period of social and cultural upheaval in the West, and a time of huge political change caused by decolonisation in many developing countries, a number of writers again also began to question and critique the relevance and benevolence of schooling, questioning whether formal education really did contribute to the type of democratic learning that Dewey was arguing for. The major arguments of 13 of these key texts, including, for example, Ivan Illich, John Holt and Carl Rogers have been explored in Harber (2009), and the following is a selective summary of some of their key critiques of formal education which are most relevant to education for democracy:

- Schools are authoritarian institutions with little serious participation by pupils in decision-making and particularly in curriculum, teaching and learning;
- Schooling is increasingly controlled from above and therefore rigid, bureaucratic and based on the principle of one-size-fits-all, rather than flexible and able to meet the needs of individuals;
- A fixed, subject-based, official curriculum does not, and cannot, educate for the rapidly changing present, let alone the future;
- Many, though not all, children are unhappy and bored at school;
- Schooling is driven by tests, examinations and 'right answers' which dictate the nature of classroom activity and cause stress and harm to pupils;
- Teacher education is part of the problem as, rather than challenging what happens in schools, it tends to socialise for it and reproduce it;
- Schooling is more about the reproduction of social inequalities than the provision of equality of opportunity – and this is so both within nations and between nations;

- Corporal punishment is harmful to learning and must go;
- Schooling tends to avoid critical and creative discussion of controversial issues;
- It is often forgotten that schooling is, historically, a relatively recent form of education and that there are other forms. However, the essentials of schooling have not altered significantly since its origins; and
- There is a great deal of 'do as I say' from adults in schools rather than 'do as I do'.

Two of these 13 writers were from developing countries and have had a particular influence on thinking about education, development and democracy. The first was Julius Nyerere, the first President of Tanzania and a former teacher. Nyerere in *Education for Self-Reliance* (1967) saw education as the key to creating a new set of values. He argued that the scarcity of opportunities for education and the characteristics of teaching and learning strongly reinforced the prevalence of individualism and competition in the education system. Many pupils went to boarding schools which removed them from contact with their communities. As a result, many were estranged from the problems of their society, wishing to obtain the privileges and comforts of salaried employment, and they increasingly adopted narrow and elitist attitudes. There was a danger that schools would become institutions of the reproduction of social inequality rather than engines of development for all. Nyerere argued that schools therefore needed to be more closely integrated with the local community through productive enterprise. Each school would possess a farm or other productive enterprise and thus schooling would not be divorced from the agricultural production of the surrounding society.

He further argued that the pressure of examinations and syllabuses based on the memorisation of large amounts of knowledge had led to classrooms that were didactic and authoritarian in nature with teachers simply transmitting information to be learned by rote. Instead, the power should be moved from the teacher to the learner by placing more emphasis on active, participatory and cooperative classroom methods, such as problem-solving and enquiry-based project work, and by adding character assessment to formal examinations. In the school as a whole, pupils should be given the opportunity to make many of the decisions about the school's productive enterprise and thus learn to value and practice participation and direct democracy. This would require school councils and more democratic forms of school organisation. Teacher training would need to be reformed so that teachers were trained for a new type of education system. Finally, the political nature of education should be recognised by introducing the subject of political education into the curriculum which would involve the teaching of controversial issues. However, while there were some successes in relation to, for example, school councils, the actual implementation of these educational principles faced considerable problems not least because at the time the wider political system was a one party state (Harber, 1989, chap. 4, 1997, chap. 6), and indeed recent studies of Tanzania itself describe a more conventional and hierarchical educational system with its fair share of resource and motivational problems (Barrett, 2005; Van Der Steen, 2011).

Paulo Freire, a Brazilian educationalist concerned with adult literacy, was both imprisoned and exiled by the military regime in the 1960s. He is perhaps best known for his book *Pedagogy of the Oppressed* (1972) which is a significant critique of existing, conventional and authoritarian forms of education. Freire begins his book by arguing that the world is marked by dehumanisation, that is many people are thwarted by injustice, exploitation, oppression, alienation and violence of the oppressors, though many yearn to recover their lost humanity by overcoming oppression. However, it is crucial that the oppressed 'must not, in seeking to regain their humanity ... become in turn the oppressors of the oppressors, but rather restorers of the humanity of both' (p. 26), i.e. that one orthodoxy doesn't simply replace another. In order to overcome oppression and realise a fuller sense of consciousness, it is important for people to critically recognise their oppression, its causes, and the possibilities for transformation both of themselves and the world around them. This can only take place through a pedagogy of the oppressed based on critical dialogue and with a proclivity to action which is forged with, and not for, the learners, recognising that the teacher is also a learner and that the learner knows many things that the teacher doesn't know. Freire recognises that all education is inherently political and that any education offered as part of the existing system in an oppressive state and society will simply reproduce the ideas and interests of the oppressors. So, he prefers educational projects working with the oppressed to official, systemic education which can only be changed by political power. However, in such projects, reflective participation (rather than monologues, slogans and communiqués) is crucial.

Freire regards the usual teacher–student relationships as having a narrative character – the teacher speaks and the objects (students) listen:

> The teacher talks about reality as if it were motionless, static, compartmentalised and predictable ... Their task is to 'fill' the students with the contents of his narration – contents which are detached from reality ... Words that are emptied of their concreteness and become a hollow, alienated and alienating verbosity. (Freire, 1972, p. 53)

So, the abstract subject matter in education is often irrelevant to the learner who memorises it for no apparent reason, turning the learner into containers or receptacles to be filled by the teacher so that, 'The more completely she fills the receptacles, the better a teacher she is. The more meekly the receptacles permit themselves to be filled, the better students they are' (p. 53).

Education of this type is therefore an act of 'depositing' and Freire refers to it as the 'banking' concept of education. He summarises the oppressive nature of banking education as follows:

(a) the teacher teaches and the students are taught;
(b) the teacher knows everything and the students know nothing;
(c) the teacher thinks and the students are thought about;
(d) the teacher talks and the students listen – meekly;
(e) the teacher disciplines and the students are disciplined;
(f) the teacher chooses and enforces his choice, and the students comply;
(g) the teacher acts and the students have the illusion of acting through the action of the teacher;
(h) the teacher chooses the programme content, and the students (who were not consulted) adapt to it;
(i) the teacher confuses the authority of knowledge with his or her own professional authority, which she and he set in opposition to the freedom of the students; and
(j) the teacher is the Subject of the learning process, while the pupils are mere objects. (p. 54)

So, the more students work away at storing the deposited knowledge, the less they develop critical consciousness about the world around them and the more they accept their place in society and adapt to the world as it is, thereby posing little threat to the established, oppressive order. In this way it attempts to control thinking and action. He further describes this as 'Education as the exercise of domination' (p. 59).

This needs to be replaced by problem-posing education where issues are approached through dialogue, reflection and mutual learning. Teachers and students become jointly responsible for a process in which they all grow and this he regards as 'Education as the practice of freedom' (chap. 3). In problem-posing education, people begin to perceive critically the way they exist in the world, not as a static reality, but in a process of transformation. For Freire, genuine dialogue involving critical thinking must take place in an atmosphere of humility, trust, hope and cooperation and be rooted in the historical and concrete reality of the participants. The themes that will co-investigated as a result of dialogue will be therefore meaningful and significant to the learners. Thus, as Torres puts it, more than 30 years after Freire's main books were published, the concept of dialogical education appears as a:

democratic tool for dealing with complex cultural conflicts in the context of unequal and combined development of Latin American education; its applicability in advanced industrial societies is well documented; and his message of a political democratic utopia in education is a political challenge to the educational establishment. (1998, p. 164)

Most recently, while Amartya Sen seems to have a firm belief in the potential of schooling to enhance democratic capabilities (Sen, 1999, pp. 216, 218; Walker & Unterhalter, 2007, p. 14), he does not really investigate what the implications of capability theory might be for the current, dominant model of formal education. However, this has been explored in some detail by Walker and Unterhalter (2007). They make the point that an education which contributes to un-freedoms, such as one that tolerates prejudice, exclusion, marginalisation or harassment, or which limits access to critical and confident participation, would not be compatible with a capability approach, and they cite Martha Nussbaum, another key writer on the capability approach, on the importance of children being taught to learn capabilities of critical thinking by debating complex and controversial social and moral issues (2007, pp. 14-15).

Capability theory also has implications for decision-making and the distribution of power in schools. If a capability is a person's ability to do what they consider valuable then this contrasts with other ideas about how we decide what is just or fair in the distribution of resources. Walker and Unterhalter argue that:

> some ideas about distribution rest on what an outsider determines is best to create maximum opportunities to achieve appropriate outcomes for, say, different kinds of schools or students. The problem is often phrased in terms of what forms of curriculum, teaching, school management and learning resources will yield the educational achievements such as examination results or skills sets, that an economy needs. Sometimes the question is posed in terms of how learners can acquire appropriate knowledge of history or religion to act as full members of a particular group which they are deemed to belong to. In both these instances the emphasis is on what kind of inputs (ideas, teachers, learning materials) will shape particular opportunities to achieve desired outcomes (economic growth or social solidarity) ... The capability approach critiques this way of posing and solving questions of evaluation. Its central tenet is that in evaluation one must look at each person not as a means to economic growth or social stability but as an end. We must evaluate freedoms for people to be able to make decisions they value and work to remove obstacles to those freedoms, that is expand people's capabilities. (2007, p. 2)

Or, as the statement in the UN Convention on the Rights of the Child puts it:

> State Parties shall assure to the child who is capable of
> forming his or her own views the right to express those views
> freely in all matters affecting the child, the views of the child
> being given due weight in accordance with the age and
> maturity of the child. (Article 12, UN Convention on the
> Rights of the Child, 1989, signed by every country in the world
> except the United States of America and Somalia)

Bates (2007) further discusses a range of contemporary theoretical literature on education which emphasises the importance of learning democratic capabilities by actually experiencing them at school and which:

> advocates an educational program quite consistent with the
> capability approach outlined by Sen and Nussbaum. It is, of
> course, a theoretical tradition that goes back to Dewey and his
> insistence that knowing comes about through doing, through
> active participation in production and active involvement in
> democratic social processes,

and that educational leadership should be based on:

> a conception of the learning society that took the development
> of capabilities centred around ideas of human development,
> agency, well-being and freedom as central, thus claiming that
> the development of a truly democratic and free society should
> be the purpose behind human activity, one to which the
> economic development of such societies should be directed.
> (2007, pp. 153, 155)

Tabulawa (2003), however, expresses an important note of caution about the use of education to spread democracy in developing countries. He argues that since the fall of the Berlin Wall in 1989, Western aid agencies have promoted more democratic forms of education because they have seen liberal democracy as inherently bound up with the free-market economy and neo-liberal competitive capitalism. According to aid agencies, one cannot happen without the other. Therefore by promoting more democratic forms of pedagogy, aid agencies have been also been promoting neo-liberalism:

> learner-centred pedagogy is a political artefact ... the interests
> of aid agencies in the pedagogy is part of a wider design on the
> part of aid institutions to facilitate the penetration of capitalist
> ideology in periphery states, this being done under the guise of
> democratisation ... This process is being accelerated by the
> current wave of globalisation which is a carrier of neo-liberal
> ideology. (Tabulawa, 2003, p. 10)

While this may be a factor, conscious or unconscious, with some aid agencies there are many both inside aid agencies and outside who do not promote greater education for democracy for this reason, but for many of the reasons discussed above – they believe that democracy is a better form of government than authoritarianism and that education can contribute to democratisation. Moreover, it is important to be careful in generalising about 'capitalism' where there are various capitalisms including, for example, the more neo-liberal Anglo–Saxon model, the more social democratic Scandinavian model, the Asian model, and the central European model (Amable, 2004). Each of these might well have different motivations in the provision of aid and the promotion, or not, of democratic education. Indeed, the changing, diverse and contradictory motivations of aid agencies, including the rise of 'philanthrocapitalism' (the provision of funding to development by rich individuals and corporations) are discussed in Colclough et al (2010). Tabulawa further argues that some of the central values of learner-centred pedagogy are individual autonomy, open-mindedness, and tolerance of alternative viewpoints, which are all in line with the individualistic Western culture. Again, while this may partially be true, many participant, group-based classroom activities used in more democratic classrooms also favour cooperation, reciprocity and collective endeavour, as well individualism. This will be further discussed later in the book. It is also important to note that while individualism is indeed a significant, perhaps dominant, trait in Western democratic histories and cultures, there are also influential cooperative movements, trade union and socialist movements, and legacies as well.

A final concern is the relationship between education for democracy and peace. While most democracies are far from perfect in practice, it can be argued that, despite their shortcomings, they offer a better long-term prospect for peace than authoritarian regimes. Historically, authoritarian regimes have tended to be marked by civil unrest, violent repression, and wars against neighbours. This has caused serious damage to the economies of developing countries and to the social fabric. On the other hand, accountable and representative government in democracies, it can be argued, minimises internal violence and the abuse of human rights and decreases the possibility (though doesn't eliminate it) of going to war without good reason. A major argument against this, of course, is the American and British led invasion of Iraq and, perhaps to a lesser extent, the invasion of Afghanistan. However, while there are many (though not all) in both the United States of America and Britain who would argue that the invasion of Iraq was indeed without good reason, those opposed to the war did at least have the right to voice their opinions in the press, in demonstrations, and in the ballot box, and the politicians responsible can be held to account through the role of legislatures, the press, and public hearings. Such public accountability and publicity may well decrease the chances of such controversial wars being launched by democracies in the future.

Education can be a significant factor in regard to peace and violence. The then Director-General of UNESCO wrote in the 1990s that:

> Wars will not cease, either on the ground or in people's minds, unless each and every one of us resolutely embarks on the struggle against intolerance and violence by attacking the evil at its roots. Education offers us the means to do this. It also holds the key to development, to receptiveness to others, to population control and the preservation of the environment. Education is what will enable us to move from a culture of war, which we unhappily know only too well, to a culture of peace, whose benefits we are only just beginning to sense.
> (Tedesco, 1994, p. 1)

Since then, it has become much clearer that education systems, primarily facilitated by their authoritarian structures and processes, can and do play a role in fostering and promoting violence, as much as promoting peace (Bush & Saltarelli, 2000; Harber, 2004, 2009; Pinheiro, 2006). A recent UNESCO report on armed conflict and education discussed in some detail the paradoxically negative and positive role of education and stressed the need to educate for essentially democratic values in order to educate for peace:

> Schools should be seen first and foremost as places for imparting the most vital of skills: tolerance, mutual respect and the ability to live peacefully with others.
> (UNESCO, 2011, p. 3)

The report further notes that the proportion of violent conflicts around the world broadly falling into the category of 'ethnic' increased from 15% in the early 1950s to nearly 60% in 2004 (p. 161), and that as the education system occupies a central role in framing identities, it has considerable potential to act as a force either for peace or for conflict:

> Education may not cause armed conflict in a direct sense, but education systems are critical in shaping the views that render societies more or less prone to violence. It is only a slight exaggeration to say that a country's future will be as peaceful, prosperous and cohesive as its education system allows. If the citizens of the future receive an education that promotes tolerance, respect for others and appreciation of the complex identities that make up multi-ethic societies, appeals to violence based on bigotry, chauvinism and distrust of the 'other' will have less resonance. That is why education should

be seen as a key element in the peace building agenda.
(UNESCO, 2011, p. 222)

The report recommends a number of specific ways in which schools could become more involved in peace building which directly involve key elements of education for democracy. One is that the teaching of history and religion should be more based on critical thinking and recognising the validity of different worldviews and encouraging respect for other faiths, asserting that 'When faith-based education is used to assert the primacy of set of beliefs and to denigrate others, it sows the seeds of potential conflict' (p. 242). Another way is to introduce civic or citizenship education in which people learn to understand what it means to be part of a diverse community and what is shared by all – universal rights, toleration and respect for diversity.

Education and Democracy: is there any evidence?

Chabbott and Ramirez note that a positive relationship between education and economic, political and cultural development is widely assumed throughout much of the modern and modernising world, even though the relationship is actually problematic for two reasons:

> First, although many empirical studies show a positive
> relationship between many forms of education and individual
> economic, political and cultural development, the effects of
> education on development at the collective level are
> ambiguous. Second, at the same time evidence for this
> ambiguity has been mounting, faith in education as the
> fulcrum of individual for individual and for collective
> development has been growing in the form of international
> education conferences and declarations and national-level
> education policies. (Chabbott & Ramirez, 2000, p. 163)

As regards the first relationship between education and democracy at the level of the individual, there is evidence of a positive relationship between levels of education and generalised stated support for democracy in those mostly more developed countries with considerable experience of democracy (Evans & Rose, 2007, p. 904). Diamond (1999, pp. 199-200) discusses empirical research in central and eastern Europe in the 1990s that suggested that education was the key variable in explaining support among individuals for democracy and rejection of authoritarianism. Education was also found to be strongly correlated with support for democracy in Taiwan, and in another study, the higher the educational level, the more likely respondents were in each of four Chinese samples (Hong Kong, Taiwan, China and urban China) to manifest pro-democratic value orientations. However, here the main concern is with the potential role of education in fostering the process of democratisation in developing countries, so we will review empirical evidence that includes developing countries to explore the extent to which the positive relationship between education and democracy holds true.

In Africa, where democracy has only relatively recently been reintroduced, evidence of the contribution of education to democratisation is uncertain. Bratton et al (2005) found that while more educated Africans are sceptical about the quality of democracy as it exists in reality, they still support democracy in preference to the alternatives. Focusing specifically on Malawi in terms of their empirical data, Evans and Rose (2007) found that there was a clear and substantial association between education level and stated preference for democracy. This difference was particularly marked between those with no primary schooling and those with some primary schooling, though there was no difference between those who had had primary schooling and those that had secondary schooling. They also found that there was a positive relationship between understanding of democracy and schooling with primary schooling, though those who had experienced post-secondary education were distinctive in having an understanding of how democracy actually works in terms of regular elections and multi-party competition. Further, in terms of three non-democratic possibilities (a single party system, military rule, and rule by presidential decree), the level of disapproval rose in a linear fashion from no formal education, through some primary, to primary, secondary and post-secondary. Moreover, they also found that education had a substantially more significant impact on support for democracy than other socio-demographic factors, such as generation, gender and region, with only party support being a stronger predictor. Overall, the strongest difference in positive responses towards democracy was between those with no education at all and all other responses. Their conclusion, in a form of human political capital development argument, is that education is a good investment for the promotion of democracy and particularly primary education. They conclude that:

> A further benefit of examining the Malawian experience in detail has been to show that education has its effects when it occurs in a non democratic system, embodying hierarchical and ostensibly illiberal values – such as was the case in Malawi during the pre-democratic era when the respondents to our survey will, overwhelmingly, have received their education. This suggests that education's impressive effects are derived from its impact on cognitive processes and values without regard to the specific content of civic education in schools. (Evans & Rose, 2007, p. 916)

There have also been a number of macro-level, cross-national studies of the relationship between education and democracy. As to whether education has a positive relationship with the existence and survival of democratic regimes, in a study of 91 countries (including developing countries) in the period 1960-2000, Glaeser et al (2007) found that education and democracy are highly correlated and that the relationship is causal – more education favours greater democracy. In their model, schooling teaches people to interact with others and raises the benefits of civic participation, including voting and organisation. They argue that as education raises the benefits of civic engagement, it raises participation in support of a more broad-based, democratic regime relative to a narrow-based dictatorship, and that this increases the likelihood of both the installation and survival of democracy. While Agemoglu et al (2005) found no relationship between democracy and an increase in the average years of schooling for the period 1970 to 1995, Castello-Climent (2008) in studying a sample of 104 countries over the period 1965 to 2000, found that an increase in the education attained by the *majority* of the population is what matters for the implementation and sustainability of democracy, rather than the average years of schooling. Thus a large mass or majority of moderately educated citizens seemed to have more influence on democracy than a restricted group of highly educated individuals.

In a study more explicitly focused on education and development, McMahon (1999) used a conceptual framework suggesting that in the long run economic growth and widespread access to primary education, and even more so secondary education, enlarges the working and middle classes and facilitates their self-organisation, thus making it more difficult to exclude them politically. Those with primary and secondary education value their improved economic status, their hard-won civil rights and their democratic freedoms. For McMahon, the causal relationship is from economic growth to the provision of greater education to democratisation, though he recognises there may be elements of a two-way flow. His empirical study of a range of developing countries suggests that education contributes to democratisation indirectly through economic growth, which he argues is related to democratisation, but that higher enrolments in secondary school contribute directly to democratisation both through concern to defend rights and through facilitating wider exposure to communications media.

In contrast, Benavot (1996) in a study using data from 1965 to 1988, and including sub-Saharan Africa, Latin America and Asia (but not including the wave of democratisations following the end of the Soviet Union in 1989), found that primary and secondary education had only a weak – and sometimes negative – effect on the emergence and consolidation of democratic regimes. However, the effects of tertiary education were positive and that this positive impact of higher education was especially pronounced among Asian, Latin American and sub-Saharan nations. He notes that his findings are surprising given previous (and, as we have seen above, more recent) findings from cross-national studies which have highlighted the positive impact of mass literacy and mass education on democracy. Thus in contrast to the emphasis given to the role of mass education in enhancing the competencies and skills of individuals by modernisation theorists, Benavot's evidence points more to the emphasis of institutional theorists on the socialisation of elites into democratic values through exposure to higher education.

While the outcomes of these studies vary, partly because they are measuring different things, the weight of the evidence seems to point generally in a positive direction between more stated support for democracy and to a positive relationship between higher levels of education and a greater chance of the existence and maintenance of a democratic system of government. However, this largely still leaves us guessing as to exactly *how* education contributes to democracy – directly through civics courses providing information about democracy and learning the skills of social interaction?; Or indirectly by facilitating economic growth and social class formation? What studies of this kind, particularly the macro cross-national ones carried out by economists and political scientists, tend to exclude is consideration of what goes on inside the 'black box' of education. This is also a criticism that has recently been made of the work of development economists who refer to education (McGrath, 2010). Crucial here is the *type* of education experienced and of particular importance in this regard the relationship between the internal micro-political structures, processes and cultures of formal education and the type of people and citizens that result. A recent study of the role of higher education in the formation of developmental elites, for example, found in both a literature review and from its own data that whilst higher education may not be a sufficient pre-condition for democratic processes and improved governance, evidence does indicate that it is a contributory factor. However, and crucially, 'The extent to which higher education institutes achieve this value added is dependent upon their structure, teaching methods and curricula' (Brannelly et al, 2011, p. vii).

In other words, if higher education is going to contribute to democracy and genuinely developmental elites, then it must operate democratically and provide experience of democratic values and behaviours. Going back to the quote from Aristotle at the beginning of the chapter, do authoritarian schools and other educational institutions tend to produce people less supportive of democracy, or supportive in more minimal ways, and more democratic schools tend to produce people who are not only more supportive of democracy, but are also democratic themselves? Do certain types of schooling contribute more directly to the possession of democratic skills and values and a proclivity towards democratic behaviour?

What we do know is that formal education and qualifications are no guarantee that a person will be a democrat. As Josef Stalin once put it, 'Education is a weapon, whose effects depend on who holds it in his hand and at whom it is aimed' (quoted in Meighan, 1994, p. 4). He should know. Stalin went to school at a religious seminary in Tbilisi, the capital of Georgia and, as one historian stated, 'From the tyrannical priests he learnt exactly the tactics – surveillance, spying, invasion of inner life, violation of feelings, in Stalin's own words –that he would recreate in his Soviet police state' (Montefiore, 2007).

It also salutary to remember that many of the leading Nazis in Germany in the 1930s and the 1940s were well-educated, as were the architects of apartheid in South Africa. Pol Pot and Comrade Duch of the Khmer Rouge, responsible for 2,000,000 deaths due to murder, torture and starvation in Cambodia between 1975 and 1979, were both former teachers and Duch had also been a teacher educator. In the religious violence that flared up in India in March 2002, a crowd of 10,000 Hindus dragged a Muslim MP, his brother-in-law, his brother-in-law's wife, and their two small sons into the street from their house and set them alight. The Police Commissioner for the city where it happened stated 'I hang my head in shame. The people responsible for all this come from the better sections of society. They are not criminals. *Many of them are educated*' (Harding, 2002). In the Rwandan genocide of 1994, when between 800,000 and a 1,000,000 people (one eighth of its population) were murdered in the space of a few weeks, teachers from a Hutu ethnic background commonly denounced their Tutsi pupils to the militia or even directly killed them themselves. Indeed, the role of schooling in this genocide poses some very serious and important questions about why and how we educate in all societies. As two commentators on the Rwandan genocide put it:

> The role of well-educated persons in the conception, planning and execution of the genocide requires explanation; any attempt at explanation must consider how it was possible that their education did not render genocide unthinkable. The active involvement of children and young people in carrying out the violence, sometimes against their teachers and fellow pupils, raises further questions about the *kind* of education they received. (Retamal & Aedo-Richmond, 1998, p. 16)

Indeed, there is now considerable evidence suggesting that terrorism is positively linked to education, i.e. people willing to use violence to pursue political ends are *more* likely to come from the higher educated sections of society. Opinion polls carried out in the West Bank and Gaza Strip, for example, suggest that the more educated sections of the population are *less* likely to support dialogue and peaceful coexistence with Israel and more likely to support armed attacks. Similarly, Hezbollah fighters and Palestinian suicide bombers tend to come from the more educated sections of the Palestinian population. The same piece of research also found that violent Israeli extremists were also disproportionately from well-educated, high paid occupations, including teachers (Krueger & Maleckova, 2003). In another paper discussing similar findings, Claude Berrebi of Princeton University comes to the important following conclusion:

> Policy makers, when trying to reduce terrorism via education or income, should focus not on the amount of education but on the content of education; changing the substance when needed in order to create positive stimulations towards democracy, moderation, appeasement and coexistence. Not all education is equal, and as Martin Luther King once said in another context, 'education which stops with efficiency may prove the greatest menace to society. The most dangerous criminal may be the man gifted with reason but with no morals'. (Berrebi, 2003, p. 38)

However, even in many countries with democratic political institutions, there exists the seeming paradox that schools educate for control via hierarchical and authoritarian school structures and curricula, as do schools under authoritarian political regimes. How does democracy survive in such circumstances? First, it has to be said that there are often differences of degree if not of kind. Forms of control in and of schools in authoritarian political systems may be more explicit and harsh than in democracies. However, schools operating in democratic political systems nevertheless on the whole socialise more towards authoritarian values in the lack of real power and participation afforded to learners. The main argument is that schools in democracies are not doing enough either to support democracy or, in particular, to deepen and strengthen it. Democracy can be created and learned and it can be lost and forgotten – and there are many historical examples going both ways. If schooling does not consciously try to contribute to the development of a democratic political culture, supportive of democratic political institutions – the political knowledge, skills, values and behaviour of a population – then democracy is always fragile and at risk. This, for example, was a key argument behind the government initiated Crick Report on Education for Democratic Citizenship in England, one of the oldest democracies in the world, which recommended that education for democratic citizenship be introduced as a key part of the curriculum. The report expressed genuine concern at levels of political alienation, apathy and cynicism among the population and the risk that this posed to democracy (Advisory Group on Citizenship, 1998).

Much of schooling in liberal democracies would help to provide the basic factors (social and political information, literacy, numeracy and modern bureaucratic skills and experience) supportive of the workings of a limited 'contemporary' model of democracy discussed in chapter one of this book, or an even more restricted version of it. A crucial difference between the two models discussed in chapter one was the commitment to develop a democratic *society*, as well as political system. Fuller versions of democracy require much greater levels of democracy and equality in our daily interactions, relationships and behaviours in the workplace and in social and domestic activities. This requires a conscious attempt to remove prejudice and discrimination on the basis of, for example, race, class, gender, sexual orientation, religion, disability, and age. It is here that the authoritarian model of schooling, with its emphasis on cognitive knowledge and a narrow range of skills and its general reluctance to engage with controversial issues, critical social and political analysis, feelings, identities and relationships, is particularly supportive of a non-democratic society under both authoritarian and democratic wider political systems.

Ramachandran also makes the point in relation to India that, while a basic level of political democracy has survived in India since independence in 1947 despite illiteracy and educational exclusion, education is still necessary for a more positive model of democracy where citizens actively engage in social and political activity:

> Education may have no one-to-one direct relationship with
> formal democracy, however, experience over the last six
> decades has shown that lack of education has affected the
> ability of citizens to engage with the institutions associated
> with the practice of democracy. It affects the ability of people
> to transcend the situation in which they find themselves at
> birth, impairs their ability to negotiate the maze of institutions
> that surround them, robs them of self-esteem and confidence
> and silences the voice of the marginalized and dispossessed.
> (2009, p. 671)

Unfortunately, and as we shall see in more detail in chapter 4, he further argues that the often poor quality and authoritarian type of formal education currently on offer in India is not likely to actually help greatly in developing the skills and dispositions required for more active forms of democratic participation.

What, then, about the converse of the authoritarian form of education – what are the benefits of more democratic forms of education? There are two ways of approaching this question, one indirect and one more direct. To a certain extent these mirror Sen's evaluative and effectiveness arguments for democracy set out in chapter 1. The indirect argument stresses the improvements to more conventional aspects of school quality that come from more democratic forms of organisation, i.e. that democracy is a more effective and efficient way of organising a school and therefore pupils themselves are more likely to actually experience and learn the organisational and bureaucratic skills and values necessary to support the operational functioning of democracy. For example, a more democratic school would be a more effective organisation because:

1. Rules are better kept by staff and students if democratically agreed to in the first place.
2. Communication in the school is improved through regular discussion.
3. There is an increased sense of responsibility as staff and students have more control over their organisation.
4. Decision-making is improved as a range of internal and external interests and opinions is considered. (Harber & Davies, 1997, p. 156)

The direct argument is that exposure to, and experience of, more democratic forms and processes of education contributes directly to specifically democratic skills, values and behaviours, and hence the wider sustainability of democratic institutions.

In terms of the first, indirect response, then, there is evidence that suggests that listening to pupils, encouraging their participation and giving them more power and responsibility (i.e. greater democratisation) can enhance school effectiveness and facilitate school improvement. In a review of the large literature on school effectiveness, for example, Dimmock (1995) argued that there are some 'generally agreed findings' which are accepted across cultures and systems' and that these are linked to student participation. Classroom organisation which encourages and rewards student involvement is linked to higher learning. Achievement is higher where students take responsibility for their own learning:

Students in effective schools are treated with dignity and encouraged to participate in the organisation of the school ... And as a result they feel valued. The effective school culture includes many of the core values associated with democracy, such as tolerating and respecting others, participating and expressing views, sharing and disseminating knowledge, valuing equity and equality and the opportunity for students to make judgements and choices. (Dimmock, 1995, pp. 166-167)

An empirical study of the practice of pupil democracy in Denmark, Holland, Sweden and Germany concluded that:

It seemed to every one clear that when pupils had a voice and were accorded value, the school was a happier place; where pupils are happy and given dignity, they attend more and they work more productively ... There was far more evidence of pupils taking responsibility for their own learning ... The link between legislation (for democracy in schools) and pupil achievement is an indirect but powerful one. (Davies & Kirkpatrick, 2000, p. 82)

Rutter et al (1979) in their major study of schools in the UK, published as *Fifteen Thousand Hours*, found that schools that give a large proportion of students responsibility had better examination results, better behaviour and attendance, and less delinquency. Trafford in his detailed study in one British school in the mid-1990s, and Hannam in his study in the early 2000s, of 12 schools which could manifestly demonstrate a claim to describe themselves 'student participative', found that there was a significant effect on both A level and GCSE examination grades, in Hannam's case a judgement also supported by Ofsted (see Trafford, 2003, p. 15).

In terms of developing countries, Harber (1993) found in interviews with Tanzanian teachers and pupils that they felt that greater pupil participation in decision-making improved communication in the school, reduced discipline problems and increased the confidence and discussion skills of learners. Lwehabura (1993) also studied four schools in Tanzania that all faced financial problems, resource shortages and low teacher morale. He found that, both in the ability to deal with practical problems of stringency, and in terms of examination success, the more democratically organised the school, the more effective (or perhaps less ineffective) it was. Similar, though more indicative, evidence exists on Ghana (Dadey & Harber, 1991, p. 15-16; Pryor et al, 2005).

The second, more direct issue is whether experience of more democratic forms lead to people with more democratic skills, values and attitudes? While there is a reasonably substantial literature on the theory, problems and practice of democratic education in relation to developing countries, much of which will be referred to in the chapters that follow, empirical research on the impact or outcome of more democratic forms of education is not common, but it does exist. There are some research findings from the United States of America and the United Kingdom which suggest that more democratic schools can contribute to both participatory skills and the values of operating democratically (Hepburn, 1984; John & Osborn, 1992). In terms of teaching methods, there is evidence that more open, democratic classrooms, which make greater use of discussion and other participatory methods, can foster a range of democratic political orientations, such as greater political interest, greater political knowledge and a greater sense of political efficacy (Ehman, 1980). Democratic and cooperative teaching methods have been shown to reduce interethnic conflict and to promote cross-cultural friendship (Lynch, 1992). A study of five racially mixed schools in the United States of America compared two more participant schools that stressed cooperative learning, interpersonal relationships, values clarification and heterogeneous groupings with three more traditional schools where students were streamed by achievement and lectured at in predominantly same race classes. The study found that cross-race interaction and friendships and a positive evaluation of different race students were significantly higher in the more participant schools than the more traditional, authoritarian ones (Conway & Damico, 1993). While there is not a large empirical research literature on the impact of democratic education on democratic values in the West, there is even less in developing countries. However, one study of a desegregated school in South Africa that had also adopted a more democratic ethos and structures found that there had been a dramatic decrease in racist comments and incidents in the schools as a result (Harber, 1998; Welgemoed, 1998).

Conclusion

There is a longstanding, historical and philosophical concern with the relationship between politics and education. Some of this has been aimed at social and political control while there is also a substantial body of literature on the potential relationship between education and democracy. While there is evidence of a positive relationship between education and democracy, sufficient attention has not been paid to how education might contribute to democracy and the type of education that can be most suitable for developing democratic values and behaviours. We know that certain forms of education are perfectly capable of leading to authoritarianism and violence, and that others may lead to support for only very limited forms of democracy, but that there is some evidence that experience of democratic relationships at school can lead to greater democratic skills and attitudes. The next chapter will consider how schools and classrooms might be organised on more democratic lines, both in principle and in terms of concrete examples from developing countries.

CHAPTER 3

Education *for* Democracy?

A much recycled joke: an educationalist who favours education for democracy dies and goes to heaven. God says to her that she can ask him any question and it will be answered truthfully. She asks God, 'Will the current model of schools ever be replaced by a more democratic form of learning?' to which God replies that there is some good news and bad news. 'The good news is, yes, schools will be replaced. The bad news is, not in my lifetime'.

In this chapter we start with the good news. Chapter 4 sets out the bad news.

Introduction

In chapter 1 we saw that in the last three decades there has been a significant global shift towards democracy as the preferred form of national government. Indeed, as the first draft of this chapter was being written, a region formerly clearly marked by non-democratic political regimes, North Africa and the Middle East, was undergoing a major political upheaval with both internal and external support for – and resistance to – greater democracy. While this shift towards greater democracy, or at least attempts at democracy, has both global and local causes, if education is to play a role in supporting, sustaining and consolidating democratic states and societies, then it will need to change in a direction that is more consistent and congruent with democratic values and practices in a number of ways and at a number of levels. This chapter then considers what the implications of education for democracy are for formal education – what might and what does it mean for:

- educational policy?
- democratic school leadership?
- whole-school decision-making and pupil voice?
- curriculum decision-making?
- methods of classroom teaching and learning?
- democratic discipline?
- democratic teacher professionalism?
- explicit programmes of civic education?

- the development of a democratic school culture?
- teacher education?
- school inspection?

Each of these key educational themes is discussed below both conceptually and, where possible, via a review of research on examples of more democratic forms of education that exist, or that have existed, in developing countries. Examples of good practice in relation to the aspects of democratic education set out above are described and discussed, as are issues of implementation to demonstrate what might be done in practice, how it might be done, and what the effects might be.

However, before we do this, it might be useful to give a more immediate flavour of what a more democratic school might look like so that each of the above themes can be set in a bigger picture. The opening chapters considered some of the main principles of, and ideas behind, democracy and democratic education. It is important to bear in mind that no two democratic schools will be identical as, by definition, certain aspects and characteristics will be decided locally within the school itself. Here we will provide a general overview or model of some key structural features and operating principles of a democratic school, then provide a pen portrait sketch of three non-state schools in developing countries which have operated along more democratic lines, before examining a major evaluation of 150 schools employing democratic principles across six developing countries.

What Does a Democratic School Look Like?

The following overview or model of a democratic school is based on a number of sources which have attempted to tackle this question in relation to both primary and secondary schools – Davies, 1995; Davies & Kirkpatrick, 2000; Davies et al, 2002, 2005; Trafford, 2003 – and which themselves have further references in them.

First of all, a democratic school would make clear and explicit its commitment to the values of education for democracy in its published documents – its prospectus, mission statement, etc. These would stress the procedural values of democracy discussed in chapter 2, including the regular, free, but polite exchange of views and opinions.

Its structures and practices would then involve a significant sharing of power over decision-making between key groups – staff, pupils, and parents. In practice, in most schools and in most countries, this would mean a significant shifting of power away from senior management and staff to others, and particularly to pupils. At the whole-school level this might well necessitate some form of freely elected school council where, depending on the size of the school, pupils and staff were represented, and some form of school governing body, where staff, pupils and parents were represented. Such bodies would have some power of decision-making and rule-making over meaningful educational areas of concern, such as budgets, staffing, curriculum, pupil and staff discipline and codes of conduct, and the use of premises, and not just more minor matters like social events or the school tuck shop. The operation of such bodies in terms of language used and scope of decision-making might well vary according to the age of the pupils involved, but age is not a reason for excluding pupils from decision-making.

A democratic school culture or ethos would also be characterised by democratic relationships built on trust and mutual respect, and therefore corporal punishment would be absent, as would other forms of physical punishment and all forms of bullying, whether staff to pupil, pupil to pupil or pupil to staff. More peaceful forms of discipline, such as peer mediation and restorative justice, would tend to prevail instead.

At classroom level, pupils would have a say in making the rules of classroom behaviour – a learning contract – and some say about curriculum content (what was to be learned and when), which classroom teaching methods were used, and which methods of assessment were used. As a result, more democratic schools tend to be characterised by more classroom variety and engagement. Also, in the classroom, teaching and learning would not shy away from controversial issues, but there would be a clear understanding of the ways they were to be discussed and debated by both staff and pupils. As well as experiencing more democratic relationships in the classroom as a result of the above, knowledge of how wider democracy works would also form part of the curriculum.

For all this to work, staff and students and parent governors would need to be explicitly trained in democratic skills or capabilities, such as speaking skills and putting a case across, listening skills, chairing skills, organising and planning skills, assertiveness, and conflict resolution skills.

No single school would probably ever completely match this model and each would have its own characteristics, some less democratic and some perhaps even more so. The brief summaries or thumbnail sketches of the characteristics of the following three actual schools in India and Ecuador is from Gribble (1998), and in these cases the emphasis is more on aspects of children's freedom of decision-making in relation to teaching and learning, and on closer, more caring and personalised classroom and school relationships. However, the distinctive nature of the schools tends to become clearer when they are compared with 'normal' or conventional schools. Another case study of a democratic school from Bolivia will be presented in the section on educational policy.

India: Neel Bagh School and Sumavanam School

Neel Bagh School was founded in 1972 and closed in 1987, but Sumavanam was founded on the same principles as Neel Bagh in 1982. Both are or were in rural areas in southern India. At Neel Bagh, school children were free to go, or not to go, to any class. Children were free to choose the kind of work they wanted to do at any particular moment. Teaching materials were geared to the attainments and abilities of each individual child and not to a mythical class average. Teaching was based on constant and cheerful encouragement. Every child was normally a teacher or the helper of other children. Every activity was meant to be enjoyable for both children and staff. No punishments of any kind were given. No dogmas, religious or political, were preached at the children.

At Sumavanam, the teaching is mostly conventional though the children are free to go, or not to go, to any class, even though in practice every child wants to go. Even though no homework is given, children want to come back to the school in the evening and carry on what they have been doing during the day. However, all children learn individually and at their own pace. There is also a stress on social equality with all children, including the 'untouchable' children, being treated exactly the same (which is still far from being the case in many Indian schools – see, for example, Harber, 2008, p. 464). The school is dominated by an ethos of mutual help rather than competition – Gribble summed up the atmosphere he observed in the class as 'eager industry' (1998, p. 123).

In order to appreciate the shift in relationships that such schools can represent, it helps to quote Gribble on the comparison both with the home background of the children at Sumavanam and with a local village school:

> Most of the children were beaten at home, some of them every day. Many of the fathers were drunkards and one of the older boys who normally slept at the school used to stay at home when his father was drunk to protect his mother. Almost all the children were undernourished, and it was not unheard of for a child to faint from hunger. One mother had recently died after her clothes had been soaked in kerosene and set alight; it was suspected it was not an accident. Shortly before my visit, a fourteen year old girl had been taken away from the school by her parents so that they could marry her to a young man who was unable to read or write. She was expected to start a family immediately and the bridegroom fiercely resented her education ... (while at the village school) ... the teachers, two well-dressed and polite women, had long canes. On the board in the classroom there were complicated equations, worked out for the top of the class to copy onto their slates ... many of them would not be able to add up but this was what was on

the curriculum for children of this age. The teachers told us
that the younger children were impossible to teach because
they did not want to learn. This was extraordinary, given the
enthusiasm of the children from the same background who
were lucky enough to go to Sumavanam. (1998, pp. 125-126)

Ecuador: the Pestalozzi School

The Pestalozzi School was opened in 1979. Here the children have
considerable freedom with the opportunity to experiment, investigate
and experience at first hand, and they are free to follow their own
interests rather than school instructions. The result, according to Gribble,
is a school overflowing with activity, but where there are no
conventional or compulsory lessons and where, consequently, disruption
and rebellion have no place. The founders of the school, in making a
connection with wider notions of democracy, believe that 'unless you
have the opportunity to make decisions for yourself as a child, when you
grow up you will never be truly autonomous; you will always be looking
for systems by which to live or leaders to guide you' (Gribble, 1998,
p. 132).

The idea is that the school provides a wealth of stimulus and
support and then the children make their own use of what is provided.
Gribble points out that the school can be compared to two famous
democratic schools in developed countries – Summerhill in the United
Kingdom, where there is a formal timetable of lessons for those that want
to follow them, and Sudbury Valley in the United States of America,
where the staff deliberately avoid guiding children even by their
provision of material. However, it also differs from these two schools in
that it is not democratically run because, although the children can make
supplementary rules themselves at both study group and weekly
meetings, the very few basic rules which concern safety and welfare are
decided and enforced by adults.

Again, perhaps the best way to understand the significance of the
freedoms involved is to contrast the experience at the Pestalozzi School
with a conventional school. One pupil said:

> I left [Pestalozzi] a year ago with a little group of friends and
> we went to try an ordinary school. We had friends outside
> who told us about the school sometimes, what an ordinary
> school was like, and they weren't happy when the holidays
> ended because they had to go to school or because they had to
> do homework, things like that. It was completely unfamiliar to
> me. So we decided to go and see what it was like and I stayed
> a year. At the beginning it was very difficult to fit in, because
> you do things they don't think of as normal, you don't behave

properly. We asked questions. It isn't right to ask questions.
You have to listen, you mustn't ask questions in an ordinary
school. Things like that. In the exams, I remember I helped one
of my friends – completely straightforwardly, I wasn't discreet
about it. I said 'You haven't got that right', and he said 'Oh yes,
I see', and then we discussed it. That was not normal. For us it
was normal ... And then I decided not to stay another year.
That was enough, I had seen what it was, that was all I
wanted. (Gribble, 1998, p. 143)

UNICEF Child Friendly Schools

In 2009, a major, multi-method evaluation, including direct observation,
took place of the UNICEF Child Friendly Schools (CFS) framework in
150 public or state schools in six developing countries – Nigeria, South
Africa, the Philippines, Thailand, Guyana, and Nicaragua – and the
following discussion is based on the final report (Osher et al, 2009). The
CFS framework recognises and supports schools in 95 countries. UNICEF
based the CFS framework on the 1990 Convention of the Rights of the
Child, as well as other international human rights instruments and
declarations. CFS are based on three interrelated principles:

- democratic participation – as rights holder, children and those who
  facilitate their rights should have a say in the form and substance;
- child-centredness – central to all decision-making in education is
  safeguarding the interest of the child; and
- inclusiveness – all children have a right to education.

Here we will report on the findings that are most directly relevant to
democratic education. Overall, they found that CFS, operating in very
different national and resource contexts, do nevertheless apply the three
key principles. There was a great deal of evidence that heads and
teachers 'speak the language of CFS'. Indeed, 'Often when asked,
teachers, school heads and families who have some comparative
perspective stated that the CFS has changed the way in which they and
others looked at education' (Osher et al, 2009, p. ii). The evaluation also
found that most schools in the six countries encouraged students' active
engagement with teachers using child-centred instructional techniques
and creating environments that encourage active learning, as well as trust
and respect. However, 'although teachers endorse active learning,
traditional notions of effective instruction persist' (p. 74) and school
heads and teachers identified the lack of trained teachers who can
implement child-centred instructional methods as a challenge in all six
countries. Moreover, specific UNICEF/CFS in-service training on
participatory and student-centred teaching seemed to have been the main
catalyst for change and was necessary because of poor quality initial

teacher education in this respect. Student or learner support for the idea that they experienced various forms of child-centred teaching ranged from 73% to 92% across countries (p. 81).

The study also found high levels of student and parent involvement in many, but not all, schools. There was also evidence of students taking an increasing role in decision-making activities through bodies like school councils or school committees, though it is important to note that the examples of activities that were used were limited to fundraising, celebratory activities, beautifying the school compound, and peer tutoring. It is also puzzling as to why students' views on students' roles in decision-making are not included in the findings of the report when those of teachers and head teachers are. Interestingly, when asked about how safe, inclusive and respectful the school was 19-56% of the students opted for 'needs improvement', while only 0-8% of head teachers and 7-53% of teachers (7-21%, excluding South Africa) did (pp. 23, 25, 26). Again perceptions of gender inclusivity and equality were much less marked among pupils than teachers and heads (p. 29). More than two thirds of students in each country reported that adults in their schools supported them, listened to them, and cared about them (though obviously a third did not think this).

These examples of attempts at more democratic forms of schooling are important in that they begin to highlight some key differences with the nature of the dominant form of mass schooling that exists in many developing societies, something which will be discussed in more detail in chapter 4. In this regard, what poses some interesting questions about such schooling is the title of UNICEF's initiative – Child Friendly Schools – does this mean that other schools, the vast majority globally, are not currently child friendly? Also interesting is that, although the CFS initiative is certainly working towards more democratic forms of education, and in some ways seems to be having some significant success, even in these schools there are still considerable problems, as particularly recorded in the responses of significant proportions of students. Moreover, the degree of sharing of decision-making power with students over matters central to teaching and learning and the running of the schools still seems somewhat limited. This may well not be a criticism of CFS, but simply a recognition of the difficulty of changing schools, especially government controlled schools, in a democratic direction, a theme that will be returned to again later in the book.

Education Policy

If there has been a shift to democracy in terms of national constitutions, statements and political practices in developing countries, is this reflected in policy statements about education? Is there officially a perceived link between education and political transition to democracy?

Although educational policies emanating from Ministries of Education in developing countries, whatever their sources and influences (Rust, 2000), may or may not be implemented in practice, they can at least set out an authoritative set of espoused goals and values which create a context and set a tone for what educationalists and educational institutions are supposed to take seriously. Put in a negative way, if clear statements about the establishment or improvement of democracy are absent from such educational policy statements, then it is less unlikely that education for democracy will be taken seriously by educational professionals and other stakeholders. A review of over 70 Ministry of Education websites in developing countries carried out for this book found that the main focus of most Ministry of Education websites is still on improving education itself and the role of education in contributing to economic development. However, many Ministries of Education do now make overt mention of democracy as a goal of education, and what follows is a selective account of some of them based both on the review of websites and published literature.

In relation to Africa, educational policy in Botswana, which has the longest post-independence record of democracy on the continent of Africa, makes explicit a connection between education and democracy, particularly in terms of the need for schools to facilitate political participation and elections based on informed choice through an appropriate curriculum (Adeyemi, 2002, p. 387). Similarly, and reflecting an aspiration towards democracy, if not always full achievement (Gyimah-Boadi, 2004, pp. 16-17), the 1998 Gambian education policy document emphasises the importance of creating through education, 'an awareness of the importance of peace, democracy and human rights, and the responsibility of the individual in fostering these qualities' (Gambian Department of State for Education, 1998, p. 10). However, it is worth noting that in both cases the emphasis is on knowledge and awareness, and little reference is made to actually experiencing democracy while at school. In Tanzania, the Education Sector Development Plan 2008-17 (http://www.moe.go.tz/) notes the importance of education for all as a requirement for democratic participation, and in Namibia, education policy since independence in 1990 has made explicit and continuing reference to the role of education in contributing to a democratic state and society (Harber, 1997, chap. 9; Zeichner & Dahlstrom, 1999), as has South Africa, which is discussed in more detail in chapter 5. But in Ghana, now considered a democratic success in Africa in that it has peacefully changed governments by democratic means on two occasions, there is no obvious reference to the potential contribution of education to democracy in either the Ministry of Education's mission statement, which stresses poverty alleviation and economic growth (http://www.ghana.gov.gh/index.php?ministry-of-education), or in the National Action Plan 2003-2015 (Ghana Ministry of

Education, Youth and Sports, 2003), which is based on the millennium development goals. An interview with a Ministry Official in Ghana in 2010 about policy on education for democracy produced a blank response (Agyemang, 2011).

As in the cases of Botswana, Gambia and Namibia, the connection between democratisation and education does seem to be made elsewhere. In Mexico, for example:

> For at least two decades now, Mexico has been in the throes of a fitful transition from a long history of corrupt authoritarian rule to a more fully democratic regime. Yet changes in civil society have not always kept pace with changes in the formal political–electoral sphere. Like so many other countries currently experiencing democratic transition, Mexico has looked to its school system to undertake the daunting task of cultivating democratic attitudes and dispositions among the new generation. (Levinson, 2004, p. 269)

Thus Objective 4 of the National Education Programme 2007-12 in Mexico is to:

> Provide a comprehensive education by balancing the formation of citizen values, the development of competence and the acquisition of knowledge, through regular classroom activities, practice teaching and an institutional environment in the support of democratic and intercultural coexistence. (http://www.sep.gob.mx/en/sep_en/)

In Colombia, and in keeping with the traditionally democratic practices of the Escuela Nueva schools (Harber & Davies, 1997, pp. 164-165):

> the Ministry of Education has carried out a thematic, conceptual and methodological revision of all areas of study in school, paying particular attention to ensuring that all aspects of human rights and participatory democracy are duly and clearly taken into account, in accordance with the draft general law on education submitted to Congress. (Meyer-Bisch, 1995, p. 106)

And in post-dictatorship Chile:

> The post-Pinochet governments of the 1990s have insisted that the teaching/learning process must be one through which the new generation will learn to live in a democracy; every effort, therefore, has been made to educate children and young people into a new culture infused with democratic values. (Aedo-Richmond, 2002, p. 194)

While in Trinidad and Tobago, the Education Policy paper 1993-2003 states that:

> there is a need to create and sustain a humanized and democratized system of education for the survival of our democracy. (http://www.moe.gov.tt/index.html)

In Indonesia:

> In 1998, in the euphoric sense of possibilities at the end of thirty-two years of authoritarian rule, the scope of citizenship education for supporting democracy was quickly seen. (Fearnley-Sander & Yulaelawati, 2008, p. 115)

In the Philippines:

> The number of Executive Orders, Proclamations of the President and Circulars and memoranda of the Department of Education, Culture and Sports attest to the strong support and recognition that the government gives to the principles of education for democracy. (Meyer-Bisch, 1995, p. 114)

While in Fiji:

> Education should holistically develop and inculcate in every child the fundamental ethical, moral, social, spiritual, and democratic values. (http://www.education.gov.fj/)

In Sri Lanka, education for democracy is also given a strong emphasis:

> Being a democratic nation ensuring and promoting democratic values and behaviour has been a priority area in government activities over many years. Despite these, terrorist activities have arisen and increased in recent history. In fact, terrorism has become the biggest threat to humanity and Sri Lanka is going through a difficult period of over 20 years facing ethnicity based terrorism. And the education system was partly responsible for this because these undemocratic activities happened mostly through the youth who left school a few years back or the youth who are still students. (http://www.moe.gov.lk/)

In South Korea, an educated person is officially, among other things:

> a person who contributes to the development of the community where he/she lives on the basis of democratic citizenship. (Kennedy & Chi-Kin Lee, 2008, p. 90)

Even in Afghanistan, Article 2.5 of the Education law states that education should:

> Strengthen the spirit of respect to human rights, protection of
> the women rights, democracy and elimination of every kind of
> discrimination, in light of the Islamic values and prevention of
> addiction to narcotics. (p. 6)
> (http://english.moe.gov.af/index.php/strategic-plan?start=2)

So, there is at least some evidence that some governments in developing countries are taking the potential role of education in supporting democracy seriously in relation to policy statements. Indeed, Nagata (2007) describes how government educational reform policy led to the creation of a democratic school in Bolivia, which provides a further useful case study of what a more democratic school in a developing country can and might look like. La Floresta School in Cochabamba was founded in 1996 by a woman teaching in a small village school in Tiquipaya on the outskirts of Cohabamba. She agreed with the basic approach of the new educational policy which stressed decentralisation and public participation in education. The policy reform called for a complete change in the curriculum with priority of learning over teaching and a focus on the learning needs of individuals. However, her own school refused to reform and continued on the way it always had based on one-sided, teacher-driven instruction. The school split into conservative and reformist factions with the latter going independent and founding La Floresta as a new public or state school.

The school, which includes children of both primary and secondary ages, was founded upon three social principles of social inclusion, tolerance and mutual respect of diversity, and the importance of social learning and practice at one-week camps (twice annually). It was also founded upon 14 educational principles which included: studying how to learn; non-directive teaching; developing autonomous learning (particularly at the secondary level in terms of individual research projects); emphasis on the real needs of children; holistic learning rather than fragmented courses and specialities; placing value on analysis rather than accumulation of information; self-evaluation and mutual evaluation by student peers; putting into practice democratic principles, such as student assemblies and self-organisation; and a Productive Month where students build up experience of the world outside the school.

The school is organised not by classes or grades but by levels, which are loosely defined age groups. Each level has its own building and these levels are the basis blocks of self-governance in the school so that pupils and teachers in each smaller unit can make age-appropriate rules. Level assembly meetings are held about twice monthly, and rules and their infringement are discussed, although essentially no punishments are imposed. Because of an earlier problem with time keeping, the one rule that comes with a punishment is for people arriving late who are then sent home. As discussed in chapter 1 on political development theory, a functioning democracy needs to be built of a relatively efficient and punctual bureaucracy.

At the school almost no traditional instruction by teachers is evident or organisation of learning by conventional school subjects – instead teachers guide or advise and facilitate children on the processes of autonomously accessing information and analysing it according to their interests and needs. Nagata makes an important observation about the democratic culture of La Floresta School. He notes that pupils respect teachers throughout Bolivia:

> However, they appear to differ considerably from students at other schools in the way that they respect their teachers. What the students at La Floresta school respect is that the adults at the school have the capacity of character and expertise to give them guidance. They do not respect the teachers simply because they are teachers, or because they have qualifications as teaching staff. In fact, in some respects the students are extremely severe in their evaluations of the adults, and they do not respect adults because they are adults. Close observation of everyday life at the school reveals that where the relationships between teachers and students are not based on status or rank, neither are they based on the equality found among friends. The relations between them are founded on trust and confidence, which is a kind of relationship found only very rarely in traditional education in Bolivia. However, this student view of adults frequently clashes with village traditions. In the village, the students of the school are seen as impudent, and it seems that they constantly come into conflict with villagers who are unable to accept their independent attitude. (Nagata, 2007, p. 1)

This latter point about clashes between traditional culture and the often new behaviours and attitudes of democracy is an enduring theme of attempts to make schools more democratic. This will be further discussed in chapter 4, and specifically in relation to subsequent changes at La Floresta, as one of the obstacles to greater democratic change in education. Here it is important to note that the school rigorously distinguishes between local cultural traditions that should be respected and traditions that are wrong in terms of human rights and children's rights.

We will now take key features of formal education in turn and consider each in terms of their potential to contribute to education for democracy, and consider any examples of good practice from developing countries in relation to principles of democratic education.

Leadership, Management and Pupil
Voice in Decision-Making in Schools

In 2005, UNESCO's annual Education for All (EFA) Global Monitoring Report focused on the quality of education. It discussed, approvingly, UNICEF's Child Friendly Schools model as part of a discussion of school improvement. It stated that:

> One implication of reforms driven by school improvement, however, interpreted and applied, is greater school autonomy. Such reforms are usually associated with decentralisation. School-based management and leadership are crucial aspects of any reform strategy in which control and responsibility are devolved.

It went on to add that this is, 'more democratic, allowing teachers and parents to take school-based decisions' – though no mention is made of pupils (UNESCO, 2005, pp. 172-173).

While the Global Monitoring Report stresses that the effect on 'learning outcomes' was equivocal, these are defined in terms of performance in tests and examinations. What is of significance for this book is that providing a democratic experience at school, and therefore developing democratic values and skills, is impossible without a certain level of decentralised school autonomy. School autonomy does not by any means guarantee democratic decision-making, however if power and control is primarily centralised with the Ministry of Education, province, or local authority, schools and head teachers do not have any power to make decisions, and therefore have nothing to share with pupils.

In the study of the Child Friendly Schools in six developing countries discussed above, the report notes that, respondents overwhelmingly recognised the importance of the school head for the success of CFS. Respondents described the school head as 'the pivot' and said 'a strong school head is critical' (Osher et al, 2009, p. 113).

The head is indeed likely to be a key figure, but his or her role in leading and managing a democratic school depends very much on how power is exercised and, most importantly, dispersed and distributed. Traditionally, head teachers have not necessarily exercised their role in a democratic manner, as will be discussed in the following chapter of this book. However, some key leadership principles in setting up and operating a democratic school are put forward by one head who has considerable experience in the matter:

– Democracy can only spread if led from the top by the school leadership group and, above all, by the head
– Start with both a clear vision and purpose as well as structures
– Plan, consult and work together: all stakeholders involved

- Democracy is about more than just asking pupils what they think about things
- School councils only thrive when the head is personally involved
- Class tutors are crucial to developing democracy through encouragement, discussion and communication
- There is also a need to promote democratic practice at the classroom level
- A democratic school removes barriers between teachers and pupils and senior managers and teachers
- Teachers and school leaders need to seek opportunities to abandon status and defence mechanisms and meet pupils on equal terms
- Everyone in the school needs to learn the skills of operating democratically. (Trafford, 2003, pp. 91-93)

In a study of democratic leadership in education, Woods (2005, chap. 9) notes that there is always likely to be resistance to democratic leadership and a more democratic school culture based on: self-interest (the power-holder who wants to maintain the status quo or those that do not have power that want to avoid responsibility); habits of deference; belief in the superior efficiency of hierarchy and governance by command and control; and apathy and reasoned scepticism. He suggests that self-interest needs to move towards, or be balanced by more, receptive attitudes of collective responsibility, deference by assertiveness, belief in hierarchy by belief in collegiality, apathy by activism, and reasoned scepticism by reasoned confidence in democratic leadership. He lists the main capabilities and skills required in democratic leadership as: status adaptability (shedding or taking on status as appropriate); communicative virtues; independence; knowledge and understanding of democratic principles and practices; skills in developing and sustaining community; respect; capacity for profound participation; critical reflection on inner potential and outer context; cultivation of 'power with'; and conflict handling.

In Thailand, for example, school principals have traditionally been viewed as the sole decision-maker in schools. Principals expected their orders to be followed with relatively little discussion or questioning from staff and with no overt dissent. Heads are therefore ill-equipped to lead change in a more democratic direction. However, Kennedy and Chi-Kin Lee (2008) cite research that suggests that change is indeed possible. The research on three case study schools suggests that after a two year training course for heads, designed to change leadership and management styles, the following occurred:

All three school directors adopted more participatory
management styles. They took specific steps including:

building widespread support for the vision of change;
reducing the 'status gap' between themselves and the
stakeholders; and gathering information that embraced a
variety of perspectives from stakeholders prior to and during
the adoption of school changes.

All school directors attempted to create an atmosphere of
harmonious group orientation (a sense of family) and
teamwork. In addition, organisational rituals such as study
visits, fairs and celebrations provided occasions for fun and a
further impetus for change through enhanced morale and
pride.

All directors encouraged voluntary participation in the
change effort first by more active and knowledgeable teachers
and, over time, initially sceptical teachers joined the project
activities as well. (Kennedy & Chi-Kin Lee, 2008, p. 125)

It is also interesting to note in the light of the discussion of teacher
education below, that the schools used action research to foster staff
learning.

So, more democratic school leadership and organisation creates a
context where pupil voice can be heard and can influence decision-
making, often through the use of different forms of school councils. Pupil
participation in classroom teaching and learning will be further
discussed below, but here the concern is more with whole-school matters
and the role of school councils and their equivalents. However, it has to
be admitted initially that the daily reality of schooling for many, if not
most, pupils globally is *not* necessarily one of participating in decision-
making about school organisation. This is despite most countries in the
world being signatories to the UN Convention on the Rights of the Child
which is supposed to guarantee to children the right to express their own
views freely in all matters affecting them. It is also despite the argument
that democracy is learned behaviour – in order to develop democratic
values and behaviours we have to see and experience democratic
practice. While there is now an increasing literature on pupils' views of
schooling, which tends to be critical about their lack of opportunities for
genuine participation (Harber, 2010), most of this is based in and is about
schooling in Western industrialised nations. However, a study of
children's views of schooling that did take place in Indonesia noted that
this was one of the first of its kind in the country because children's
views on education are not usually taken into account by researchers or,
as the study established, by teachers and educational policymakers:

parents and policy makers at all levels make decisions and
formulate policies generally on the basis of adult perspectives.
Their policies related to children's necessities are mostly
focussed on the provision and the protection of the children

based on adult views whereas children's right to participation
is neglected and remains a formality. (Wibowo, 2005, p.190)

There are nevertheless exceptions and positive examples of how pupil voice can be a structured part of school decision-making. Khan (2006) provides a useful overview of who participates in school councils in developing countries and how, with a particular focus on Africa. For the present discussion, the main concern is with the role of pupils or learners in school councils and out of the seven countries in Africa cited by Khan as having functioning school councils, only three (Ethiopia, South Africa and Tanzania) involved pupils in their deliberations. Historically, as discussed in chapter 2, Tanzania has had a record of involving pupils in school decision-making via school councils, as part of the policy of education for self-reliance between the late 1960s and the 1990s (Harber, 1997, chap. 6). Moreover, post-independence reforms in Namibia also established school councils with pupil representatives (Angula & Grant Lewis, 1997; Harber, 1997, chap. 9), and there have been some attempts at involving pupils in school councils in Ghana (Pryor et al, 2005). However, South Africa is the country in Africa where a policy and practice of pupil involvement in school councils has perhaps been most developed and this will be discussed in detail later in the book.

Kahn also notes that pupils are increasingly playing a role in school councils in schools in Latin America, and this is indeed the case as the following three examples from Brazil demonstrate. They are based closely on Paulo Freire's ideas of dialogue and conscientisation, as discussed above. First, McCowan (2010a, b) describes the Plural School initiative of Belo Horizonte, a city with over five million inhabitants. Here the explicit aim is to develop democratic citizenship by providing pupils with an experience of a democratic school culture. McCowan uses the term 'prefigurative' to describe the initiative as it describes forms of political organisation that reflect the qualities of the ideal society that is being aimed for – schooling becomes a microcosm of the ideal democratic society and state based on a new relationship between teachers and pupils. As the Municipal Secretariat of Education puts it:

It is necessary that a dialogical relationship is established in
the classroom, where all can put ideas forward, ask, exchange,
negotiate meanings, share. It is necessary to break with the
monological pedagogy in which only the teacher speaks.
(Cited in McCowan, 2010b, p. 28)

However, another aim of organising schools more democratically was to provide a more inclusive environment so as to combat 'school failure', represented by drop-out and repetition of whole school years which affects some, poorer, social groups more than others.

All schools in the initiative have direct elections for head teachers, and pupils are part of the electorate. Pupils in the Plural Schools participate in three bodies. First, the school assembly with representatives from the whole school community has the function of making decisions on key issues, such as arrangements during a teachers' strike. Second, the smaller school council with pupil, teacher and community representatives has a more executive role, including responsibility for the school budget. While there are state guidelines on the curriculum, individual schools have a large degree of freedom regarding what is taught and therefore they construct their own distinctive politico-pedagogical plans for the curriculum. The third is the *gremios* which are associations which organise cultural, sporting and political activities and which are elected by the pupils themselves. These have an organising committee of up to 12 or so pupils, but involve much greater numbers at meetings and events.

McCowan notes that pupils do change school rules, such as not wearing school uniform or being able to leave school at lunchtimes, but that the main difference was that students were more aware of their rights and were able to articulate them, both in particular classrooms and the wider school. Moreover, participation in the school context led to political action outside, student campaigning being instrumental in getting funding to improve school buildings, soundproofing from traffic noise and extra teachers to make up for a shortfall.

Second, McCowan (2010b) also describes the network of 1500 schools belonging to the Landless Movement. Again, pupils participate in the election of head teachers. They also have representatives on the school council which is the highest body of school management, with responsibilities for financial resources, the school calendar, the politico-pedagogical plan, and guaranteeing the responsiveness of the council to the wishes of all members of the community. Within classes, pupils are encouraged to organise class councils, assemblies, establish classroom rules, evaluate and change the educational process and teaching styles, propose voluntary work, and generally debate the direction of the school. As with the examples from India and Ecuador discussed above, the deputy head of one of the schools spoke of the difference between these schools and many others. Speaking of pupils who had gone on to study in other schools, the deputy head said that the pupils said that in their previous school they could complain, they could change things, influence and participate – 'there they don't let us do anything' (McCowan, 2010b, p. 35).

Third, are the Citizen Schools of Porto Alegre which are all situated in the most impoverished parts of the city. Gandin and Apple (2003) note that:

> Education in Brazil, as a rule, is centralised. In the majority of
> states and cities there are no elections for the city or state
> council of education (traditionally a bureaucratic structure,
> with members appointed by the executive), let alone for

> principals of schools. The curriculum is usually defined by the
> secretariats of the cities and states. Since the resources are
> administered by centralised state agencies, schools have very
> little or no autonomy. (2003, p. 163)

However, the Citizen School project represents a sharp contrast with this description. The principles behind the Citizen Schools was decided on in a democratic and deliberative forum known as the Constituent Congress of Education, composed of key members of school communities – parents, pupils, teachers, and administrators. The key aim that emerged was a radical democratisation in the municipal schools in terms of management, access to the school and access to knowledge. The whole school community elects the head teacher by direct vote and the head is therefore someone who represents the school community rather than the interests of government. A key aspect of this is curriculum and what counts as knowledge. Action research is carried out by teachers, pupils and parents in the community to establish the main concerns, interests and worries of the community. Then the most significant ones are constructed into interdisciplinary 'thematic complexes' that will guide classroom learning for a period of time. Thus, the curriculum is based on the real problems of the pupils and the community rather than 'official' knowledge determined from above.

Each school has a school council composed of teachers, other school staff, parents, pupils and one member of the administration, usually the head teacher. Seats on the council are divided equally, 50% for teachers and staff and 50% for parents and pupils, and training is provided for all participants. The school council discusses school administration, the curriculum (as part of the process described above), the allocation of economic resources (in a context of significantly increased school financial autonomy), and monitoring the implementation of decisions.

Sometimes the need for more democratic change in the organisation of schooling and a greater role for student voice are only brought home when an emergency leads to the disruption of 'normal' educational structures and practices. Indeed, as has been argued in relation to post-emergency education in South Asia, if schools are to fully and truly become safe learning spaces for children traumatised by an emergency then in many cases they must be changed in some fundamental ways so that children at the very least are not beaten there, sexually abused by pupils and other students, and not discriminated against because of their caste or ethnicity (Davies et al, 2008). At the moment it is automatically assumed by many concerned with emergencies that for vulnerable groups, like AIDS orphans, traditionally organised schools are uncontroversially a 'safe space' and the main need is simply to ensure that children attend school. Consequently there have been few large-scale discussions about the need to transform the school environment itself to better serve such vulnerable groups of children to give them a voice and a meaningful, safe and supportive experience in school. Kendall makes this point strongly in relation to AIDS orphans:

> It will not be easy to rethink the roles and forms that education and formal schooling might play in vulnerable children's and communities lives, as it will require destabilising international and state definitions, theories, frameworks for actions and relational practices that are well-established and relatively comfortable for those in power. If the international development community is to play a just role in this epidemic, however, this is exactly what must occur. (2008, p. 382)

This was just the case in Mindanao in the Philippines where the conflict has disrupted and interrupted schooling for long periods of time. As a result, Oxfam have implemented a programme called 'Partnership in Education for Community Empowerment'. Aikman comments that:

> Through reform of schools, and supporting and training a new generation of caring teachers, the programme set out to transform schools into places able to protect children from violence and the fear of violence, respect their rights, promote new and deepening forms of democracy and become a beacon for wider community change. The Mindanao programme came about because different actors – NGOs, local communities and government – identified the school as providing an opportunity and space for change and saw young people as the catalysts for peace-building beyond its walls. In its approach it is strengthening the school as a place for peace and learning, classrooms as social spaces for democratic and peaceful relationships, and drawing on a consensus that radical change is needed to break decades of conflict and deepening poverty. (2010, p. 27)

Sometimes pupil voice can be useful in helping to stop some of the negative features of schooling in less fundamental ways. In Nepal, corporal punishment, though illegal since 2005, still persists in schools. However, since the 1990s, there has been a strong growth of children's clubs in schools in Nepal often facilitated by international NGOs supportive of a rights-based approach to development, such as Save the Children. Bhattarai (2010) describes how two such clubs have campaigned against violence against children in schools, including corporal punishment both by speaking to, and negotiating with, teachers and parents, and by trying to take responsibility for non-violent discipline in the schools themselves. Bhattarai notes that in the two cases he examined corporal punishment was significantly reduced due to children's persuasive efforts and comments that 'One of the major impacts felt among children is that they speak out and their level of confidence is higher' (2010, p. 54).

The Children's Village School in Thailand also arose out of a context of violence. Nagata (2007) describes how the rapid economic growth in Thailand from the mid-1980s to the mid-1990s brought with it a number of social problems, including increasing rural–urban migration and the spread of slums in which levels of poverty led to increasing child labour and child physical and sexual abuse. The Children's Village School was started in 1979 as a refuge for orphans and other children who had suffered in such circumstances. The idea was to provide a secure, safe and caring environment in which children could begin to recover from the violence and deprivations which they had experienced. The school was inspired by the practice of Summerhill School in the UK and its emphasis on self-determination by children. The school therefore has a school council as a form of self-government where:

> children who serve as jurors and secretaries name and assign appropriate punishments to those – not only students but also staff – who have inconvenienced (trespassed on the freedom of) other people. Punishments are on the order of forbidding them to watch videos, not allowing them sweets, or not allowing them to leave the school grounds. No corporal punishment is ever imposed. Like Summerhill School, too, the self-government assembly has the important function of amending and abolishing school regulations, creating new regulations, and so on. (Nagata, 2007, p. 29)

While in some of the positive case studies of school councils described above, pupils have had an influence on the core business of schooling – what is taught, learned, and how – through the school council, this is unusual. Khan (2006) in her survey of school councils in developing countries concludes that most school councils 'tend to limit themselves to administrative functions. Decisions related to classroom pedagogy and curricula are infrequent' (p. 100), a point that is also true of Asian countries (Kennedy & Chi-kin Lee, 2008, p. 98), and more globally (Harber, 2010). However, while pupils only rarely get a say on the composition of the school curriculum as a whole, there are many smaller and day to day ways in which pupils can be involved in influencing and shaping what is taught and learned in classrooms, through more participatory and diverse forms of teaching and learning.

Curriculum, Learning and Teaching

It is important to note at the beginning of this section that democratic education means greater variety in teaching and learning methods with pupils being actively engaged in learning on a regular basis. Discussion, group work, projects, visits, simulations and independent study will all be used more often than in a traditional, authoritarian school. However, while democratic education implies variety and regular participation in learning, it does not necessarily mean constant participation. Learners need to experience many different forms of learning and interaction if they are to develop as flexible, self-sufficient and democratically skilled people. At times this means being able to digest, organise and analyse information provided by others (e.g. teachers, visiting speakers and other pupils); at other times it means knowing how to look for information oneself, and at other times it means knowing how to discuss in order to clarify one's thinking about a controversial issue or to argue a case coherently. However, in the traditional authoritarian school such variety is not possible as the emphasis is overwhelmingly on teacher-dominated transmission.

Any move away from sole reliance on teacher-led instruction in the classroom involves a small shift of power from the teacher to the learners. When pupils are encouraged to ask questions, and feel safe doing so, rather than simply answering questions asked by teachers, then the agenda and content of learning has shifted in a small way in their direction as the teacher is no longer in complete control. The same goes for classroom discussion and group work. When pupils do projects or an independent study, or prepare for a presentation to the class, although within the boundaries of a school subject, they nevertheless play a part in deciding what will be researched, how it will be researched and how it will be presented.

Therefore greater classroom participation and activity is an important aspect of a more democratic education. Does it happen in schools in developing countries? Generally, the answer – as we shall see in chapter 4 – is not as much as it ought to or would be desirable. However, there are examples of good practice where the barriers to more democratic forms of classroom interaction have been overcome, or overcome at least partially.

The 2005 EFA Global Monitoring Report on the quality of education describes the difficulty of moving away from the dominance of:

> rigid, chalk-and-talk, teacher centred/dominated, lecture-
> driven pedagogy or rote learning ... Such pedagogy places
> students in a passive role, limiting their activity to memorizing
> facts and reciting them to the teacher ... Such teaching
> practices are the norm in the vast majority of classrooms in
> sub-Saharan Africa and elsewhere, even in the most affluent
> countries. (UNESCO, 2005, p. 152)

The report then contrasts this with more desirable 'open-ended and discovery-based pedagogies' which is participatory, interactive, child-centred, and characterised by cooperative learning and inquiry, and which fosters conceptual understanding, critical thinking, and problem-solving skills. It cites a number of programmes that have adopted such pedagogies, for example, the Escuela Nueva programme in Colombia, the non-formal primary education programme of the Bangladesh Rural Advancement Programme, the Escuela Nueva Unitaria programme in Guatemala, the Fe y Alegria schools in Latin America, convergent pedagogy in Mali, and the Aga Khan Foundation-supported Dar es Salaam Primary Schools Project. In addition, such programmes are also described as having some or all of the following characteristics: peer tutoring among learners, carefully developed self-guided learning materials, teacher – and student – constructed learning materials, and a school focus on learning, rather than teaching (UNESCO, 2005, p. 153).

As this list of programmes suggests, pedagogical reform in a more democratic direction has tended to be based on specific programme interventions, usually with a strong element of in-service teacher education. The nature and impact of such programmes will be discussed in the next section. However, while child-centred pedagogy has become one of the most pervasive educational ideas globally, and in sub-Saharan Africa specifically, partly at least through donor encouragement (Chisholm & Leyendecker, 2008, p. 3), it is important to note that classroom practice is often very different and is sometimes neither 'teacher-centred' nor 'child-centred', but a mixture of the two. In a study of primary school classroom practice based on interviews with, and observation of, teachers in Tanzania, Barrett (2007) argues against a simple polarisation of teacher-centred versus child-centred pedagogy in systems in which teachers work in a context of significant resource scarcity, such as very large classes, low salaries, understaffed rural schools, a heavy workload, the absence of professional development opportunities, and hence demoralisation. A long school day and an overcrowded syllabus also do not help and nor does the ranking of all schools according to the school leaving examinations, which also tends to orient teaching to examination performance. Thus, 'these conditions erode teachers' willingness and ability to invest extra time and energy into their work' (p. 280), and teachers are therefore unlikely to take on more participatory forms of teaching and learning that are expensive and demanding of teacher time on a large scale. Question and answer was used extensively in every lesson observed and teachers saw this as 'participation' contrasted with 'theory' or 'lecture' methods. However, Barrett also notes that there was also some degree of mixing of teaching styles which challenged some assumptions that are made about the dominance of explicitly controlled, whole class teaching in Africa:

> Some believed it was important to understand pupils
> conceptualisation of subject-matter, to make use of the
> knowledge children acquired outside of school and that
> primary education should be useful and relevant to children's

present contexts as well as their future life-careers. These
ideals could all be described as features of constructivist
pedagogies. Many teachers readily adopted the discourse of
participation and recognised the importance of praise,
although not all practiced it. They also recognised the
individuality of children and several claimed they gave
personal counselling to those suffering neglect at home.
(p. 288)

Even though overall teaching was characterised by explicit teacher
control and the absence of personalisation, Barrett's study is an
important reminder that classroom realities are likely to be more mixed
in contexts which are classified as either more 'democratic' or more
'authoritarian', and that there are good contextual reasons why teachers
work the way they do. Altinyelken's study of the introduction of child-
centred pedagogy into Uganda makes a similar point. Noting that
attempts to introduce child-centred pedagogy have occurred in Ethiopia,
Tanzania, Namibia, The Gambia and South Africa, she concludes overall
that:

These case studies seem to suggest that prescriptive
instructional behaviour is so deeply embedded in the
professional culture that even if child-centred approaches are
initially embraced, they disappear with time and are replaced
with traditional instructional behaviour. (2010, p. 156)

The Ugandan government introduced child-centred pedagogy into the
curriculum in 2000. By this it means:

1. Children should have a chance to interact with each other
and with the teacher during the lesson
2. Class activities should be organised so that children learn by
doing. They should be able to move around from time to time
and to use their hands
3. Activities should be organised around a variety of learning
materials and children should be able to handle those
materials
4. Children should have the opportunity, from time to time, to
have influence in the direction the lesson (or day) takes. Allow
the lesson to reflect the interests, abilities and concerns of
children. (Cited in Altinyelken, 2010, p. 158)

Interviews and observation in eight schools suggested there was a high
level of receptiveness to, and approval of, the ideas of child-centred
pedagogy. However, observations suggested that the pedagogical reforms
actually permeated the classrooms to a lesser extent because of perceived
contextual obstacles similar to those discussed by Barrett (2005). Though
in a minority, some teachers had a superior ability to engage students

75

with the lesson, and used a variety of teaching techniques and learning approaches to stimulate and reinforce learning. Also, some aspects of the pedagogical reforms, such as organising students into groups and using teaching aids, were more readily adopted than others. Others, such as facilitating interactions among pupils, allowing them to influence the direction of the lesson or the day, or organising meaningful group activities in mixed achievement groups, were ignored. Altinyelken agrees with Barrett in rejecting a polarised view as the teachers in her sample revealed a hybrid of traditional and reform-oriented practices.

Writing on her research on teacher education in Ghana, Dull (2006, p. 27) also notes that lessons that she observed had humour, performance and questions to engage children and that 'Their classrooms were rarely the dull and autocratic environments caricatured by aid-givers and scholars of African education'. In a seminar discussion on a number of lessons that all members of the group of student teachers had observed, they were asked whether or not they thought the lesson was democratic. One lesson was thought to be democratic because 'every child was asked to and allowed to bring out his/her view', and the lesson was thought to be child-centred and activity oriented since the pupils were involved in activities through which a concept was developed, rather than being spoon-fed. The student teachers consistently defined lessons as democratic when teachers asked questions of the children. Dull, however, comments that despite this participation and interaction:

> the teachers questions elicited facts and information, not opinions or ideas or critical analysis. Part of this related to children's facility with English. However, even in upper-level classes, open-ended discussions were avoided ... Teachers were therefore expected to lead students to correct answers and definitive conclusions about a topic ... Many teachers told me that they would never admit that they were wrong or did not know an answer to children. If teachers did not know an answer they would ignore the question or scold the child for distracting the class. (2006, pp. 29-30)

Understanding the contextual obstacles to more democratic forms of teaching and learning, and the resulting hybridity of teaching methods, is important in appreciating the gains and small steps that teachers make in situations of resource scarcity and either insufficient or poor quality teacher education. Often such hybridity marks a step forward from sole reliance on teacher-centred methods and may even be a step on a longer journey. Vavrus (2009, p. 303) studied a teacher education college in Tanzania actually founded on the principles of social constructivism, which encourages student teachers to view themselves as facilitators who elicit pupil knowledge and who enable independent and peer to peer learning in the classroom. This is opposed to the formalism of traditional, teacher-centred pedagogy. As a result of the mixed responses and behaviours from staff and students she calls for what she calls a 'contingent constructivism' which is more attuned to a country's cultural, economic and political conditions. She concludes that:

> it is critical that policy makers recognise that the examination system, the material infrastructure of schools and the length and quality of teacher education programmes limit the likelihood of a fundamental shift from formalism to constructivism ... If a 'cognitive revolution' through the use of social constructivist pedagogy were truly sought by international financial institutions, then they would need to promote the conditions for such as approach to flourish. This would include lowering, not raising, teacher/student ratios and increasing, not shortening, the length of teacher education programmes to allow time for the transition from formalism to constructivism ... [but] ... the international financial institutions that influence teacher education reform policies do not appear prepared to devote the necessary resources for them to succeed. (2009, pp. 309-310)

However, while realistic and understandable in the contexts of many developing countries, it is still nevertheless open to question whether such hybridity or contingency actually represents a significant enough shift to contribute in any meaningful or widespread way to the learning of democratic skills and values via teaching methods. It also remains true, as will be discussed in more detail in chapter 4, that more straightforward, teacher-led and essentially authoritarian forms of classroom practice remain dominant in most education systems. However, there are positive examples of significant pedagogical reform in a democratic direction stemming from specific in-service teacher education programmes and it is to these that we turn in the next section.

Teacher Education and Professional Identity

At the heart of the problem of creating more democratic schools is changing teacher professional identity and practice. In the context of education for democracy, Davies et al describe three ideal types of teacher professionalism which tend to have the following characteristics:

> 1. *Unprofessional* – not doing the job properly – teacher absenteeism, unplanned lessons, lack of punctuality, the teacher has more than one job, instances of sexual abuse, strong use of corporal punishment, not collegiate, hostility to, and distance from, children.
> 2. *Restricted professional* – teachers that do the basic job but are primarily concerned with the mastery and exercise of

technical skills in the classroom, a concern with basic competence, teacher-centred, tend to blame children for not learning, little CPD, unimaginative or routine teaching, occasional use of corporal and psychological punishment, rigid, individualised, instrumental. Essentially minimally competent in an authoritarian manner. Personal rewards to teachers primarily extrinsic.

3. *Extended professional* – uses autonomous and independent judgement to reflect on what they are doing, they don't just follow the rules but take active responsibility for themselves and their pupils, child-centred, variety of methods, collaborative, trusting, no corporal punishment, part of CPD support system, adaptive and flexible. Personal rewards to teachers primarily intrinsic. (2005, pp. 35-39)

The problem for democratic education is not just moving from unprofessional teachers to restricted professionals, who at least turn up and plan their lessons, but operate in an authoritarian manner, but to create new, more democratic forms of extended professionalism. Certainly, as argued in chapters 1 and 2, competent and functioning, but authoritarian teachers and schools can help to teach the values and behaviours necessary for the modern bureaucratic organisation that forms the social basis on to which democracy is to be built. As Dull (2006, p. 30) puts it in relation to Ghana, lessons may not be critical or philosophical, but they do teach 'practical and "modern" behaviours and skills', such as hygienic practices or scientific explanations for natural phenomena. However, if teaching is also to contribute to the development of democracy more directly, then pupils will also need to be exposed to more explicitly democratic practices as well. For example, in Bolivia a teacher is expected to be a 'democratic person who stimulates student participation not only in learning activities but also regarding decisions that concern them while generating a climate of respect where different opinions and criteria are heard' (cited in Avalos, 2000, p. 10).

Vulliamy (1998, p. 12) doubts whether it is possible to change the teaching styles of teachers in developing countries 'unless there are massive in-service training programmes to support them'. He further argues that if such programmes are absent then it might be better to concentrate on producing more effective and efficient authoritarian teachers:

in developing countries, where both the prior level of educational attainment of teachers and their degree of teacher training are low, the quality of teaching is better enhanced by making improvements in formalistic teaching, such as better

> textbooks, than by attempting to convert teachers from such
> teaching to the progressive approaches. (p. 13)

As will be discussed in more detail in chapter 4, in many developing countries (and elsewhere) initial teacher education is indeed a part of the problem of lack of democracy in education, rather than the solution. Moreover, if later in-service teacher education programmes are to help to break the cycle of authoritarian initial teacher education and authoritarian schools, then their methods must be congruent with their desired outcomes, i.e. teacher participants must themselves learn in a more democratic way if they are to work in a more democratic way in schools in the future. This section examines examples of positive practice, and attempts at positive practice, which have achieved varying degrees of success. First, in relation to an attempt to change and reform initial teacher education in a democratic direction in The Gambia, then in relation to programmes of in-service education for serving teachers, before concluding with a discussion of the possibilities of action research and reflective practice for facilitating more democratic modes of pedagogy amongst existing teachers. Further discussion of the limitations to some of these approaches will take place in chapter 4 on the nature of obstacles to democratic educational reform.

Initial Teacher Education

Schweisfurth (2002a) discusses the processes and outcomes of a two-year project in The Gambia which aimed to foster greater understanding and skills in democratic education among lecturers and students undergoing initial teacher education at the School of Education of The Gambia College. The College was the sole provider of teacher education in this small West African nation, and as such it had considerable influence over education in the country. The project consisted of workshops at the College with staff and students on education and democracy. Concurrent with the three workshop visits, and in two subsequent trips, research was carried out into local perceptions of democracy and democratic education, and into the impact of the workshops on the attitudes and teaching practice of the participants. Over 45 people were interviewed, and over 30 lessons were observed at the College. A total of 10 of the student participants were visited at their school placements. A survey was conducted among all workshop participants of opinions regarding the College itself and democratic management and structures. Additionally, six participants – three staff and three students – acted as case studies over the year period, and were interviewed and observed at each phase of the project. They were also given disposable cameras to document what they perceived as democratic or non-democratic aspects of college life.

In terms of impact, most of the lecturers interviewed professed that the experiences had 'opened their eyes', and that they had a generally positive perspective on democratic modes of education. Lecturers also, as part of the first workshop, completed 'personal action plans' which reflected a clear commitment to change their practice to become more democratic, and optimism about the potential for this change to take place. Some examples of their plans include: 'delegate responsibility to students'; 'be less autocratic in my behaviour towards students' ; 'ensure that at all times and situations, I make myself a guide, learner and a facilitator rather than a Mr Know All'; 'endeavour to include more students in planning and decision-making'; and to 'not allow male students to intimidate female students'.

Their positive perceptions and intentions were unanimous and clear, but despite these positive responses, quite a lot of teaching practice within the College appeared to have been little affected by the intervention. It remained true that some lecturers were highly authoritarian in their teaching approaches. There were examples of people refusing to answer student questions, and plenty of sessions which were based almost exclusively on the teacher talking and students copying notes from the board. When asked to identify 'democratic moments' in these types of observed lessons, lecturers were usually able to respond, but did not tend to identify these behaviours as new. One student teacher struggled to remember anything about what had happened at the workshop six months before, although he remembered enjoying the atmosphere. This constituted the second-largest category of participant: those who participated enthusiastically and verbalised agreement with the principles of democracy, but whose practice revealed little or no sustainable impact. The existence of the optimistic 'personal action plans' from these same lecturers further suggested that the lack of observable change was not a question of conscious resistance.

There were many examples of teaching where there was evidence of some change, but where the innovations had been mediated to fit existing practice and preferences, or had been incorporated into routines in ways which left long-standing practice the predominant force. This constituted the largest group. This was true not only of lecturers with decades of experience, but also of student teachers who had been steeped in many years of authoritarian role models. Two examples are:

- a lecturer who talked to students about democratic education, while they copied notes he made on the subject from the board
- a student teacher who introduced learning contracts not through active creation and negotiation by the pupils, but through posting in his classroom the rules of conduct created by the participants of one of the workshops.

The teachers involved considered these to be good examples of democratic education. It was acknowledged by some teachers that they would have liked to be more radical in their implementation, but that constraints of time, syllabus, resources, student numbers and student attitudes limited their potential. Other teachers were already using methods that they perceived as democratic before the workshops. However, learners were unused to such approaches and not trained in how to get the most from them in a democratic way. For example, a Gender Studies session used a very open debate format for discussing controversial issues, but it was dominated by vociferous male students making derogatory comments about women.

At the other end of the scale of impact, there were examples of lecturers who appeared to experience something akin to a 'sea change' in the course of the in-service training. The evidence of this came not only from them, and from observing their sessions, and several students attested to changes in their behaviours, providing triangulating evidence. As two students observed:

> Having certain lecturers attending the workshop was a
> blessing. We could see the changes. The next day, students
> were blowing questions at the lecturer, very open. The lecturer
> was sharing his experiences as a student in the UK. He
> admitted that he had learned about democracy but did not put
> it into practice! ... In [One lecturer] ... the way he was
> behaving, the way he was treating the poem – trying to take on
> what the students had in their mind, they had a different point
> of view from the lecturer. He had never done this before. It
> was just after the workshop. This made the poem so lively.

This research also raised an important question concerning issues of compatibility between, and adaption to, education for democracy and local culture. Do the concepts associated with democracy and democratic education need to be adapted to fit local capacities and local culture? And where would one draw the line, and say 'that no longer constitutes democracy', regardless of the cultural imperatives? Is democracy, ultimately, negotiable democratically? Participants in the project were clearly sensitised to the potential of undesirable transfer from projects from the north, and were protective of their own culture. For example, in answer to a pre-workshop questionnaire item, 'Do you think Education for Democracy is important?', one participant replied, 'could be, if it takes into account the cultural and social background of the society in which it is practised'. Three lecturers answered the question, 'Is there anything further you would like us to take into consideration in planning these workshops?' as follows:

> Try to know more about the history of education in The
> Gambia, the various policies in education and the

environment in which we teach, to determine whether this approach (i.e. democratic education) is possible.

Cultural differences in education; the pros and cons of democracy; putting democracy in a contextual form.

You must consider the ethos of the society.

This issue has been discussed in some depth in relation to Africa by authors who pose the question 'Should education for democratic citizenship be seen as amenable to a Universalist approach or must we rather find local or regional foundations on which to base it?' (Enslin & Horsthemke, 2004). The authors argue strongly and in some detail for the former approach as there is no distinctly or uniquely *African* democracy, so that while democracy is certainly interpreted locally in Africa, if this interpretation is not merely structural (i.e. parliamentary versus presidential, simple majority versus proportional voting systems), but contradicts the basic tenets of democracy (equality in participation, transparency, genuine electoral choice, freedom of opinion and association, individual accountability and autonomy, for example), then it ceases being democratic.

In-service Teacher Education

In Namibia, Zeichner and Dahlstrom (1999) describe in some detail how since independence in 1990, both initial and in-service teacher education has been seen as the key site for breaking the cycle of authoritarianism in education, including consideration of the need for congruence between what is experienced in teacher education and what is expected of teachers in schools:

> Much effort has been devoted to creating conditions in the colleges of education where future teachers experience in their education for teaching the same kind of teaching and learning that is envisioned for schools in the country. To accomplish this a great deal of effort has been devoted to professional development for teacher educators ... The preparation of teacher educators willing and able to prepare teachers in a manner that is consistent with national and educational goals has long been a neglected element of educational reform in Third World countries. (1999, p. xv)

The learner-centred philosophy that has guided post-independence educational reform calls for the breaking down of authoritarian teacher–student relationships of the past and encourages both an understanding of learners' existing knowledge, skills and understandings, and the active involvement of learners in the learning process with the explicit goal of preparing citizens for a democratic society through democratic learning. It was also decided that education had been too examination driven and that new assessment policies should reward demonstrated performance rather than penalise mistakes. In Namibia, the learner-centred education in schools that was the ultimate aim of the reformed teacher education system was understood to have the following features among others:

1. Active student participation in learning
2. Conceptual learning beyond factual learning
3. A willingness by teachers to let go of some of the old ideas
4. An emphasis on problem-solving
5. Continuous assessment
6. Accountability for the results of teaching and learning
7. Learning integrated across subject areas
8. An emphasis on the whole learner
9. Systematic use of valuable life experiences
10. Sufficient curriculum time for teacher and student initiated activities
11. Encouragement of creativity on the part of the learner
12. Encouragement of trial and error learning
13. Encouragement of choice
14. Encouragement of flexibility and balance – the teacher as guide or coach, not as expert
15. All teachers and learners are both learners and teachers
16. Peer teaching by students
17. Stress on the joy of teaching and learning
18. Patience on everyone's part
19. Opportunity and time for small group work
20. Mutual respect and cooperation of all teachers and learners. (Namibia Ministry of Education, 1993, pp. 81-86)

Zeichner and Dahlstrom add an important further point that:

> In a multicultural, multilingual and stratified society like Namibia, post-independence policy makers realised that if teachers were to become the agents and implementers of change, then they must grapple with multiple points of view, raise root questions, deal rationally with controversy, learn to distinguish between substantiated and unsubstantiated opinion, make fair and flexible evaluations and explore personal beliefs. (1999, p. 38)

As will be further discussed below in relation to in-service education, the reforms of teacher education in Namibia were firmly grounded in the promotion of reflective practice, action research, and teacher as researcher among student teachers. The idea was to engage students in practices that encouraged critical reflection on their own practice and that of others, and to provide opportunities to experiment and try out new ideas, learn from the experience through reflection and research, and then change and improve practice accordingly. Teacher education was to provide experience of reflective practice through action research projects, critical reflection on observation of teaching, and engagement in reflective writing through diaries and journals. As Stephens (2009, pp. 53-54) points out, such practices have a strong democratic impulse with traditional roles of research and researcher transforming into facilitator and researcher–practitioner.

At least one teacher educator who carried out research on his own students in a college in northern Namibia felt that he could see a change in his students:

> After each activity I observed that there was a behaviour change in my students. For example, female students would voluntarily decide to take roles in the class. They started to be involved in reporting group findings, asking questions and critically challenging a friend's idea whenever there was a class discussion ... During microteaching lessons the students demonstrated their ability to use a combination of activities, ranging from individual to pair and group work ... On controversial issues, females were beginning to participate in substantive arguments ... In conclusion I have come to learn that students in general have the potential and ability to participate in activities as long as there are clear guidelines, teacher encouragement and learning opportunities that are free from stereotypes. (Tubaundule, 1999, p. 155)

In a study of the implementation of the in-service version of the programme to reform teacher classroom practices in Namibia over a three-year period in the mid to late 1990s, O'Sullivan (2004) found that initially the teachers were still heavily using teacher-centred methods and that, because of contextual factors, they found it hard to understand the meaning of, and therefore implement, learner-centred education. She therefore decided to focus on some basic learner-centred activities which took the realities within which teachers worked into account in the hope that this would lead them away from the teacher-centred, didactic approaches they were using and 'could potentially lead to the successful development of teachers' capacities to implement learner-centred education in the future' (2004, p. 596). This reflects a less polarised and more hybrid or contingent pedagogy approach of the types discussed above. While all the time taking care that her own teaching approaches were congruent with those she wished the teachers to be able to use in the classroom, she stressed four basic strategies:

- ask the learners their opinions on the lesson topic or on a particular text;

- ensure that the learners understand the topic of a lesson through examples, demonstrations and visual aids. Ask them if they understand by asking them questions;
- give learners time to take in a new idea and do not continue with a new step until they are ready, i.e. if learners do not understand the concept of fractions, there is little point in teaching them the addition of fractions; and
- do not waste any time, be on time for lessons, attend all lessons, and ensure that the learners are busy at all times.

In this way the teachers were working within their professional capacity and they came to view learner-centred education as using whichever teaching methods bring about effective learning. O'Sullivan notes that in follow-up lesson observations, teachers no longer exclusively used rote methods, but instead used a variety of methods and, moreover, that learners' reading skills improved partly as a result (2004, p. 597).

In Guatemala, following decades of armed internal conflict, active learning approaches are seen as directly contributing to democratic behaviour (De Baessa et al, 2002). The government-backed Nueva Escuela Unitaria (NEU), based on the Escuela Nueva model of Colombia (see, for example, Torres, 1992; Rojas, 1994), has been designed to improve educational quality for children in rural schools. Teachers have attended a series of three one to two week in-service training workshops at which they are provided with a package of activities to encourage collaboration between teachers, pupils, and parents. At the workshops, the teachers reflect on their own experience as pupils in schools and as teachers; develop materials to be used by pupils; form teachers' circles that meet regularly with each other to help one another with implementation issues; carry out parent involvement activities; develop a series of active learning strategies, such as the use of self-instructional guides, learning corners, small group work and peer teaching, as well as participation in elected school government. The NEU programme stresses the role of teacher as facilitator who encourages learners to be active and creative through working in small groups and in a variety of learning contexts:

> Such learning experiences are seen to lead to both the construction of knowledge through social interaction and democratic attitudes and behaviours such as comradeship, co-operation, solidarity and participation. (De Baessa et al, 2002, p. 206)

A study compared 116 children from NEU schools with 104 children from the more conventional escuelas unitarias (EU) schools, based on observation to examine the extent to which they exhibited democratic behaviours, such as turn-taking, assisting others, expressing opinions, and directing and leading others (De Baessa et al, 2002). The study found that participation in student-directed small groups encouraged democratic behaviours, and as NEU schools had a relatively high use of small groups, they also had a greater frequency of democratic behaviour among pupils. The authors conclude that:

> For countries wishing to develop democratic behaviour in primary school, decentralised classrooms that promote active learning by offering children the opportunity to engage in a variety of learning contexts, especially those of small group student–student interaction, appear essential.
> (De Baessa et al, 2002, p. 217)

However, they go on to warn that in countries such as Guatemala this requires a radical departure from the typical pedagogy of lectures to large groups and individual seat work, which means a substantial investment in in-service training that allows teachers to build knowledge through social interaction, as was carried out in the NEU.

In India, according to Sriprakash:

> Pedagogic renewal in Indian government primary schools has sought to reform dominant modes of textbook-based, rote-oriented, authoritarian and didactic instruction with the promise of more child-friendly, democratic learning environments. (2010, p. 297)

Sriprakash goes on to discuss the Nali Kali or 'joyful learning' in-service training programme in the Indian state of Karnataka which was implemented in some 4000 rural primary schools in the late 1990s, and which was supported by the Indian government and sponsored by the World Bank. She describes the 'democratic ideals' of the programme in trying to reform the non-participatory, teacher-centred instruction of the traditional system requiring the teacher to 'transform herself from an authoritarian figure to a fun loving and creative facilitator' (2010, p. 299). Nali Kali pedagogy is organised around an individualised pedagogy of exercises and activities on learning cards which children work on in small groups. So, while children are not necessarily given more control over the selection and sequence of knowledge, they can progress at their own pace so that there is no pressure to rote learn large amounts of knowledge. It was hoped that group work on learning cards would create a more informal, friendly and less hierarchical atmosphere in the classroom, with more open and equal relationships, and that this would help to develop self-confidence, self-esteem and a sense of security in children. However, teachers were also expected to continue to teach according to a state syllabus with content that has to be completed each month, which pulls in the opposite direction of individual children learning at their own pace. Through detailed classroom observations of one teacher, Sriprakash comments on the separation between the somewhat successful attempt to create a friendlier and happy classroom environment, and the continuing emphasis on government and teacher-centred construction of what counts as knowledge. While pupils were treated in a more caring way, the affective or relationships dimension of the classroom was distinct from learning and knowledge which children had little say over. This contributed to a continuing hierarchical social order and forms of control which competed with the democratic ideals of child-centred pedagogy expected from the programme.

An earlier study of 234 teachers who had participated in the District Primary Education Project (DPEP) in the same state of India (Clarke, 2003) came to a similar conclusion. The DPEP was implemented in 226 districts in 18 states in India, and its aim was to move from rote learning and memorisation in an atmosphere of fear and deference, to a more enjoyable, active, student-centred pedagogy. Teachers went through intensive periods of training for a few weeks, and then subsequently professional support was provided once or twice a month by a coordinator who visited the classroom and who observed teaching and helped teachers reflect on what was observed. Sessions were also held once a week at Cluster Resource Centres. The study found that as a result of the project the teachers now successfully used a greater variety of teaching aids and activities. However, as in the Sriprakash's study above:

> Teachers' use of instructional aids, activities and
> demonstration during instruction have not integrally
> transformed teaching and learning in the classroom. They have
> skilfully integrated activity and joyful learning into their
> traditional rote method of instruction where knowledge is
> transferred en bloc and memorised. Knowledge continues to
> be 'given' in demonstration and activity and learning
> continues to be based on repetition ... The teacher continues to
> be the primary player in that she or he continues to be in
> control and define the parameters for student participation.
> (Clarke, 2003, p. 28)

Action Research and Reflective
Practice in In-service Teacher Education

As discussed above, action research has been seen as an important method of teacher education in democratic educational reform in Namibia. However, it has been utilised elsewhere with some success as well. Jabr reports on a small-scale project using action research in Palestine, but warns that 'It is not easy to enhance thinking, to increase openness, to promote cooperation and to encourage democratic values when students and teachers are under occupation' (2009, p. 724).

Noting that lecturing, rote learning and memorisation are still the dominant modes of teaching, Jabr discusses an in-service project with four teachers in two government high schools in Ramallah that used collaborative action research to develop a problem-solving approach with pupils:

> Traditional school education engages learners in problem solving that focuses on problems that are clear and possess correct, convergent answers. However, problems in real life are ambiguous and have various ways of solving them. These problems demand people to make judgements to defend the most appropriate solutions. (2009, p. 725)

Using the problem of 'saving the dead sea' the teachers learned to work in a way with the pupils that did not determine what they would learn, but which would help them to inquire, coach their thinking, and facilitate their decision-making. While the author admits that the female pupils that worked with the teachers already wanted to be independent, hoped to take an active role in their society, and were critical of the school system, the author nevertheless concludes from the evidence of participant observation, interviews and diaries that the project:

> fostered self-learning and enquiry skills; improved creative and critical thinking skills ... Students learned cooperatively to fully understand the problem, its causes, consequences and solutions. The learning process oriented them to meaning-making over fact-collecting. They expressed their own views and opinion ... In spite of the enormous challenges in Palestinian schools, our attempt to teach problem solving was successful and contributed to personal, social and academic development of participant teachers and students. (2009, p. 734)

Jabr concludes, two years before the 'Arab Spring' that:

> In the Palestinian context, where the lives, safety, well-being and dignity of people is endangered by the conflict, it is a priority to focus on promoting education, giving the youth a voice and handing some power to our students ... Such pedagogy will influence our future; it will contribute to rebuilding the society, healing the psychosocial wounds of conflict, promoting understanding and democracy and enhancing social development. (2009, p. 735)

In chapter 4, we shall consider existing cultural patterns as one possible obstacle to developing more democratic forms of education. However, in an article on teacher education in the United Arab Emirates, Clarke and Otaky (2006) remind us that culture is neither completely homogenous nor fixed for all times, and that culture has the capacity for adaption and change. They reject the arguments put forward in an earlier article

(Richardson, 2004) that Emirati teacher education students are programmed by 'Arab–Islamic culture' which is not congruent with the underlying assumptions of action research and reflective practice. The article examines evidence from face to face conversations and online web communications technology conversations. They argue that in fact the students embraced critical thinking and reflective practice, demonstrating considerable self-awareness of their capacity for growth, development and change. They conclude that:

> culture can be usefully understood as a never-finished site of competing historical and social discourses rather than as a received set of beliefs and values. We wish to emphasise the 'given and the possible' rather than just the 'given' in order to resist what we see as another form of cultural imperialism. We advocate a view of reflection as a human capacity akin to our abilities to create and use language and other 'tools of the mind', even though the particular forms it take will inevitably be shaped by historical, cultural and social factors.
> (Clarke & Otaky, 2006, p. 120)

Hardman et al (2009) report on an in-service programme with 47,000 primary school teachers in Kenya aimed at increasing active learning through the use of new textbooks designed to facilitate the diversification of teaching methods. Central to the programme was school-based training and the concept of the reflective teacher encouraging critical reflection on beliefs and classroom practice. Through this the in-service training sought to get a better balance between teacher-led interaction and pupil-centred activities, such as collaborative forms of learning, problem-solving, learning by doing, and independent research. A baseline study by the programme showed that, in line with previous studies, teaching in Kenya is dominated by rote, recitation and the transmission of 'facts' through teacher explanation. The post-programme study found that the use of group work and paired work had increased significantly. Lesson planning had improved with teachers making more use of teaching aids from the local environment with less reliance on talk and chalk. Classroom layouts were more varied to meet the requirements of the different learning tasks. Those who had received most training were also the most interactive and gender sensitive and made greater use of praise rather than criticism. However, as with a further study discussed immediately below, the 'cascade' model of school-based training, whereby teachers who have been part of the project work with other colleagues to pass on their training, did not work as well as hoped because of the heavy workload of teachers – they simply did not have the time to train their colleagues. Crucial to the success of the programme was the opportunity for teachers to have the opportunity to think through new ideas and to try out new practices, and that the head teacher moves beyond the traditional role of administrator to provide collaborative leadership of pedagogic change.

Save The Children Norway's Quality Education Project (QEP) in four African countries (Ethiopia, Zambia, Mozambique, and Zimbabwe) has a particular view of quality in education based upon both processes and outcomes. This involves the capacity building of teachers and teacher educators in terms of skills of critical reflection, action research, problem-solving, planning and executing a more diverse range of more child-centred, non-authoritarian methods of teaching and learning, based on the needs of children. It is based on a human rights philosophy and encourages local ownership for the responsibility of improving quality based on existing resources. The ultimate aim of the QEP is to improve the learning outcomes and conditions of children by listening and responding to all those involved (particularly the pupils) in the delivery of quality education. The training provided by the QEP therefore attempts to move away from authoritarian forms of teaching and learning and classroom relationships, towards more democratic forms. An evaluation of the impact of the QEP's action-research based training (Harber & Stephens, 2009) found that in interviews with teachers and teacher educators, there was regular and consistent verbal testament made to changes in professional identity, a new concern with problem-solving, the use of a more diverse range of teaching methods and not just lecturing content, self-criticism, the rejection of a tendency to blame others, less of a 'I know it all' attitude, a more open-minded attitude, a realisation that the teacher was part of the problem and part of the solution, a new pride, interest and enthusiasm in the profession of teaching, a new willingness to collaborate and engage in conflict resolution, and a different view of children and student teachers as participating in learning rather than just vessels waiting to be filled. Observations of teaching in schools in the countries concerned suggested that the average level of quality of teaching in the QEP schools pointed more in the direction of extended professionalism, as discussed above, than the average for non-QEP schools. When the QEP training was done well, with motivated participants and in a sustained supportive environment, it produced significant changes in classroom teaching and relationships in a more participant and child-friendly direction.

Taught Programmes in Education for Democratic Citizenship

If the political goal of a society is democracy then explicit education for democracy is one thing that the education system cannot leave to chance or choice. This suggests that somewhere or somehow the curriculum should teach the knowledge, skills and values necessary for democratic citizenship. There are many possible ways in which this could be done (Davies et al, 2002, p. 24), but most commonly it is through a curriculum slot called 'social studies', 'civics', 'citizenship' or, perhaps less often, through 'social science' or 'government and politics'.

UNESCO's Global Monitoring Report on the quality of education said that citizenship and global citizenship education, or educating for democracy and peace, had increased as a curriculum subject in almost all grade levels since the 1980s (UNESCO, 2005, p. 150). In an article on civic education in Costa Rica and Argentina, Suarez (2008, pp. 485-487) notes that in the last few decades schools in more countries have spent more time teaching citizenship and that these have been primarily concerned with democracy, human rights, equality, participation, social cohesion, solidarity, tolerance of diversity, and social justice. Indeed, formal civic education courses were widely promoted by organisations in the USA, Africa, South America and Asia in the 1990s in order to promote the transition to democracy (Carothers, 1999, p. 232). Suarez (2008, p. 488), for example, points out in relation to South America that regional organisations such as the Organisation of American States and the Inter-American Development Bank have been active in promoting education for democratic citizenship, and that this has been part of the shift from authoritarianism to democracy that began in the 1980s.

So, the good news is that more and more governments are introducing courses specifically and overtly aimed at increasing education for democracy. However, there are also potential and actual problems. One is that such courses can be used as a form of political socialisation to simply reinforce the duty to respect for those in power, as well as promote an uncritical sense of patriotism. Also, as noted by Divala (2007) in relation to Malawi, such courses can in practice equally be used to undermine, or at least restrict, the development of the very same democratic values that they are supposed to support by an presenting only a minimalist and elitist view of democracy of the sort discussed in chapter 1. Another important point is that if such courses are to stand a chance of being successful they too must exhibit the democratic forms of teaching and learning discussed above within them – sole use of the teacher-centred methods of lecturing on the nature of democracy is unlikely to have much impact on pupils as present and future democratic citizens. This has long been a criticism of such courses in the West (e.g. Stacey, 1978, pp. 67-68) and with social studies programmes ostensibly aimed at critical awareness in Africa (Harber, 1997, chap. 5). Evaluations of such civic education programmes in countries such as the Dominican Republic and Zambia found only limited impact in terms of participation, knowledge, skills and values, and one of the reasons seemed to be the use of conventional and formalistic teaching methods (Carothers, 1999, pp. 233-234), a point also noted by Suarez (2008, p. 496) in relation to Costa Rica and Argentina. Similar contradictions between the introduction of a subject called 'Civic and Ethical Formation' aimed at education for democracy in Mexico, and the ongoing authoritarian nature of classrooms and schools, was noted by Levinson (2004). Likewise, in Cambodia where, although the good news is that, following years of authoritarian rule, the subject of 'Civics and Morals' is now taught in schools where students learn about concepts such as democracy, elections, human rights and freedoms, the bad news is that everything else that pupils learn in schools contradicts the message of the subject itself (Tan, 2008).

Apart from the issue of the variety of teaching methods used there and the question of congruence between what is taught and how it is taught, there are also important dispositions that need to be fostered in a course on citizenship or civics education if it is going to make a contribution to education for democracy. One of these is the development of critical thinking. A study of education in the town of Pelotas in southern Brazil (McCowan, 2006) contains an unusual extension of this concept and quotes the official documentation on citizenship education policy to the effect that:

> Citizenship is ... a political practice based on values like ...
> disobedience towards any authoritarian power. Education for
> citizenship requires the possibility of creating educative
> spaces in which the social subjects may be able to question,
> think, adopt and critique the values, norms and moral rights
> belonging to individuals, groups and communities, including
> their own rights. (2006, p. 466)

When asked about what was meant by 'disobedience towards any authoritarian power', the Secretary of Education for Pelotas explained that Brazil had come through long periods of dictatorship which had created a culture of obedience so that, even under the subsequent democratic regime, there is a need to rebel against or confront peacefully any authoritarian exercise of power where decisions have not been made democratically. McCowan comments that government policy in Pelotas proposes not only autonomy and critical thinking, but also disobedience towards any authoritarian power, but the extent of such disobedience is not altogether clear. However, he thinks that while it clearly means that armed rebellion is not permissible: 'Direct political mobilization and, in some cases, non-violent civil disobedience would, however, be justified' (2006, p. 467).

Also, essential in developing a democratic society and state is the disposition and ability to discuss controversial issues and the possession of the procedural values that underpin democratic debate. At the heart of democratic debate is the recognition of the legitimacy of diversity, difference and disagreement. For example, the Crick Report on education for democratic citizenship in England, which heralded citizenship as a compulsory subject in secondary schools for the first time, argued that:

educators must never set out to indoctrinate; ... to be completely unbiased is simply not possible, and on some issues, such as those concerning human rights, it is not desirable. When dealing with controversial issues, teachers should adopt strategies that teach pupils how to recognise bias, how to evaluate evidence put before them and how to look for alternative interpretations, viewpoints and sources of evidence; above all to give good reasons for everything they say and do, and to expect good reasons to be given by others. (Advisory Group on Citizenship, 1998, p. 56)

The Report also defined a controversial issue as:

about which there is no one fixed or universally held point of view. Such issues are those which commonly divide society and for which significant groups offer conflicting explanations and solutions. There may, for example, be conflicting views on such matters as how a problem has arisen and who is to blame; over how the problem may be resolved; over what principles should guide the decisions that can be taken, and so on. (1998, p. 56)

And this is a concern elsewhere as well:

Controversial issues are a must in African schools because, without them, African children are not likely to form citizenship dispositions that are vital to the health of their communities. (Asimeng-Boahene, 2007, p. 241)

Yet, despite the many very good reasons for teaching controversial issues in the classroom and the existence of a number of published practical guidelines, there are many obstacles to teaching controversial issues. Asimeng-Boahene (2007) found that students in Botswana, for example, enjoyed learning about controversial issues, including rival and contradictory opinions, and found it useful in helping them form their own opinions as critical citizens. However, he noted that African teachers may well avoid sensitive topics and that:

Conducting beneficial discussions on controversial issues is an art that requires skills and practice. However, studies have shown that most African teachers lack this very ingredient, as there is a great shortage of trained and experienced teachers versed in issue-centred approaches to teaching.(2007, p. 236)

A further study in Botswana (Koosmile & Suping, 2011) found that final year pre-service teacher education students were generally reluctant to debate contemporary controversial issues in science education and that their contributions generally lacked critical reflection and thorough analysis. Indeed, the students were challenged by the participatory and interactive thrust of the course and this has implications for the overall nature of teacher education currently being provided in Botswana. Partly because of a lack of training, many teachers are afraid of teaching controversial issues, even in countries where there is well-established system of political democracy in place like England or a relatively new one like South Africa (Chikoko et al, 2011). This is perhaps less surprising in some developing countries where the wider political system is still authoritarian or only semi-democratic, such as Zimbabwe where teachers have expressed fears that teaching about some controversial issues could lead to victimisation (Sigauke, 2012).

Assessment

Kennedy and Chi-kin Lee, writing on education in Asia, argue that:

> Assessment is not only an educational tool – but a political one as well. Rigid assessment regimes usually focus on pre-specified outcomes stressing knowledge rather than action. This kind of assessment is unlikely to support the development of individuals who can take their roles in civil society as informed citizens capable of understanding complex citizenship issues. Yet in the future, all citizens will need to have knowledge, skills and dispositions that will enable them to engage with civic issues. (2008, p. 64)

Another issue for education for democratic citizenship therefore is the types of assessment that are used in schools. There are in fact many different types of formal and informal assessment relationships that actually take place in schools, or might usefully take place in schools, between key actors, such as, for example, pupils, teachers, and inspectors (Meighan & Harber, 2007, chap. 13). However, the dominant one in practice is that teachers assess pupils. Indeed, the 'backwash' effects on classroom teaching methods of traditional, and very common, forms of teacher assessment of pupils, based on examination of knowledge memorisation, are usually seen as an obstacle to more democratic forms of teaching and learning. Discussing the context of Africa, Hawes wrote that:

> It is by no means surprising, therefore, to find that the vast majority of items in Social Studies and Science papers demand straight recall of specific facts and that teaching is adjusted accordingly; in one paper analysed in Botswana out of fifty questions forty-nine required only factual recall of information. (1979, p. 103)

In an education for democracy it is important to assess skills and values, as well as knowledge, if these are all to be taken seriously in learning and teaching. Moreover, more diverse forms of assessment will also encourage more diverse forms of learning and teaching. A range of the different ways in which political knowledge, skills and values can be assessed by teachers are discussed in the handbook on education for democracy by Davies et al (2002). Also of importance is how pupils can be more involved in assessment through such practices as: encouraging a pupil to start the lesson by recalling key points from the previous lesson and recapping the main points at the end of the lesson; by discussing with pupils at the end of the school day what they have learned and how they feel about it; by discussing with pupils at the beginning of a topic or course what outcomes they want from it, what criteria they want to be assessed against and how they would like to be assessed; by using more projects where pupils decide what is to be researched with the help and guidance of the teacher; by using records of achievement where pupils play a part in recording and reflecting on their own progress; by asking pupils to write a self-assessment at the end of a topic or course (Alexander, 2001).

UNESCO (2005, p. 158) distinguishes between formative assessment (which looks at how each learner learns and the problems she or he encounters) and summative assessment which relies on a one-off examination and is used to determine whether pupils are promoted to a higher grade or level or awarded certificates or diplomas. Discussing formative assessment, UNESCO also notes that 'Where practical it should also draw on learner self-assessment, which can empower learners to assess their own progress and reflect on how they could improve their learning' (2005, p. 158).

UNESCO is optimistic that Ministries of Education are increasingly opting for continuous assessment which is a combination of formative and summative assessment, citing Sri Lanka, South Africa and Ghana as examples with the idea 'to facilitate more holistic judgement of learners' progress and achievement and lessen incentives to teach to exams' (2005, p. 158). However, it is also noted that in practice, because of resource issues, lack of training, and the pressure of external summative assessment, such continuous assessment 'often amounts to repeated summative assessment with teachers filling in record forms while no specific feedback is given to learners' (2005, p. 158).

School Inspection: a case study

Little appears to have been published on the potentially important role of school inspectors in developing more democratic education. Here therefore we will draw extensively on one study of a project designed to work with the school inspectorate in The Gambia to help to put education for democracy on a more sustainable footing (Harber, 2006). As a result of discussions with the Gambian Department of State for

Education during an earlier project on education for democracy and teacher education (Schweisfurth, 2002a), it became clear there was a need to move beyond teacher education to work with those involved in a supervisory relationship with teachers, such as inspectors and advisers. It was argued that if education for democracy was to be put on a more sustainable footing then it was important that not only those who educate new teachers experienced professional development in the field of education for democracy, but also the inspectorate who regularly go into schools to evaluate and advise teachers. This is because teachers need ongoing support and monitoring needed to be done by inspectors to see whether teachers and schools were operating in a democratic fashion and whether this was making any difference to educational quality.

'Quality', however, is not a neutral term and judging the quality of education depends on the aims set for education in the first place. In this project it was understood as improving the nature and processes of schooling by moving them in a more democratic direction based on equal human rights. However, the workshops in the six educational regions of The Gambia that formed a key part of the project also examined whether quality understood in this way also enhanced quality understood in other ways, such as better examinations results, less drop-out and less truancy. This also required discussion and agreement on what was meant by a 'professional' teacher and in particular what was meant by the 'democratic professional'.

However, materials and training for the development of supervisors and inspectors in Africa is lacking. The International Institute for Educational Planning (IIEP) and UNESCO report 'School Supervision in Four African Countries' (2001) commented:

> The need for more and better training – both at the beginning and during their career – is a recurring demand of supervisors in the Eastern and Southern African region ... While a number of in-service courses take place, they are not integrated within an overall capacity-building programme, neither do they focus sufficiently on supervision issues ... Not unimportant is the availability of a number of instruments, such as manuals and guidelines, which help them to fulfil their tasks effectively and break to some extent the feeling of isolation ... some instruments are available, but few go beyond the rather administrative forms and circulars. (De Grauwe, 2001, pp. 72, 75, 76)

The project therefore aimed to provide such training and to produce a manual or guidebook as a result. Workshops were held with inspectors and supervisors in all six educational regions of The Gambia to enable discussion among inspectors and supervisors as to what democracy and democracy in education might be and how it might relate to improved quality. A particular issue addressed in the workshops was how do inspectors *know* that schools are of good quality and their teachers professional or not? In particular, how can we evaluate the quality of schools in terms of democracy and human rights, and teachers in terms of democratic professionalism – what are the observable and measurable indicators of good quality democratic education? Lists of observable indicators of quality in schools often include indicators that might be judged as being more democratic in nature. For example, a list provided by Rameckers (2002, p. 86) in relation to secondary education in Africa, includes not only conventional indicators concerning school organisation (e.g. 'There are norms of operation/conduct known by heads, teachers, students and parents'), but also 'There are student organisations such as student government, student commissions or clubs'. The list on children's well-being included, 'Teachers dialogue with children showing respect for them', 'The school promotes the rights of children (children learn their rights, posters/pamphlets available)', 'Teachers combine lecturing with work in groups or individual work' and 'Teachers motivate children to take initiative, ask questions, work on projects, seek information, explore their surroundings and use reasoning'. In the project under discussion *democratic* indicators were a key consideration in discussing school quality.

While earlier work had been done on possible indicators of democratic schools internationally (Davies, 1995), an important aspect of the workshops was to discuss and decide upon possible principles of democracy and to see if there were indicators that could provide evidence of their existence in schools and classrooms in The Gambia. For example, Table I sets out some indicators that emerged from a workshop.

Principle of democracy	Observable indicators and appropriate evidence to self and an inspector
Participation	Regular group work and discussion sessions are planned in writing and executed Students participate in drawing up their own work plans The number of students who ask and answer questions in class is high or increasing
Respect for human rights	Lessons are planned and executed around rights and responsibilities Children can talk about rights and have produced materials There is a decline in recorded instances of children or teachers abusing others (physically or verbally) There are few or no instances of corporal punishment

Table I. Principles of democracy and possible indicators in schools.
Source: Davies et al, 2005, p. 27.

This then raises the issue of the nature and characteristics of the democratic professional teacher, and the guidebook resulting from the workshops explores this, as well as tools of self-evaluation for schools and teachers, the nature of democratic relationships in inspecting and supervising, and the democratic skills required by teachers, students and inspectors (Davies et al,2005).

In terms of the impact of the project, workshop participants were asked to state one way in which they would improve their practice, and both they and the workshop organisers kept a copy. Participants from each region were then interviewed on a subsequent visit (usually about three months later) about any changes to their attitudes and practices stemming from the workshop – for example, participants in region three would be interviewed on the next visit after the workshop had been carried out in region four. At the end of the project, a final workshop was held in the capital, Banjul, where representatives from the participants from all regions were invited to read, discuss and comment on the draft guidebook stemming from the project. A final evaluation sheet was used with all participants at this workshop to explore whether those who participated in the project had embraced democratic values as defined by the project's orientation.

When asked about whether they had ever attended a workshop on this theme before the overwhelming majority of participants said 'no'. This therefore does not seem to be a topic or approach that has been widely discussed in The Gambia. Indeed, the very positive, even revelatory, tone of many of the responses to the other questions (e.g. 'The workshop has really opened a new page in my life') suggests that this was indeed an innovatory theme and approach to continuing professional development in education in The Gambia.

When asked about the most useful things they had learned in the workshop, some respondents simply said that they found all aspects useful or that they had learned to 'be more democratic in their job', but most respondents mentioned specific aspects of the content of the workshops, such as:

- principles of democracy;
- the basic concept of democracy in education;
- the use of learning contracts;
- ways of involving staff and children in learning and teaching;
- self-evaluation as a way of improving performance;
- the use of democratic indicators in inspection;
- the nature of the democratic professional;
- ways and means of sustaining democracy;
- links between school effectiveness and democracy; and
- how to operate democratically as an inspector.

Others commented not so much on the content of the workshops, but on the way that they had been organised and run – learning by doing:

- The practical aspects, diverse views, tolerance and participation which characterises the presentation.
- Respect for each other's views as enshrined during the session.
- The group activities/work, and the democratic atmosphere throughout.
- The free exchange of ideas throughout.
- The participants were able to share ideas, skills and experiences throughout.
- Everyone had the opportunity and was encouraged to participate.
- Democracy in education really prevailed.

Perhaps revealingly, one respondent stated 'In most Gambian workshops participants are "talked at". You "talk with" participants and this is key in effectiveness'. This reinforces a key point made in relation to teacher education above about the need for consistency and congruence between the methods of teacher education (initial and in-service), and the skills and values that a teacher educator wants teachers to have in the classroom.

As mentioned earlier, workshop participants were asked to state one thing in their practice that they would change as a result of the workshop. The responses summarised here are perhaps instructive of current inspection and supervision practices in The Gambia and very possibly elsewhere:

- listen more attentively to teachers
- use more dialogue with teachers and pupils
- allow teachers to talk about the constraints they face
- be more transparent and open
- give teachers a chance to think for themselves
- give feedback after my inspection
- liaise with the school authorities before I go into the classroom
- discuss observations with person I have inspected
- observe at random children's workbooks and interview pupils about teacher performance
- discuss with students how to achieve improvement
- I will let them know I am not there to find faults but to share and express ideas and opinions
- when there has been conflict between teachers and pupils I don't normally listen to the pupils ... after the workshop I see the need for dialogue with both
- positive reinforcement of teachers – minimise fear
- more mutual respect
- more respect for evidence in making judgements
- do to others as you would like others to do to you.

Overall, the responses suggested a strongly felt need for more openness, dialogue, trust and collegiality aimed at school improvement, and a move away from more hierarchical, authoritarian and fear and blame-led approaches to inspection.

Roughly three months later, did the workshop participants feel that they had changed their practice in any way? Participants interviewed after the workshops generally had clear memories of the workshop and could name and describe features which they found particularly useful. For example, respondents noted that in order to be able to have a vivid picture of what is in a school, you need to make sure you contact *all* concerned and not just the head; that learning contracts were important so that everybody is reluctant to deviate from the rules; that there is an important line between professionalism and prying into someone's private life as part of inspection. In terms of changing their practice or introducing new ideas as a result of the workshop, respondents noted the following :

> Before you wanted to do things but there was no reference point. But now I can say I can do this and this is wonderful ... I knew it was right but I didn't have a vocabulary and the workshop provided reasons and enabled you to defend your position.

> I used to just turn up to school but now warn ahead. We were seen as a threat, a witch hunt, now they are ready for us and are happier as previously they were very uncomfortable.

> Now talk to people more, urge them to attend meetings, use the phone and visits to show that each and every one is important. I urge people to collaborate and consult. This is an idea coming from you people ... but it needs sacrifice. Inspectors used to go to the village in the night and then sneak into the school to spy, now it is more collegial and there is more fair play.

> Now when I go to a school I look for gender equality ... my colleagues say I am pressing too hard.

> I been involved in a survey using a score card to try to get the views of student teachers and the community about what makes a good school – they score the school in terms of priorities they expressed and this sometimes leads to a hot debate. It helps participation and is a good way of identifying problems ... it helped to solve a problem concerning PTA meetings.

> I have become more accommodating and the workshop is at
> the back of the mind ... I think, this Principal is not delegating.
> Our methods are becoming more democratic, involving the
> people we inspect. Although we wanted to do this anyway but
> we didn't know how to do it.

> I give people a chance to come up with their own thinking
> more.

Although the same person who made the last comment also noted that efforts by the regional office to promote more democracy in schools was meeting resistance from some PTAs who were 'scared of children's rights'.

One head teacher who was also an inspector said that he now works more closely with teachers in running the school – 'A headteacher alone cannot run the school'. On the other hand, one inspector noted that 'We have some headteachers who are dictators' and that he was now working with heads to try to bring about better treatment and more involvement of staff.

One respondent said that he had been thinking about a self-help group that took one chapter at a time from the teacher education guidebook distributed at the workshops (Davies et al, 2002). Another said that he was organising a cluster level workshop for six schools on education for democracy and that the inspiration had come from the workshop – he wanted new ideas about democratic decision-making and openness to be debated in the cluster. One inspector noted that he had said that he wanted to get involved in promoting AIDS sensitisation and that he had now managed to get funding and had organised meetings on the subject since the workshop.

Interview respondents were therefore generally positive about the impact of the workshops and many could provide specific examples of changes in outlook and practice.

Conclusion

This chapter set out our understanding of what a democratic school would look like and showed that democratic practice is possible, and does exist, in schools and teacher education in developing countries. This is so at various levels from the whole school to particular teachers and classrooms. Moreover, democracy now features as an explicit aim for education in a range of developing countries and this could set a policy framework for educational change in a more democratic direction. However, if practice in schools is to change away from the more authoritarian modes that are currently prevalent, then new or different ways of educating teachers will be necessary, and this chapter showed that there are positive examples in this regard and that action research and critical reflection might offer a particularly useful way forward. However, throughout the discussion of positive examples of what can be done, it had to be noted that these remain in a minority and that there remain many obstacles to the democratic reform, or perhaps democratic transformation, of education in developing countries, and it is to these obstacles and barriers that we now turn in more detail.

CHAPTER 4

Obstacles to Greater Democracy in Education

Introduction

Although chapter 3 looked at examples of good practice in relation to education for democracy in developing countries, it was already clear that these are still very much in a minority and that there is a range of factors hindering change or progress in this direction. This chapter examines the historical nature and purposes of schooling as a fundamental obstacle to greater education for democracy in schools in developing countries and how this plays itself out within schools and teacher education. It then asks what other factors make change in a democratic direction so difficult.

Examining the origins of mass formal schooling is important because it has changed very little in essence since the late nineteenth century:

> Over the past century or more, we have come to learn much
> about how human beings, young and old, actually learn best.
> Yet very little of this knowledge has penetrated the standard
> practices of formal schools, which generally carry out the
> rituals and traditions associated with the conceptions of how
> learning occurs and what is worth knowing that were
> developed over a century ago, first in Western Europe (Prussia
> in particular) and then around the world following a
> combination of colonial imposition and cultural borrowing.
> (Farrell, 2008, p. 200)

The world may well have moved on, but much of schooling has not.

The Bureaucratic Legacy in Schools in Developing Countries

The organisational model of schooling bequeathed by history is essentially bureaucratic. The German sociologist Max Weber argued that bureaucracies had the following characteristics:

1. Staff are personally free, observing only the impersonal duties of office.
2. There is a clear hierarchy of offices.
3. The functions of the offices are clearly specified.
4. Officials are appointed on the basis of a contract.
5. They are selected on the basis of a professional qualification.
6. They have a money salary and pension rights. The salary is graded according to position in the hierarchy.
7. The official's post is his or her sole or major occupation.
8. There is a career structure and promotion is possible either by merit or seniority and according to the judgement of superiors.
9. The official may appropriate neither the post nor the resources that go with it.
10. The official is subject to a unified control and disciplinary system. (Albrow, 1970, pp. 44-45)

Shipman (1971, chap. 2) has argued that schools have been organised bureaucratically to teach the impersonal skills, contractual values and relationships that typify the transition from agricultural to modern industrial society. Thus the values which are enforced in the school are those needed from the efficient functioning of bureaucratic organisation – obedience, abiding by the rules, loyalty, respect for authority, punctuality, regular attendance, quietness, orderly work in large groups, working to a timetable, tolerance of monotony, the ability to change readily from one situation to the next, and the ignoring of personal needs when these are irrelevant to the task in hand.

As was argued in chapter 1, while not democratic in itself, this bureaucratic model of schooling is nevertheless important for democracy because it can help to provide the values and skills necessary for the modern organisational basis upon which democratic structures and practices can be built and developed. However, in practice in developing countries, many schools do not actually exhibit the bureaucratic characteristics outlined above.

Harber and Davies (1997) used Riggs's theory of 'prismatic society' to argue in some detail that many schools (and other modern organisations) in developing countries have both 'traditional' and 'modern' organisational, social, cultural, economic, and behavioural characteristics coexisting side by side within them. Riggs (1964) used the analogy of a fused white light passing through a prism and emerging diffracted as a series of different colours. Within the prism there is a point where the diffraction process starts but remains incomplete. Riggs was suggesting that developing societies contain both elements of traditional, fused types of social organisation and elements of the more structurally differentiated or 'modern' societies. The result is an organisation that seems like a modern, bureaucratic school, but this is often something of a façade as the school functions quite differently in reality in terms of marked features, such as, for example, teacher absenteeism, lateness, un-professionalism, sexual misconduct and corruption, as well as cheating in examinations and violent conflict (Harber & Davies, 1997, chaps. 3, 4, 6). On October 6, 2011, for example, the front page of the *Windhoek Observer* in Namibia had three headlines: 'Rogue Lecturer Suspended' (sexual misconduct at the University of Namibia), 'Pastor in Court for Incest' and 'Bogus Nurse Sentenced'. In Tanzanian schools, Van Der Steen (2011, p. 162) found the following examples of such practices:

- A teacher being physically assaulted by an education officer at the municipal office when complaining about a work-related issue;
- A teacher reportedly not being paid salary for five months as she refused to pay 'commission' to the accountant in charge;
- Teachers ordered to carry out demographic surveys in their neighbourhood on behalf of the municipal office without financial compensation;
- The monthly payment of teacher salaries rarely being on time;
- A teacher using her influence in the municipal education office not to be transferred to a school she did not want to go to;
- Reporting of inaccurate information of progress, such as exaggerating the provision of education to disadvantaged children and the number enrolled in schools;
- Punitive action against a head teacher who refused to use school funds to provide visiting officials with meals; and
- Bribery in the allocation of secondary school places to primary school leavers.

In a detailed and systematic study of educational decentralisation in Uganda which used prismatic theory, Oryema (2007) explored the wider question of why so many well-intended and modern educational policies fail in developing countries. He identified a number of key traditional features of Ugandan society that radically affect the actual implementation of organisational change on the ground in Ugandan schools. These he describes as: family size and structure: the unavoidable burden; blood link solidarity: the who, where and what questions; superstition and witchcraft: the invisible intimidation; perceptions of authority: the cock of the village; specialisation problems: a jack of all trades and master of none; who is who?: age and gender issues; the documentation and records vacuum: are witnesses sufficient?; precision and the danger of proximities. As these headings suggest, educational decentralisation did not work as it was supposed to in Uganda because in practice key actors locally – teachers, officials, parents, heads, contractors, villagers – had traditional loyalties, responsibilities, priorities, fears and practices that were at odds with the essentially modern bureaucratic assumptions of the policymakers in Uganda and among its international advisers and supporters.

Interestingly, Dull (2006) found that an awareness of such issues meant that teachers and student teachers in Ghana were primarily focused on school discipline as a contribution to national discipline, rather than any democratic approaches to education: 'the democratic way of teaching would give room to pupils to misbehave by saying anything at all' (student teacher, quoted in Dull, 2006, p. 1).

In her case study of a teacher education institution in Ghana, Dull found that student teachers' greatest fear was indiscipline, which explained why they teach the way they do. She also makes the wider link to a perceived need for national discipline in that:

> by enforcing a strict morality and hard work among schoolchildren, teachers appear to 'consent' to the terms for development set by the international aid community. Ghana's leaders have decided, under strong pressure, to adopt institutions and values promoted by the United States government and the World Bank as necessary for development: neo-liberal economics and liberal democracy, Christian morals and work ethic, scientific rationalism. Teachers are keenly aware of these demands and understand that acts of indiscipline, such as election fraud and civil unrest, scare away tourists and investors. In school they work hard to prevent the indiscipline they attribute to fellow citizens ... teachers become the 'partners' that donors and lenders seek to carry out their impositions. (2006, p. 1)

In the teacher education college Dull worked in, the trainees used the language of democratic education to critique their own schooling and society as authoritarian, but there was a contradiction between teachers' critical words and their rather more traditional and authoritarian actions: 'The need for social order prevented teachers from using questions or methods that could lead to rowdiness or aberrant thinking' (Dull, 2006, p. 15). Hard work and moral discipline was seen as more important than democracy in the classroom. Similarly Stephens (2007, p. 181) in his study of teacher education in Ghana found that dedication to work, such as being punctual and a commitment to teaching and learning, were seen as admirable teacher attributes. Such teachers' concern with professionalism, if essentially restricted authoritarian professionalism, may well be helping the development of modernised, rational-bureaucratic norms and behaviours necessary for the institutional foundations or organisational infrastructure of democracy. However, as will be further discussed below, it is doing little at present to contribute to more democratic values and skills in Ghanaian society.

The Authoritarian Legacy

What is also significant for present purposes is that the historical model of schooling that persists in its fundamentals today was not only bureaucratic, but also essentially an authoritarian one, and that this was not accidental, but based on a perceived need for control and compliance. Green's historical study of the origins of formal schooling systems in England, France, the United States, and Prussia in the nineteenth century argues that a key purpose of their construction of a subject citizenship was that:

> It helped construct the very subjectivities of citizenship, justifying the ways of the state to the people and the duties of the people to the state. It sought to create each person as a universal subject but it did so differentially according to class and gender. It formed the responsible citizen, the diligent worker, the willing tax payer, the reliable juror, the conscientious parent, the dutiful wife, the patriotic soldier and the dependable or deferential voter. (1990, p. 80)

Schooling thus provided a means of social and political control, in particular to counter the threat to the state of increasingly industrialised, urbanised, and potentially organised working populations. As Green's study argues, 'The task of public schooling was not so much to develop new skills for the industrial sector as to inculcate habits of conformity, discipline and morality that would counter the widespread problems of social disorder' (1990, p. 59). Schooling would be organised to prepare future workers with the subordinate values and behaviours necessary for the modern bureaucratic, mass production workplace and the existing social order – regularity, routine, monotonous work and strict discipline. Its organisational form would therefore need to be both bureaucratic and authoritarian in order to inculcate habits of obedience and conformity (Shipman, 1971, pp. 54-55). As Toffler wrote:

> Mass education was the ingenious machine constructed by industrialism to produce the kind of adults it needed ... the solution was an educational system that, in its very structure, simulated this new world ... the regimentation, lack of individualisation, the rigid systems of seating, grouping, grading and marking, the authoritarian style of the teacher – are precisely those that made mass public education so effective as an instrument of adaptation for its time and place. (1970, pp. 354-355)

This authoritarian model of schooling with its origins in state formation, modernisation, and social and political control, gradually extended globally from European societies and Japan through colonisation where the key purpose of schooling was to help to control indigenous

107

populations for the benefit of the colonial power. Even if it was not always entirely successful in this, and indeed in the end helped to sow the seeds of its own destruction, the organisational style of schooling bequeathed by both the needs of industrialised mass production and then colonialism, remains as a firm legacy in many post-colonial societies. Moreover, this, authoritarian style, even if not spread directly through colonisation, was adopted and imitated by other nation states as *the* only 'modern' mass model of education.

So, built into the structures and processes of the dominant model of formal schooling historically is a deeply rooted authoritarian ideology which, as we have seen, it is possible, but not easy, to change – and particularly in any large scale manner. This interpretation of the history of schooling is certainly supported by contemporary evidence on the distribution of power in the majority of schools in developing countries, and often elsewhere. However, it is important to bear in mind that, because of the 'prismatic' factors discussed above in relation to bureaucratic school organisation, this authoritarianism often operates in what has been termed a 'messy and incoherent way' (Harber & Davies, 1997, p. 50). We shall now examine a series of ways in which schools operate in an authoritarian manner in developing countries.

Whole School Organisation, Ethos and Culture

Stating that most education systems in Arab states exist in the context of authoritarian political regimes, Massialas and Jarrar comment that 'the Arab classroom teaches reverence to authority figures and complete submission to their will; it teaches not to question traditional sources of knowledge and wisdom' (1991, pp. 144-145).

Despite the 'Arab Spring' of 2011, it will be some time before the majority of schools in North Africa help to build, develop and sustain democracy, even if the authoritarian states above them are reformed in a more democratic direction. While Herrera and Torres (2006, p. 8) cite some positive examples of educational projects grounded in a more critical pedagogy in the Arab region, a nevertheless recurrent theme in almost all chapters of their book on Egypt, is the overwhelmingly authoritarian nature of relationships in schools and universities based on control and submission. As one contributor put it, schools are characterised by 'The inflexible state curricula, rigid examination processes, heavily bureaucratic school administration and constant inspections, all [of which] reflect the authoritarianism school governance' (p. 12).

Similarly, in a study of the potential of shared decision-making involving pupils in schools in Egypt, Hammad (2010) found that the egalitarian ethos necessary to promote democratic decision-making was not there. The centralised, hierarchical control, lack of trust, excessive emphasis on enforcing rules and regulations, the bureaucratic and authoritarian mode of teacher education, and the autocratic style of head teachers, were all part of a school culture of compliance and passivity, and were serious obstacles to progress.

A study of schooling and violence in Colombia for UNESCO's International Bureau of Education argued that the function of schools was control, homogenisation and reproduction. Time is controlled by strict timetables where everyone does the same thing at the same time and physical space is used as a means of controlling and watching over all of the activities undertaken at the school. Absolute power is incarnated in the image of the teacher and this fluctuates between the strict application of the rules to the administration of judgements, and condemnation of the students' attitudes, behaviours, feelings and abilities at times at the teacher's whim. Students have no say in the curriculum which is taught in a dogmatic and authoritarian manner generating discrimination, school failures and drop-outs (Bernal, 1997, pp. 36-37).

In Vietnam, Saito et al found that although government policy was entitled 'child-centred education', there was a huge gap between the policies and the actual practices:

> In reality, children who need to be at the centre of the
> educational policies were still oppressed and regarded as
> marginal. Moreover, there was a severe lack of trust among
> colleagues in schools despite the fact that it was imperative to
> develop teacher collegiality; without professional collegiality
> in schools it would be impossible to promote child-centred
> education. In sum, based on what was observed, primary
> schools tended to be institutions which lack a certain amount
> of care and concern pertaining to the students. (2008,
> pp. 101-102)

A key figure in creating the processes and ethos of a school is the head teacher. The role of the head in schools in many developing countries has been described as that of a 'despot' (Harber & Davies, 1997, chap. 4). Using examples from Nigeria, Malaysia, Thailand, Indonesia, South Africa, Kenya, and Latin America, Harber and Davies argued that:

> in developing countries headteachers emerge from the
> teaching population and have had little or no training for the
> job. Classroom teaching experience is the key factor in the
> selection of heads ... evidence from a wide range of developing
> areas strongly suggests that classroom teaching is
> overwhelmingly authoritarian in style. Given the nature of
> school organisation, their own identities as teachers and the
> top-down, highly centralised systems of education in most
> developing countries, it would be unlikely for the majority of

headteachers to be anything other than despots, benevolent or otherwise. (1997, p. 61)

Likewise, in a section of a review of a wide range of published literature on school principalship in developing countries, entitled *A King in His Realm?*, Oplatka argued that:

A major ideal characteristic of principalship in developed countries is a participative, democratic leadership style ... Conversely in many developing countries the degree of autocratic leadership style displayed by the principal is relatively high. (2003, p. 437)

These autocratic styles range from 'army like' control, where principals demand from subordinates unquestioning obedience to authority, to a pseudo-participative leadership style, where the last word always belongs to the principal. Citing studies from Singapore, Mexico, Thailand and China, Oplatka also partly attributes this to cultural scripts based on a high level of 'power distance values' (Hofstede, 1991) where the expectations of the less powerful is to accept that power is distributed unequally. In Tanzania, Van Der Steen comments that:

In terms of management, state primary schools are hierarchically organised, with headteachers as the highest authority as well as personally accountable with regard to running the school as required by ward and district education officers ... They can hardly diverge therefore from the 'top-down' directives, guidelines and values imposed by education officers and school inspectors. (2011, p. 35)

In a study of both public and private schools in Pakistan, Nazir found that power was very much concentrated in the hands of the 'higher-ups' – the heads and, in the case of private schools, also the owners, and that:

In both cases the tendency of the teachers is to accept the authority without challenging it. In private schools, this submission seems to come from job insecurity, and in government schools, from the fear of transfer to undesirable areas and schools. The teachers have not reported any democratic practice to legitimise authority in educational settings. (Nazir, 2010, p. 339)

Also in Pakistan, an in-service education project to develop teachers who used more participative classroom styles and worked with other teachers to help them diversify their teaching was hampered by school managements who saw the teachers as a threat (Shamim & Halai, 2006, p. 62). Moreover, in the same project, one teacher stated that 'Once my students were busy in discussion and there was noise in the class, the head entered the class and scolded the students about discipline and asked me to stop this game and start to teach as before' (cited in Dean, 2006, p. 97).

Rather than a democratic ethos which values and practices equality, fairness and respect, authoritarian schools can have an organisational culture which favours inequality, unfairness and disrespect. One form of this is racism against a particular group. Violence against lower caste people or Dalits in India, for example, is widespread (Human Rights Watch, 1999). Schooling, however, not only exacerbates prejudice against lower caste people, it also acts in a directly violent way towards them. A national report in 2002 found that many lower caste children are regularly beaten at school by teachers who regard them as polluting the class. The India Education Report compiled by the National Institute of Educational Planning and Administration (Behal, 2002b) noted that lower caste pupils were verbally and physically abused. Teachers in schools often refused to touch them and made them targets of their anger and abuse. They were punished at the slightest pretext and often humiliated. They were made to sit and eat separately. Their exercise books or writing slates were not touched by the higher caste teachers. They were made to sit on their own mats outside the classroom or at the door. In many cases they were beaten up by children from the higher castes. Many lower caste children were not allowed to walk through the village on their way to school and were denied their right to free textbooks, uniforms and a midday meal. In rural Karnataka, children from the lower castes were referred to as *kadu-jana* (forest people) by teachers who claim that they would not learn anything unless they were given a severe beating (Behal, 2002b). Padma Yedla, head of Save the Children's education programme in Orissa and Andra Pradesh, said there remained ingrained prejudices against lower caste children in Indian state schools:

> Instead of finding out why a child hasn't completed their homework, or recognising that they cannot get help from an illiterate parent, the teachers resort to verbal abuse and humiliation. It's a vicious circle that only gets a bad response from the child. (Bancroft, 2006, p. 15)

This was further confirmed by Sayed et al's (2007) study of schools in India which found that teachers did not have any relations with Dalit pupils inside or outside the classroom, and there was no sharing of food observed across castes among teachers or pupils.

Another form of widespread non-democratic discrimination is against females. In 2008, for example, Amnesty International published a report tellingly entitled *Safe Schools: every girls right*. In the introduction it states:

> Every day, girls face being assaulted on their way to school, pushed and hit in school grounds, teased and insulted by their

classmates, and humiliated by having rumours circulated about them through whisper campaigns, mobile phones or the internet. Some are threatened with sexual assault by other students, offered higher marks by teachers in return for sexual favours, even raped in the staff room. Some are beaten or caned in the name of school discipline ... Violence against girls takes place in and around many educational institutions all over the world. It is inflicted not only by teachers, but also by administrators, other school employees, fellow students and outsiders. The result is that countless girls are kept out of school, drop out of school, or do not participate fully in school. (2008, pp. 1-2)

While the phenomenon is certainly not only located in developing countries (Harber, 2004, chap. 7, 2009, pp. 128-134), PLAN (2008, pp. 22-33) cites evidence of significantly high levels of sexual violence against girls by students and staff in Uganda, South Africa, Zambia, Botswana, Ghana, Malawi, Zimbabwe, Ecuador, the Dominican Republic, Honduras, Guatemala, Mexico, Nicaragua, Panama, Thailand and Nepal.

One aspect of fairness and equality in a more democratic school culture and ethos would be the consistent application of rules. However, schools are often marked by a culture of one rule for us (the pupils), but another rule for them (the teachers). In his research on Tanzanian primary schools, for example, Van Der Steen found that:

– Both teachers and pupils were expected to be in school on time but while only a quarter of teachers managed this there were no consequences while pupils were punished.
– School rules stated that pupils were to abstain from abusive language but he regularly heard teachers making derogatory remarks about, and to, pupils in lessons – and teachers made such remarks about each other as well.
Pupils were supposed to keep their uniform neat and tidy. A boy who had lost his brother to AIDS had drawn the AIDS awareness symbol on his school shirt and was severely and unlawfully beaten by a teacher for having done so.
– Pupils were not supposed to do any business in school (such as selling food or water) yet pupils were sent on errands by teachers during school time such as delivering messages, collecting water, lighting the charcoal burner for making tea, washing up and cleaning.
– During the showing of a UNICEF promotion film on Children's Rights after school hours pupils who tried to watch without paying were caned by the organisers. (2011, p. 235)

School Discipline and Corporal Punishment

> Teachers always hold a stick. Once I argued with a teacher. I
> was instructed to lean against the wall and I was hit three
> times by a stick. I was so stressed out and I perspired heavily.
> (Quotation from young person in Thailand, PLAN, 2008, p. 11)

Historically, authority and order in schools has consistently been
associated with violent imposition:

> From their inception, formal schools in Western capitalist
> societies have been designed to discipline bodies as well as to
> regulate minds. A key purpose of modern state schooling has
> been the formation and conduct of beliefs, as well as the
> acquisition of prescribed knowledge. School discipline has
> frequently been overt and physically violent, with students
> most often the target of teacher-administered punishment.
> (Rousmaniere et al, 1997, p. 3)

A form of violence institutionally still sanctioned in many schools
around the world is corporal punishment. In 90 countries out of the 197
monitored by the Global Initiative to End All Corporal Punishment of
Children (endcorporalpunishment.org), corporal punishment remains
legal despite evidence of its harmful effects and being incompatible with
the United Nations Convention on the Rights of the Child. In other
countries where it has been officially banned, it still continues,
suggesting that corporal punishment in school still exists in at least one
third, and perhaps as much as half of the countries of the world. This
rarely makes pupils feel enthusiastic about schooling and there is
considerable evidence of the physical and psychological harm that it
does (Parkes, 2009).

The World Health Organisation, which explicitly includes corporal
punishment in school as part of child abuse, states that:

> Importantly there is now evidence that major adult forms of
> illness – including ischaemic heart disease, cancer, chronic
> lung disease, irritable bowel syndrome and fibromyalgia – are
> related to experiences of abuse during childhood. The
> apparent mechanism to explain these results is the adoption of
> behavioural risk factors such as smoking, alcohol abuse, poor
> diet and lack of exercise ... Similarly there are many studies
> demonstrating short-term and long-term psychological
> damage. Some children have a few symptoms that do not
> reach clinical levels of concern, or else are at clinical levels
> but not as high as in children generally seen in clinical
> settings. Other survivors have serious psychiatric symptoms,
> such as depression, anxiety, substance abuse, aggression,

> shame or cognitive impairments. Finally, some children meet
> the full criteria for psychiatric illnesses that include post-
> traumatic stress disorder, major depression, anxiety disorders
> and sleep disorders. (WHO, 2002, pp. 69-70)

So while there is no evidence that corporal punishment improves behaviour or academic achievement – quite the opposite (PLAN, 2008) – there is considerable evidence of its harmful effects, including physical harm and even death. For example, in Bangladesh, where corporal punishment is common despite a 1995 government order banning it, police investigated a teacher accused of caning eight of her pupils so hard for forgetting to bring their pencils to class that they needed hospital treatment (*The Independent*, March 9, 2010). The authoritarianism in schools in Egypt is also violent with instances of teachers beating, insulting and humiliating children on a regular basis (Herrera & Torres, 2006). Corporal punishment was outlawed in Uganda but only after one incident where five students were admitted into hospital with severe head injuries after being assaulted by their teachers. The students had failed to report a fight between two other students and so the teachers decided to punish the entire dormitory. Two weeks before this a 20 year old female student received severe back injuries after a beating by her geography teacher for failing to complete an assignment. She was also admitted to hospital and could not walk unaided (Kigotho, 2006). In Tanzania, a survey found that approximately 80% of teachers regularly resort to physical punishment to maintain discipline and to 'promote' learning (Sumra, 2004, cited in Van Der Steen, 2011, p. 32). A further study of teachers and pupils in Tanzania found that corporal punishment was the most common form of punishment used in secondary schools (Feinstein & Mwahombela, 2010). In Pakistan, teachers in both private and government schools expressed complete ignorance of either the UN Charter of Human Rights or the UN Convention on the Rights of the Child, and in government schools the teachers reported violence and humiliation for students as punishment for being absent, late, not wearing school uniform or forgetting to bring a textbook to the class (Nazir, 2010, p. 341). In Mexico, Martin (1994) reports that between a quarter and a fifth of the pupils he interviewed said that corporal punishment contributed to pupil drop-out and Trippett et al (2010) reports a study that 51% of children in Peru had experienced aggression at schools from teachers. In India, Sayed et al describe physical punishment as 'a normal and daily occurrence' in most of the schools they studied (2007, p. 98). In Nepal, corporal punishment is an important reason for school drop-out (Bhattarai, 2010), while in Botswana:

> The more obvious effects of corporal punishment included
> increased student anxiety, fear or resentment in class. Girls, in

particular, remained silent, and were mistakenly dubbed as 'lazy' or 'shy' by some teachers, and so did some boys. Other boys absconded or refused to cooperate in female teachers' classes ... Other studies have also found that excessive physical punishment, generally of boys, can prompt truancy. (Humphreys, 2006, p. 68)

In Ghana:

During morning assembly, the principal or a designated teacher stand in front holding a switch to be used for punishments. For example, the principal of the demonstration school caned pupils who did not bring their school fees or who forgot their cutlasses and brooms for ground keeping. At another school, the teacher on duty caned the children who arrived late for school, checking they were not wearing extra clothing to soften the blows ... one of the trainees, Koffie, worried that 'the slightest mistake the pupils make, some teachers use that as an excuse to whip pupils mercilessly', which speaks ill about democracy in the classroom. (Dull, 2006, pp. 18-19).

Stephens (2007, p. 181) also notes that student teachers in Ghana said that their worst school experience was being caned.

A major factor in the global spread of corporal punishment was colonialism, particularly British colonialism. In Africa, for example, it has been argued that although corporal punishment is now sometimes justified on the grounds that it is 'part of African culture', evidence on pre-colonial education systems suggests that this is unlikely. As Tafa argues in relation to pre-colonial Botswana, where corporal punishment is still widely used in schools, 'There is no evidence to suggest that children were flogged every step of the way' (2002, p. 23). He notes that when neighbouring Zambia banned caning in 2000 it was described as 'a brutal relic of British rule'. He argues that:

Caning became ingrained in the popular minds as critical to school discipline hence the common refrain that its abolition equals classroom disorder and failure. The result is a cycle of caning transmitted from one generation to another and justified in on the basis of experience and sentiment ... In a class of 35-40 authoritarianism is a means of orchestrating 'mob control'. Instant punishment and military style parades typical of Botswana schools are all about social control. Teachers are saddled with systemic constraints of large and mixed class sizes for which no extra resources were made available. (Tafa, 2002, p. 23)

Classroom Methods and Assessment

It was noted in chapter 3 that pupils very rarely have any say over the content of curriculum. It also remains true that, despite the examples of good practice cited in chapter 3, the dominant teaching style in developing countries remains firmly teacher-centred. A study of schools in Papua New Guinea found that:

> The three major requirements that students must display in order to be considered a 'good' student by the majority of teachers included: (1) that the student is obedient and listens to the teacher, (2) that he or she behaves well in class and (3) that he or she is a quiet person who concentrates well ... Not one teacher, for example, suggested to me that a good student might sometimes question a teacher's or anyone else's authority. (Fife, 1997, pp. 102-103)

Similarly, a study of school improvement in Indonesia found that 'Observing lessons showed that teachers still practice whole-class instruction. Students are not encouraged to participate actively' (Van Der Werf et al, 2000, p. 353). Alexander's (2000) detailed study of primary school classroom practice in five countries included India. Here the teacher-centred, transmission model of teaching is overwhelmingly predominant, described as the 'rite of rote'. There was a large gap between teachers' espoused theory (activity method, group work, individual attention and joyful learning) with observed classroom practice. Instruction was 'unremittingly didactic with students seated in rows, taking notes and repeating what they had been told'. Overall, Alexander describes Indian primary education as characterised by 'regimentation and ritualization' (2000, pp. 307, 334, 387). This was further supported by Sayed et al (2007, p. 95) whose study of schools in India confirmed a traditional and authoritarian approach in classrooms. In Cambodia, the teaching of civic and moral education in schools tends to be characterised by teachers reading passages from textbooks and asking students questions about them to get 'correct' answers with little use of discussion and little participation (Tan, 2008, p. 567). A study of rural schools in China found that teachers mainly used factual or close-ended questions which required students to give replies or read from the text and:

> There is very little opportunity for the students to express their own understanding or to comment about the author. Discussions that require student initiative and critical thinking do not exist. (Xiao 2006, cited in Kennedy & Chi-kin Lee, 2008, p. 111)

A similar style of teaching was also found to be dominant in the Philippines (Kennedy & Chi-kin Lee, 2008, p. 115). Teaching in the

Philippines tends to be characterised by Freire's 'banking' education with teachers pouring knowledge into the students who are expected to regurgitate it later in examinations within a context of hierarchical student–teacher relationship so that:

> This banking model of learning has produced graduates who lack the capacity of critical thinking, but are very useful in maintaining the social and political status quo. Sadly they are not very useful at transforming society. (Toh & Floresca-Cawagas, 2003, p. 218)

In Pakistan, teaching is considered by most teachers as:

> the transmission of information by the teacher to the student and tends to be heavily teacher-centred. At the secondary level, the focus of education is primarily on high stakes exam performance. Teachers, relying on the textbook, normally give lecture notes to students who are expected to memorise them with little or no attention given to understanding the content. Thus teachers have become textbook dependent and are overwhelmingly concerned to complete the syllabus so that their students have at least 'covered' the course content. (Khamis & Jawed, 2006, p. 175)

In a project designed to encourage more participatory methods in the classroom in Pakistan, the teachers selectively encouraged the use of one method – listening actively and using quiet voices supposedly as part of the strategy for more cooperative learning – because it resulted in a quiet and orderly classroom, and promoted the transmission of knowledge (Dean, 2006, p. 94).

In Africa, schools have been characterised by hierarchical organisation, transmission teaching and teacher-centred classrooms. Evidence on this comes from Malawi (Fuller, 1991, p. 68), Botswana (Prophet & Rowell, 1990; Tabulawa, 1995; Tafa, 2002), Ghana (Hedges, 2002), Nigeria (Harber, 1989), Zimbabwe (Nagel, 1992; Davies, 1993; Bourne et al, 1998) and Zambia (Serpell, 1993). In Mozambique, one study ranked different pupil activities by the amount of time pupils spend on them. Ranked first was listening to teachers – the probability is that a pupil will get to speak once every second day and even then will be repeating the teacher's sentences or sentences from the textbook. Second in importance is waiting – for the teacher to begin the lesson, for the teacher to write things on the board, for their classmates to finish exercises, which they have already finished, and for their work to be corrected. The third most common activity was copying. The author comments that 'The dominant classroom interaction pattern, then, seems to be that of overwhelmingly passive pupils whose activities are limited to be almost entirely reproductive in nature' (Palme, 1997, p. 196). In an

117

observational survey of classroom interaction in Kenyan primary schools, the main finding was that the prevailing pedagogy was the transmission of facts and that:

> there was an overwhelming predominance of teacher-directed question-answer exchanges and that the vast majority of questions were 'closed' (i.e. calling for a single response or offering facts) as opposed to 'open' (i.e. calling for more than one answer) questions which accounted for only 2% of the total ... As a result, real discussion in which there was an exploration of the topic and interchange of ideas to enable higher order thinking, seemed to be rarely practiced. There was virtually no pupil–pupil interaction. (Ackers & Hardman, 2001, pp. 250, 256)

Despite the positive impact of the subsequent in-service education programme in Kenya discussed in chapter 3 (Hardman et al, 2009), the authors of this later study still point to the traditionally authoritarian nature of the education system, the fact that it did not reach three quarters of primary school teachers, and that there remain considerable pedagogical issues to overcome (Hardman et al, 2009). A further observational survey of classrooms in Nigerian primary schools found a prevalence of teacher explanation, recitation and rote in the classroom (Hardman et al, 2008), while in Ghana, 'In classrooms, children sit in rows facing a teacher who sits or stands at the front directing lessons and monitoring behaviour' (Dull, 2006, p. 18).

In Palestine:

> lecturing is still the dominant pedagogy in most schools. Teachers introduce knowledge as a set of fixed and discovered truths. They tend to cover material in the textbooks and do not have much time to engage students in discussion and cooperative work. As a result, the teacher is placed at the centre of the educational process while the students are considered passive receptors rather than active disseminators of knowledge. (Jabr, 2009, p. 724)

Schools in Colombia outside of the Escuela Nueva Programme have been described as rigid, authoritarian, favouring rote learning and discouraging inquiry, questioning and a critical approach (Abello, 1997, pp. 459, 461).

In Guatemala, De Baessa et al report that, while an experimental programme, as reported in chapter 3, proved successful in getting children engaged in more democratic behaviours:

> in countries such as Guatemala this requires a radical departure from the typical pedagogy of large group lecture and individual seatwork, characterised by the non-experimental

schools and the less well-implemented schools in this study.
(2002, p. 217)

The negative effects of over-testing have been known about for a long time. Dore (1976) and Oxenham (1984) both detailed on a global scale the way that tests and examinations distort the quality of the educational experience, encourage concentration on some parts of a curriculum at the expense of others, encourage a cramming of facts, and creates an overwhelming dependency on extrinsic goals, rather than intrinsic ones. As we discussed in chapter 3, sole focus on rote, retention and regurgitation in examinations can have a narrowing and authoritarian backwash effect on teaching. Part of this means that teachers feel the need to stick strictly to the syllabus and get it covered in time for examinations. This has the effect not only of teachers delivering rather than exploring or discussing subjects – and at their pace rather than that of the learners – but also of seeing the knowledge that is taught as safe and 'factual' rather than, as is often the case in all subjects across the curriculum, containing values, points of view and omissions which need to be debated and discussed rather than simply consumed. This is a particular problem for more child-centred, participatory forms of teaching as they are attempting to develop skills and values that are not normally assessed in traditional examinations. For example, teachers in Ghana are:

> expected to lead students to correct answers and definitive
> conclusions about a topic ... a teacher warned his junior
> secondary school students to 'ask about real situations' when
> they grew curious about political matters that the teacher felt
> were unrelated to his lesson on the Mamprusi ethnic group.
> (Dull, 2006, pp. 28-29)

Moreover, a survey of assessment in Asia (China, Indonesia, Malaysia, Philippines, Singapore and Thailand) argued that there was no evidence that assessment reform was systemic or part of a broader educational reform agenda and that on closer inspection:

> What the Southeast Asian Ministers of Education Organisation
> (SEAMEO) refers to under the guise of 'formative' assessment
> is really a regime of testing geared to preparing students for the
> final examination ... Examinations continue to reign supreme
> as the dominant mode of assessment in Asia.
> (Kennedy & Chi-kin Lee, 2008, p. 79)

Teacher Education

In many countries, including many developing countries, teacher education tends to help to perpetuate authoritarian practices rather than be a source of more democratic ones. This is because teacher education tends to perpetuate traditional, unreflective and teacher-centred pedagogy rather than challenge it. Some 30 years ago Bartholemew put forward the idea of the 'myth of the liberal college' – that it is a myth that there is a contradiction between the liberal, progressive and democratic college or university on the one hand, and the traditional, conservative and authoritarian school on the other (Bartholemew, 1976). This myth suggests that student teachers are exposed to more radical, democratic forms of teaching and learning during their courses in higher education with a high emphasis on learner participation, but are rapidly re-socialised into more authoritarian understandings and practices during their teaching practice and their subsequent employment in education. However, rather than there being a contradiction between the two, in terms of power over what is taught and learned, how and when, it is argued that in reality, teacher education is often an authoritarian and reproductive preparation for teaching in schools. There is a contradiction in teacher education between 'do as I say, and 'do as I do'.

In Africa, the myth of the liberal college in teacher education means that there is often a gap between what teacher educators say they do and the perceptions of student teachers of what actually happens. One publication on Africa, citing evidence from Uganda, Botswana and Zimbabwe, described teacher education as an 'un-virtuous circle of authoritarian reproduction' (Harber, 1997, p. 93). While, as we saw above, there have been some attempts to introduce more democratic methods into teacher education, elsewhere in Africa not much seems to have changed. The Multi-Site Teacher Education Research Project (MUSTER) was the first major study of teacher education in developing countries – including Ghana, Lesotho, Malawi and South Africa – since the 1980s. Its findings (Lewin & Stuart, 2003) very much correspond with the above analysis. Teaching in teacher education resembled traditional high school teaching methods and was lecture-based, with most teaching following a transmission style with question and answer. Overall, the studies found that the curriculum in teacher education was informed by a conservative, authoritarian ideology where debate and critical reflection was not encouraged. This reality was at odds with the principles of participatory, learner-centred and enquiring pedagogy frequently espoused in curriculum documents of the teacher education institutions. Indeed, there seemed to be a kind of collusion between tutors and trainees, who knew little else from their schooling, to maintain the transmission mode because students found project work 'difficult' and group work 'less useful'.

MUSTER published three case studies from Africa. Without it being the central research focus, each of these commented on the seeming predominance of lecturer-centred, transmission teaching, an emphasis on recall and a discouragement of independent learning and reflective practice. There is also a significant gap between the priority given to abstract academic theoretical knowledge in colleges and universities, as opposed to the practical skills and application of knowledge also required to succeed in the reality of the classroom.

The study on Ghana noted:

> Both student teachers and newly qualified teachers stressed that the most commonly used instructional approach in college was 'lectures with tutors dictating notes'. Rarely, it appears, were opportunities created for more interactive 'small group' work or discussions that would place much of the responsibility for developing personalised understanding of teaching on trainees. (Akyeampong, 2003, p. viii)

Indeed, in her study of Peki Teacher Training College in Ghana, Dull (2006, pp. 20-21) also noticed that while tutors at the college taught about progressive methods, they did not really use these methods in their classrooms. Most relied on lectures and some discussion.

In teacher education in Malawi:

> Much learning is undertaken in a transmission style where information is projected with few opportunities for students to engage in debate and reflection. Questions were often informational and recall-based and much of the teaching appeared examination-driven, rarely departing from material likely to be found in assessment tasks. Few attempts seem to be made to capitalise on trainee insights into teaching and learning based on their experience in schools.
> (Kunje et al, 2003, p. xiii)

While in Lesotho:

> Classroom observation confirmed the conservative nature of the programme in that, in practice, most teaching at the College is transmission-oriented, and there is little emphasis on independent learning, critical analysis, creative thought or learning to exercise professional judgement. The interaction between students and tutors during lectures involves a question-answer approach but questions are restrictive and do not allow for full independent thinking for students.
> (Lefoka & Sebatane, 2003, p. x)

Lewin and Stuart make a distinction between teacher education as preparing the 'teacher as technician' and training the teacher as a 'teacher as reflective practitioner':

> The technician is seen as having a restricted role, her job being to deliver the curriculum – which is prescribed at a higher level – as effectively as possible, while the reflective

practitioner is expected to play a more extended role, that may
include developing the curriculum to suit the context,
evaluating and trying to improve her own practice, and
mentoring new teachers. (2003, p. 63)

Within teacher education, the whole ethos of institutions can be as
authoritarian as schools. Teacher education students at the college
studied by Dull (2006) in Ghana were treated as though they were school
children in a regimented manner. The students at Peki College were
expected to do manual labour such as sweeping or farming in the
mornings, afternoons and at weekends, and were punished if they failed
to do it by being made to do more hard labour. Lights out was signalled
at 10.30 by drums and if they wanted to leave campus they had to get
permission from the head tutor, and off-campus visits were limited to
two per term. Strict rules were also applied to the appearance of students
in terms of jewellery, haircuts and clothes. The students wore uniforms
which were believed to part of keeping indiscipline at bay. This is
corroborated by Stephens (2007, pp. 187-188) who describes the
'authoritarian environment' of teacher training colleges in Ghana and
quotes one student teacher in Ghana as saying, 'We are treated like
primary school pupils. We are not allowed to regulate our lives'.

Agyemang (2007) analysed teacher education in Ghana according to
four principles of democracy – equity, rights, participation and informed
choice. Generally, the structures and processes were not democratic. For
example:

- Students have the right to ask questions during teaching and
  learning, but this is entirely controlled by the tutors and some do
  not encourage questions from students. Students have no rights in
  suggesting the kind of teaching methods they might like.
- Students can elect prefects and can choose their programme of
  study, but the student representative council is mainly concerned
  with social activities and planning menus. Students have no say in
  administrative decisions – they are just informed – they play no
  part in making rules and regulations.
- Some punishments contradict human rights, e.g in one college,
  students were given a one-week internal suspension with hard
  labour for not attending morning devotion. They were made to wear
  white clothes and dig out a blocked drain. There is no appeal
  process. Most of the colleges did not have student handbooks where
  disciplinary procedures are explained.
- Students play no part in curriculum decision-making to suit their
  individual needs.
- Every student is subjected to the same daily routines which are
  compulsory and they do not enjoy freedom of movement.

In a study of teacher education in the Commonwealth Caribbean, Jennings (2001) found that, while government policies stressed more child-centred approaches to teaching, a sample of teachers across eight countries who were asked to rank what teacher type their teacher education college put most emphasis on, responded in terms of two more teacher-centred approaches – giver or imparter of knowledge first and organising and managing the learning process second. Jennings cites Ratnavadivel (1999) as having similar findings in Malaysia and comments that this is not a surprising finding in the context of the Caribbean, quoting the principal of a teachers' college to the effect that:

> The enduring cultural preference among students of being lectured to and talked down to. Teacher trainees do not possess the spirit of self-directed learning. They wish to be merely recipients of knowledge at all times. They do not seem to want to have interactive learning. (Jennings, 2001, p. 122)

Jennings comments that:

> What we have here is a vicious circle. The trainee teachers themselves were taught in school by teachers who saw themselves as knowledge givers. Because they were never imbued with a spirit of self-directed learning, they expected their college lecturers to continue in like vein. (p. 124)

Jennings argues that the culture of teacher education in the Caribbean is itself often authoritarian and that there is a need to train the trainers if teacher education is going to contribute to more learner-centred teaching in schools, quoting Griffin to the effect that 'We must model with our teacher education students those practices that we hope they will carry with them to their own classrooms' (cited in Jennings, 2001, p. 131).

However, the issue is not confined to Africa and the Caribbean. In educational reform in Peru, for example, 'Many teacher training events followed a top-down approach that contradicted the very changes being promoted' (Balarin & Benavides, 2010, p. 316).

Politics, Resources and Culture

In chapter 3, we saw that change in a more democratic direction was possible in schools in developing countries. However, in this chapter we have argued that the dominant inherited existing power structures and practices of schooling and teacher education are still essentially authoritarian. Why are they so difficult to change?

One obvious factor is that those in power may explicitly not actually want democracy as an aim for education and they may overtly use schooling as part of a system of political control via political indoctrination or socialisation, as discussed in chapter 2. In Shanghai in

China, for example, the first regulation for secondary students is 'love the nation, love the people, love socialism and love the Communist Party of China' (Law, 2007, p. 29), while in Malaysia, there is a:

> political agenda that emphasises loyalty and obedience to the incumbent administration ... Far from being taught a critical attitude to authority, pupils are constantly barraged with terms such as respect (*hormat*), loyalty (*kesetiaan*) and obedience (*taat*). (Brown, 2007, pp. 229, 327)

In Pakistan, a history of military governments and behind the scenes military influence on democratic governments has hardly been conducive to the development of more democratic forms of education (Nazir, 2010, p. 330). Moreover, if an educational system, such as that in Pakistan, is predicated on a political system founded exclusively on a sole religion, then there can be problems for education for democratic citizenship because there is an overall, preordained right answer, thereby seriously reducing the scope for free discussion. Indeed, Ahmad (2008) provides an interesting discussion of tensions between two competing visions of the relationship between religion and the state in regard to citizenship education in Pakistan – the theocratic, according to which only an orthodox Muslim can be a good citizen, and the liberal democratic, which draws a line between the state and religion. However, Ahmad is clear that the theocratic interpretation remains dominant in Pakistan, a point reinforced by Dean who puts it that:

> The nature of the aims and objectives indicates that the curriculum makes no distinction between Islamic education and citizenship education. Social studies education must produce true practicing Muslim citizens who will work to strengthen the Islamic state. (2005, pp. 40-41)

In Iran, the situation is even more clear-cut and less democratic:

> The religio-political leaders of Iran have used education as an agent of politicisation and Islamisation since they came to power in 1979. Iranian schools are openly and avowedly religious and ideological and have been assigned the task of politicising the young and transforming them into the soldiers of Islam and the revolution. (Mehran, 2003, p. 324)

A key obstacle to more democratic teaching methods often cited by teachers in developing countries, and discussed in chapter 3, is a shortage of material and human resources – books, teaching aids, class size, and teacher skills and capacity (see, for example, Altinyelken, 2010, pp. 164-167, on practical obstacles to the introduction of child-centred pedagogy in Uganda). While these are important issues, and having sufficient resources is certainly helpful (and in relation to teacher skills and capacity, probably essential), there is some disagreement about whether a more active and participatory approach ultimately requires a plentiful supply of material or physical resources, or whether it can still take place in conditions of resource stringency (Harber & Davies, 1997, pp. 24-25; Schweisfurth, 2011, p. 428). Certainly, the converse is not true – contexts with a plentiful supply of teaching materials do not guarantee the existence of more democracy in schools (Harber, 2004).

We also argued in chapter 3 that, while culture can be a barrier to change in education, it can also be changed in a more democratic direction by educational efforts. In this chapter we examine how, with all the caveats about culture expressed in chapter 3, cultural values and practices can still nevertheless present barriers to be overcome in achieving more democratic practices. Writing on Namibia, O'Sullivan, for example, writes that:

> Learner-centred approaches were developed in the West and are appropriate to the Western focus on the individual. This raises questions about their potential relevance in developing country societies. In many of these societies, including the case study district, the interests of the individual tends to be subsumed under the group. (2004, p. 595)

A common obstacle to greater participation by young people in their schooling in many cultures is the adult view of the role of the child in society. Writing about Zambia, Chiwela notes that:

> children are brought up to believe that they should remain silent in the presence of adults. Hence the child may be hesitant to speak, while the adult is uncomfortable with the child who expresses an opinion. (2010, p. 66)

And Altinyelkin comments that:

> in traditional Ugandan culture, children are brought up to respect adults and those in authority. Questioning or challenging them are not often considered appropriate behaviour. (2010, p. 167)

In chapter 3, we described La Floresta School in Bolivia as a case study of a state school working in a more democratic way (Nagata, 2007). However, the school was harassed by conservative local opponents of its atmosphere of freedom and because children were behaving more independently and were less conformist. Some parents withdrew their children from the school. In 2000, the school moved and set up as a private school so that it could still operate according to its democratic principles, though unlike other private schools in Bolivia, it accepts children from all social classes. As Nagata concludes:

> The experience of La Floresta School reveals how difficult it is
> for alternative education which advocates innovativeness to
> survive in the midst of traditional institutions of education
> and in a conservative region. (2007, p. 23)

Stephens (2007, chap. 8) presents an interesting study of action research and in-service teacher education in Laos in respect of cultural dissonance. He asks the question:

> What happens when you introduce a research approach that
> has as its overt agenda one of change and democratic
> involvement of practitioners into a culture hierarchically
> ordered and growing out of political traditions of obedience
> and consensus? (2007, p. 203)

Action research's encouragement of self-reflection, self-evaluation, and the belief that the change process is owned by the practitioners involved, was difficult to reconcile in Laos with a culture of Buddhism with a strong sense of communalism where no-self is to be attained, and a socialist political culture of centralism and authoritarianism emphasising imposed consensus and conformity. Even though there were elements of action research (e.g. its collaborative nature) that fitted quite well, the vignettes of critical moments described by Stephens illustrate well potential problems of compatibility between Western liberal democratic values and some existing cultures.

In Cambodia, a cultural preference partly influenced by a particular interpretation of Buddhism, for social harmony, conformity and passivity has proved to be a considerable obstacle to the introduction of civic and moral education in schools, which is designed to teach students about concepts such as democracy, elections, human rights and freedom, and to promote active citizenship (Tan, 2008).

In discussing the introduction of a programme of educational reform in India aimed at more active, student centred pedagogy, Clarke (2003) outlines four cultural constructs that influenced the success or failure of implementation:

1. A shared holistic worldview that stresses interdependence and supports the acceptance of regulation.
2. Intertwined with openness to regulation is the conception of instruction as duty – duty is part of the natural order and we must do what is our duty regardless of whether we feel like it or not.
3. A social framework defined by structural hierarchy in terms of caste promotion and this is reflected in the display, at least superficially, of respect, esteem and even reverence expected by teachers from students.
4. Knowledge as collectively accumulated, attested and transferred – individual choice and decisions are shaped and constructed by the

community. In this process, an individual constructing his or her own knowledge becomes less significant.

Clarke argues that numbers 1 and 2 appeared to be conducive to reform, whereas numbers 3 and 4 did not.

The 'prismatic' culture of a society and schooling discussed at the beginning of this chapter can also be a barrier to change. Tan (2008), for example, points out that another cultural challenge for Cambodians in terms of a process of political democratisation is the historical, but still powerful, patronage system. She cites St. John (2005) to the effect that 'Modernisation is promoted in Cambodia within an authoritarian political model, with patronage at the heart of the Cambodian political system' (Tan, 2008, p. 568). This is a winner-takes-all system where no opposition is tolerated towards a ruler or ruling group, and where the ruled are expected to maintain the patronage relationships by accepting the patron's authority:

> On the other hand the patron is expected to maintain his network of clients in order to neutralise his opponents and keep the loyalty of his followers by funding them ... Such a system, where people secure jobs and favours from their patron, interferes with the development of democratic institutions such as parliamentary institutions, independent judiciary and a strong civil society. (Tan, 2008, p. 565)

Similarly, in Africa, where regime transitions to democracy have been only patchy in their success, some newly elected regimes have reverted to the more established cultural patterns of authoritarianism, patrimonialism, and clientelism of the recent past. Indeed, some have argued in detail that the very way that politics operate in Africa mean that there is little chance of success for the institutionalisation of democracy, despite the economic harm authoritarianism has done to the continent (Chabal & Daloz, 1999). So, in both contexts, what students are supposed to learn about democratic institutions and behaviour in schools is often contradicted by their daily experience in the wider society.

Finally, corruption in education is an issue confronting the introduction of education for democracy in many developing countries (as sometimes elsewhere) because it contradicts some of the basic tenets of democracy, such as openness, fairness and social equality. As a book on corruption in schools and universities in a range of countries puts it, there is no lack of data illustrating the diverse forms that corruption can take in the education sector (Hallak & Poisson, 2006). As the authors of the book also point out, educational corruption and malpractice undermines one of the main potentially positive purposes of education, the promotion of universal values including integrity, citizenship and ethics. A report by Save the Children in Mongolia, for example, noted that teachers had started hidden businesses forcing pupils to buy textbooks, handouts, and charging illegal fees, thus pricing out many from attending school. This, incidentally, is also coupled with widespread physical and emotional violence against children by teachers in school, also a major disincentive to attend (Save the Children, 2006). The study of civic and moral education in Cambodia cited above noted that:

> It is important for teachers teaching Civics and Morals to be role models, be respected by their students, and work in partnership with the students' families to inculcate civic and moral values in the students. However, the relationship between the teacher and the students (as well as parents) is hampered by the prevalent practice of teachers openly charging money for supplementary tutoring and other contributions. (Tan, 2008, p. 563)

Teachers deliberately cover only part of the syllabus in order to promote, or even force, their students to attend after-school supplementary private lessons. Bribes are also paid by parents for students to pass exams.

In Pakistan, a study found that government school teachers perceived most officials of the education department to be corrupt and that there were no effective mechanisms for dealing with this. Favouritism, bribery and embezzlement were reported as widespread and thrived in an authoritarian atmosphere of insufficient open accountability (Nazir, 2010, pp. 339-340).

Conclusion

Schools can potentially contribute to democracy and democratisation in a number of ways. If efficiently organised and run, pupils can learn the bureaucratic organisational skills necessary for the functioning of any modern institution. On top of this, or as well as, schools can also operate not only in an efficient and competent manner, but also more democratically through the shared power of decision-making. Unfortunately, as this chapter has demonstrated, many (probably the majority) of schools in developing countries do not at present provide a sufficiently robust or consistent model or experience of a well-organised democracy to make a significant contribution to the development of a more democratic political culture. There are still many barriers and obstacles to overcome before formal education can play a significant part in exposing the majority of young people to education for democracy. However, one developing country that has tried to transform its education system in a democratic direction at all levels is South Africa and it is to a detailed study of that country that we now turn.

CHAPTER 5

The Roles of Education in Relation to Political Development: South Africa as a case study

Introduction: development goals for education in post-apartheid South Africa

This chapter uses post-apartheid South Africa, ranked 123rd on the UNDP's Human Development Index (out of 187 countries) in 2011 (UNDP, 2011), as a more detailed case study of the different possible roles of education in relation to democratic political development. Schooling was a significant site in the struggle against apartheid and there is no doubt that post-apartheid governments since 1994 have attached considerable importance to educational reform.

The first White Paper on education and training set out the key goals of the new education system (Harber, 2001). First, there was considerable emphasis on education as human capital as a meritocratic attempt to move away from unequal social and economic reproduction of apartheid to more equal opportunities for all. An integrated approach to education and training was key to human resource development as the old academic/applied or 'head and hand' distinctions were seen as having helped to reproduce occupational and class distinctions. There was a need for a form of education that provided the skills and predispositions for continual learning, moving flexibly between occupations, and taking responsibility for personal performance as a contribution towards developing a successful economy (Department of Education, 1995). This emphasis on the role of education in providing the skills necessary for economic competition in the global market place has continued (McGrath & Akoojee, 2007) and was reflected in the Revised National Curriculum Statement (NCS) of 2001, where two key developmental outcomes for schooling that are relevant to the economic role of education, for example, are to explore education and career opportunities, and develop entrepreneurial capacities (Department of Education, 2001a).

Second, and in line with modernisation theory as discussed earlier in this book, there is an emphasis in the original White Paper on creating a 'modern' society through education by means of an efficient, professional and well managed education system (Department of Education, 2001a, pp. 15, 44, 69, 74). Some of the attributes of a modern person are spelt out in the NCS where the kind of learner envisaged will, for example, display a developed spirit of curiosity to enable creative and scientific discovery, display an awareness of health promotion, use effectively a variety of problem-solving techniques that reflect different ways of thinking, and make informed decisions and accept accountability as responsible citizens in an increasingly complex and technological society (Department of Education, 2001a, p. 13).

Third, and finally, post-apartheid education policy has had an overwhelming emphasis on the role of education in helping to create a more democratic and peaceful society:

> The realization of democracy, liberty, equality, justice and peace are necessarily conditions for the full pursuit and enjoyment of lifelong learning. It should be a goal of education and training policy to enable a democratic, free, equal, just and peaceful society to take root and prosper in our land, on the basis that all South Africans without exception share the same inalienable rights, equal citizenship and common destiny, and that all forms of bias (especially racial, ethnic and gender) are dehumanising. (Department of Education, 1995, p. 22)

That this new philosophy based on democracy and human rights would mean changing all aspects of the education system was also recognised:

> The letter and spirit of these rights and freedoms should inform the intellectual culture in all schools and educational institutions, and professional services in departments of education. This has unavoidable implications for curricula, textbooks, other educational materials and media programmes, teaching methods, teacher education, professional supervision and management culture. (Department of Education, 1995, p. 43)

Based on the above quote, an effective school in South Africa is one that operates democratically in order to promote democracy in the wider society (Mncube, 2005).

Subsequently, education policy was changed to introduce a curriculum aimed at encouraging more active and participant classrooms, creating more independent and critical thinkers, and introducing new governance structures in which parents, teachers and learners are involved in more democratic forms of decision-making and school organisation (Harber, 2001; Carter et al,2003).

As this book is primarily concerned with political development, and in the light of the earlier analysis in chapters 1 to 4, this chapter will focus on two developmental aspects of educational reform – modernisation and democratisation.

Modernisation or Disorganisation?

We have argued in this book that democracy needs to be built on an effective, functioning modern organisational and institutional base. If schools are to be a key source of 'modern', bureaucratic organisational attitudes and behaviours then young people must experience them through the effective operation of schools as organisations and the professional behaviour of staff. For example, Bloch has argued in relation to South Africa that:

> It is clear that honesty, reliability, determination, leadership
> ability and willingness to work within the hierarchies of
> modern life are all characteristics that society rewards. These
> skills are, in part, formed and nourished by schools. (2009,
> p. 19)

There are many effective and well-organised schools in South Africa. Importantly, there are many examples of such schools in areas affected by poverty and poor resources which function effectively and achieve good examination results (Harber, 2001, pp. 66-68). Bloch (2009, chap. 5) provides further positive examples. He quotes the head of Bhukulani High School in Soweto, which has a matriculation pass rate of over 90%, to the effect that schools work simply because there are people who are prepared to work, who turn up for class on time and teach effectively. As Bloch comments, comparing this school to another equally successful school in a poor area, 'There is a detailed set of planning processes and systems to ensure success, no magic formula'. The role of the head is important as 'Teachers need the administrative efficiency and ordered predictability of a well-run school' (2009, pp. 136-137). He further cites a Ministerial committee that examined the nature of successful schools in South Africa which found that the key to success was doing the basics well:

> Firstly, all of the schools were focussed on their central tasks
> of teaching, learning and management with a sense of purpose,
> responsibility and commitment. Secondly, they and a strong
> organisational capacity, including leadership and management
> and professionalism was valued. Thirdly, all of the schools
> carried out their tasks with competence and confidence; all
> had organisational cultures or mind-sets that supported hard
> work, expected achievement and acknowledged success. And
> lastly, all had strong accountability systems in place which

enabled them to meet the demands of external accountability, particularly in terms of Senior Certificate achievement. (2009, p. 138)

However, the problem of disorganised schools has also been recognised as a serious issue in post-apartheid South Africa for some time. In 1997, the Deputy Minister of Education said:

> In many of our education departmental offices, there is a chronic absenteeism of officials, appointments are not honoured, punctuality is not observed, phones ring without being answered, files and documents are lost, letters are not responded to, senior officials are inaccessible, there is confusion about roles and responsibilities and very little support, advice and assistance is given to schools ... Many of our parents fear their own children, never check the child's attendance at school, are not interested in the welfare of the school, never attend meetings, give no support to the teacher or principal ... Many of our teachers are not committed to quality teaching, their behaviour leaves much to be desired, are more interested in their own welfare, are not professional and dedicated, are never at school on time, pursue their studies at the expense of the children, do not prepare for lessons ... Many of our children are always absent from school, lack discipline and manners, regularly leave school early, are usually late for school, wear no uniform, have no respect for teachers, drink during school hours, are involved in drugs and gangs, gamble and smoke at school, come to school armed to instil fear in others ... Many of our principals have no administrative skills, they are the source of conflict between students and teachers, sow divisions among their staff, undermine the development of their colleagues, fail to properly manage the resources of their school, do not involve parents in school matters. (Mkhatshwa, 1997, pp. 14-15)

In 2000, the then Minister of Education made a surprise visit to a school in Soweto which had one of the lowest pass rates for the school leaving exam in the country (13%). He found pupils milling in the street, empty classrooms and teachers absent. He blamed the teachers for a lack of discipline and organisation (McGreal, 2000). More recently, the State President of South Africa, Jacob Zuma, called on teachers to be 'in class, on time and teaching' and to spend the rest of the day on 'preparation and marking' (*Mail & Guardian*, September 2-8, 2011), a theme he returned to in his 2012 State of the Nation Address. In the same vein, Duncan Hindle, a senior education official in South Africa, has argued that school accountability is lacking when even the basic minimum terms of employment are not being complied with. He describes a situation where:

> teachers are absent without good reason, some arrive late or leave early, and others are perhaps at school but not in class. Funerals, council duties and union meetings provide convenient excuses. Fridays become 'early closing' days and on paydays non-attendance is the norm in many schools. Pupils display similar traits. (*Mail & Guardian*, September 2-8, 2011, p. 12)

Academic research has supported these political statements. Christie (1998) analysed schools as '(dis)organisations' in the 'poor and disrupted communities spawned by apartheid'. She notes that the list of characteristics associated with such schools (absenteeism, low morale, violence, etc.) is an inverse of the 'lists' of features so popular in effective schools research, and uses social psychology and the idea of 'social defence' to analyse and explain the way dysfunctional schools operate. School organisations need to contain the anxieties associated with learning and teaching. Rituals, school rules, formalised social relations and adherence to the boundaries of time and space provide a form of containment for learners and teachers. However, when the organisation itself is collapsing – when authority structures have broken down and the boundaries of time and space no longer exist for staff and learners – then social defences cannot contain the anxieties of the organisation's members. She argues that when the organisational context of schools breaks down, teaching and learning as basic group tasks in a school are subordinated to unconscious group activity, whereby social relations and office politics get more attention than substantive work. Instead of being able to focus on teaching and learning, schools have become caught up in forms of conflict, aggression and uncertainty that cannot be contained in a weak organisational structure. This, she argues, goes some way to explaining 'the apathy, depression, impotence, anxiety about physical safety, lack of agency, disempowerment and projection of blame onto others' (p. 291) that she and other researchers found in the dysfunctional schools they visited.

A later research report of 2007 noted that educator attendance varies widely between schools, but is known to result in significant loss of learner time. Apart from arriving at school late and leaving early, reasons for educator absence include strikes and stay aways, examinations, and sporting events and municipal activities. The report also noted that loss of learning time will undoubtedly adversely affect achievement, outcomes and progression (Motala et al, 2007, pp. 58-59).

Further recent evidence also suggests that these problems persist. The South African Human Rights Commission report on the right to basic education in 2006 described a dysfunctional schooling system for the majority and a privileged, functional sector serving a minority. The report followed public hearings in October 2005 on a litany of problems that schools face, including low teacher morale, lack of accountability and non-attendance of children. Teacher absenteeism and lack of enthusiasm also remain as problems (Nelson Mandela Foundation, 2005; Hunt, 2007). Moreover, various forms of corruption are also not unknown in South African schools (Harber, 2001; Fataar, 2007).

In their research in schools in three provinces of South Africa, Hammett and Staeheli noted that:

> On multiple occasions during our work at a township school
> in Cape Town we witnessed educators either arriving late or
> leaving early from class or even remaining in the staffroom for
> the duration of the teaching period (despite being timetabled
> to teach) ... On a number of occasions at other schools, it
> appeared that educators were drunk. At many schools,
> educators used learners to run personal errands – primarily to
> fetch food or drinks from the school tuck shop or neighbouring
> street traders. (2011, p. 275)

In a sustained analysis of what he terms 'dysfunctional' schools, Bloch (2009) relates in some detail evidence of poor educational outcomes in South Africa to poor internal organisation. Acknowledging serious problems of infrastructure in schools in relation to the supply of electricity, libraries, laboratories, computers, clean water and suitable toilets, he also notes the enormous difficulty of recruiting competent heads to manage all 27,000 schools in South Africa. As a result:

> Schools are often not well organised, timetabling is poor,
> institutional process is arbitrary and ineffective. At a teaching
> level, haphazard planning and time management are often
> reflected in a poor ability to plan and timetable teaching plans
> for the curriculum over the year. (2009, pp. 82-83)

Bloch argues that the dysfunctional nature of many schools in South Africa is not only a problem for success in terms of outcomes, such test scores and examination results, but also has implications for democracy. First, in terms of the Zuma administration's commitment to creating an efficient 'developmental state', as discussed in chapter 1 of this book, because:

> There are too many tales of salaries not being paid by
> departments, of strikes being unfairly monitored by officials,
> of transport for poor scholars not being in place, of corruption
> and theft, of non-transference of moneys to fee-free schools,
> and so on. The disappearance of millions in school nutrition
> money in the Eastern Cape is the most extreme and perhaps

the most shocking example, but it is not entirely
unrepresentative. (Bloch, 2009, p. 117)

Second, in a more direct way, he quotes Taylor to the effect that:

More disturbing is that dysfunctional schools are unable to
socialize young people into the attitudes of mind required for
citizenship in a democracy ... school leavers are easy prey to a
life of crime, poverty, corruption and inefficiency. (cited in
Bloch, 2009, p. 68)

Democracy and Peace or Authoritarianism and Violence?

Democracy and peace were at the forefront of the new, post-apartheid
educational policies, given South Africa's authoritarian and violent past.
South Africa is governed by the Constitution, the supreme law of the
country. The Constitution of the Republic of South Africa (RSA) aims at
ensuring democracy, and as such is permeated by democratic principles.
For example, the Constitution of the RSA (1996) in its preamble
emphasises a new set of values in moving away from the past so as to:

heal the divisions of the past and establish a society based on
democratic values, social justice and fundamental human
rights; lay the foundations for a democratic and open society ...
improve the quality of life of all citizens and free the potential
of each person; and build a united and a democratic South
Africa. (Republic of South Africa, 1996a, p. 1)

The Constitution therefore sets out the foundations for a state and society
based on human rights, democracy, social justice and freedom. South
Africa is a transitional society attempting to progress from
authoritarianism to democracy and it is the Constitution that provides a
framework for democracy in the country (Naidoo, 2012). Democratising
schools was believed to be a vehicle of fostering democracy (Mncube,
2005). In a study of the leadership and management of democratic
schools conducted by Naidoo (2012), the principals at both the case
study schools felt strongly that schools should support democracy
because it was enshrined in the Constitution of the country. In 2001, the
Department of Education in its *Manifesto on Values, Education and
Democracy* set out the fundamental democratic political values
stemming from the Constitution that should form the basis of the
education system (Department of Education, 2001b). These values and
their educational implications are set out in Table II.

Fundamental value	Educational implications
Democracy	Empowerment of population to exercise democratic rights; provision of skills to participate, think critically and act responsibly.
Social Justice and Equity	Access to education is the most important resource in addressing poverty – only then will liberty be achieved. Reconciliation requires social justice to address past injustices – education for all is an essential element of social justice.
Equality	Access for all to an educational provision that does not discriminate on any grounds. Equality in the treatment of all, by all.
Non-sexism and Non-racism	Regardless of race or gender, learners afforded the same opportunities and the same degree of security.
Ubuntu (Human Dignity)	Mutual understanding and active appreciation of the value of human differences.
Open Society	Participation rather than observation; empowerment to think and act; a culture of dialogue and debate.
Accountability	Power and responsibility for all involved in education – learners, educators, managers, parents, etc.
Rule of Law	Rules within which learners, educators, managers, parents, etc. operate – including the law of the land.
Respect	Precondition for communication and teamwork – schools require mutual respect between all partners.
Reconciliation	Acceptance of all individuals through learning about each other, valuing differences and diversity.

Table II. Fundamental values and their educational implications in South Africa. Source: Carter et al, 2003, p. 16.

As argued above, such democratic values and their concomitant structures and practices need to be built on top of, or in parallel to, an already functioning school. In a study of three schools operating in a more democratic manner at the end of the 1990s:

> the schools were clearly and recognisably carrying out their basic functions as schools in a consistent and reliable way, something which cannot necessarily be taken for granted in South Africa. All three schools exhibited an orderly, purposeful and calm atmosphere with clean premises and businesslike behaviour. Teachers and students were in

classrooms when they were supposed to be and learners experienced a full day's planned curriculum each day. However, the schools were also interesting in that they went beyond these possible minimum level indicators of functional effectiveness in their willingness to embrace change and in their commitment to implementing a new educational ideology aimed at fostering a non-violent, non-racist democratic society. (Harber & Muthukrishna, 2000, p. 430)

Here we will briefly describe each school participating in this research in order to give a flavour of their interpretations or emphases of democratic education, before going on to examine a number of key themes of attempted democratic educational transformation in South Africa in turn. The principal at the first school, for example, described the democratic, participative culture at the school where all stakeholders have a meaningful role to play and where they participate fully in defining the goals of the school and in implementing policy. Learners participate democratically through a learners' representative council which is represented on the school's governing body. This was quite clearly aimed at enhancing racial integration in the school because the school was the only place where racial tolerance could be learned, given that the pupils still lived in racially segregated areas. Ensuring fair racial representation on school decision-making structures was an important issue. The goals of the school have been decided on jointly by learners, parents and teachers, and the school's mission statement contains a clear stand on the need to educate for democracy and the need to reject any form of racism, sexism or sectarianism.

The second school, which has been described and discussed in more detail elsewhere (Harber, 1998; Welgemoed, 1998), began to change its school structures in a democratic direction before government legislation was passed, as a response to the changing racial balance in the school. The school had begun to desegregate in 1991, but desegregation is not the same as integration – simply putting people of different racial backgrounds together in the same school says nothing about the nature and quality of racial interaction. The first results of racial desegregation were hostility, conflict, name-calling, and even violence between pupils. Realising this, the head teacher began a process of democratisation which involved a student representative council and student representation on the school governing body. Democratic skills, values and behaviours are learned and do not necessarily develop naturally or by chance, so training was provided for all class representatives on the nature and responsibilities of their role. The school also embarked on a process of writing a new set of basic values, code of conduct and set of disciplinary procedures and staff, students and teachers were all involved in the process. Democracy, mutual respect and peaceful conflict resolution were at the heart of the values underpinning the new code of conduct. Interviews with the head teacher, staff and students suggested that enhanced communication, openness and trust had resulted from the democratisation process, and that there had been a marked, even dramatic decline in racial conflict as a result of the change in the school's ethos.

Interviews with the head teacher, staff and students at the third school suggested that within overall democratic structures particular emphasis had been given to peaceful conflict resolution. The Community Dispute Resolution Trust, a non-governmental organisation that trains in the area of conflict resolution, was invited into the school and learners who were trained in the skills of peer mediation of conflicts then formed the conflict resolution committee which attempts to settle conflicts in the school without resorting to violence. This had reduced violent conflict significantly in the school and improved staff–learner relationships, which had also improved teaching and learning. Of the six schools in the immediate locality, all with pupils from identical (low level) socio-economic backgrounds, this school had a matriculation pass rate of 79%, whereas the next most successful school had a pass rate of 59% despite being a better equipped school. The other four schools ranged from 11 to 43% (Harber & Muthukrishna, 2000, pp. 430-432).

A Democratic Curriculum?

A democratic curriculum emphasises access to a wide range of information, acknowledging the right of those with alternative opinions to have their viewpoints heard. Educators in a democratic society have an obligation to help young people identify a range of ideas and to voice their own opinions on issues. However, such freedom of self-expression is still not the general rule in many schools, with many educators still persisting in avoiding open discussion, even though a democratic and participatory curriculum implies that learners are encouraged to ask critical questions and to discuss controversial issues. Beane and Apple (1999) assert that a democratic curriculum includes not only what adults think is important, but also the questions and concerns that young people have about themselves and their world. Such a curriculum invites young people to shed the passive role of knowledge consumers and to assume the active role of 'meaning makers', which entails their being encouraged continuously to explore such issues, to imagine appropriate responses to problems, and to act upon such responses (Beane & Apple, 1999). For example, the curriculum includes learning experiences enabling them to learn about how to cope with contemporary problems and to be able to discuss controversial issues.

Kelly (1995) argues that education in a democratic society should promote openness of knowledge and freedom of opinion, and both Lewis (1999) and Knight (2001) contend that, at the present time, important knowledge is sometimes still overlooked in the classroom. 'School-sponsored knowledge', (a National Curriculum) is that which can be regarded as official or high-status knowledge, which is produced or endorsed by the dominant culture (Apple, 1993). Such knowledge has been used in the past as a means of silencing the voices of those outside the dominant culture, particularly those of people of colour, women and the young. Knight (2001) argues that a democracy must emphasise the development of important knowledge, which is used by all and not by the select few (the elite), and such knowledge should be the basis for decision-making for the public good. Further, Pearl and Knight (1999) argue that the knowledge developed at school should meet, at the very least, the following goals:

- the preparation of an informed, responsible and involved democratic citizenry;
- the realisation of active participation in the economic life of the community;
- the realisation of meaningful participation in the development of a democratic culture; and
- the development of healthy human beings capable of fulfilling the responsibilities of a parent, mate, friend and contributing member of the community.

In South Africa, the Outcomes-Based curriculum, known as Curriculum 2005 and introduced in 1997, was designed to facilitate more active, participant and democratic forms of learning (Harber, 2001). As argued in one article:

> The principles which guided the new curriculum are
> purported to be based on cooperation, critical thinking and
> social responsibility, thus enabling individuals to participate
> in all aspects of society. Concomitant with this is the
> envisaged need for teachers to change their pedagogy from one
> that is more didactic and teacher controlled to one which
> encourages more active learner participation.
> (Scholtz et al, 2008, p. 22)

The initial version of the curriculum reform was criticised for being over complex and demanding for teachers and was subsequently reviewed and revised in 2001 and replaced by a revised National Curriculum Statement (NCS), which was written in plainer language, and

> gave more emphasis to basic skills, content knowledge and a
> logical progression from one grade to the next. It combines a
> learner-centred curriculum requiring critical thought and
> emphasising the democratic values embedded in the
> Constitution, with an appreciation of the importance of
> content and support for educators. (Motala et al, 2007, p. 22)

139

The National Curriculum Statement Grades R-12: Curriculum and Assessment Policy emphasises aspects like teamwork, human rights, inclusivity, active and critical learning (DoE, 2011), and is an approach to curriculum which still emphasises the active participation of learners, thus making teaching and learning more learner-centred.

However, in line with the NCS, the Curriculum and Assessment Policy Statement (CAPS) has recently been developed to improve the quality of teaching and learning. The CAPS clearly advocates 'an active and critical approach to learning, rather than rote and uncritical learning of given truths' (DoE, 2011, p. 3). The CAPS is not a new curriculum, but part of the NCS. The focus will be on content to be taught per term and the required assessment tasks for each term, though in some subjects there will be more curriculum changes than in others. Under the CAPS, every subject in each grade will have a single, comprehensive and concise document. It appears therefore that the CAPS is placing a greater emphasis on content than outcomes-based education (OBE) and is going back to terminology that was used in education in South Africa before OBE was introduced. It is also seemingly avoiding the jargon that was used when OBE was implemented. Liebenberg (2011) describes succinctly the key changes of the CAPS:

1. CAPS will mean less group work and more individual work.
2. Learning Areas and Learning Programmes will be called Subjects.
3. Learning Outcomes and Assessment Standards will be replaced with Topics.
4. The CAPS will break down each Subject into teaching weeks and outline the topics that need to be covered per week.
5. The number of Subjects in the Intermediate Phase (Grade 4 to 6) will be reduced from eight to six.
6. The number of projects for learners will be reduced from the year 2010.
7. Annual National testing of Grade 3, 6 and 9 will be fully implemented by the end of 2011.

Curriculum reform is therefore one of the key initiatives of democratising education in South Africa as it emphasises the need for learners to think critically, to analyse and to solve problems arising in the classroom, school and society (Mncube & Harber, 2010). In a study of educator perspectives on democratic schooling in South Africa by the authors of this book, one of the respondents affirmed the need for active engagement of learners in lessons, stating that, unlike in the past when the learners had merely to listen to the educator, engage in rote learning and eventually write tests on the material with which they had been provided:

the present system of education in South Africa requires learners to be active participants in a lesson so that they can raise their concerns/views/opinions coming up with new ideas. This is a demonstration that, in quality education, freedom of expression exists, which is another aspect of democracy. This is what leads to quality education. (Mncube & Harber, 2010, p. 620)

Asked about what they understood about democratic education another educator said:

Learners do have a say on what to learn and on how learning should take place. [An] individual excels at that which he or she wants to do, rather than at what he or she has to do. The learning content that is provided in the NCS (National Curriculum Statement) is linked with what the learners experience in their everyday lives. For example, in a Science lesson, learners relate that when the iron is left in the rain, it will rust and they will better understand the meaning of oxidation, etc. Learner participation will be encouraged through allowing them to ask questions that are relevant to the content taught. Further, they will be asked to demonstrate wherever possible and encourage them to share their views even if different from mine. I always ensure to create an environment which is conducive to teaching and learning by always treating them with respect. (Mncube & Harber, 2010, p. 620)

In the view of the above educator, a democratic classroom is one in which learners have a say in matters pertaining to their teaching and learning. Such a classroom is also one in which the educators link the content of the NCS to learners' experiences, ensuring that their teaching inspires learners at all times. This is the type of classroom in which learners are allowed to ask questions, as well as to engage in open discussions about controversial issues, and in debate and dialogue. Such engagement is only possible if the educators concerned are willing and determined to create an environment that is conducive to effective teaching and learning (Mncube & Harber, 2010).

Another educator explained further how teaching was now more learner-centred and described how activities were developed to involve the learners. A further educator also referred to the content of the lessons, emphasising that it should be meaningful and relevant to the learners. The educator also stated that the learners should be able to relate to what is being taught. One of the other respondents referred to adapting teaching and learning to accommodate the differing needs of all learners in the classroom by organising teaching to take into account 'the learners and the different levels they are at' (Mncube & Harber, 2010,

141

p. 621). There signals a shift in focus towards the appreciation of human diversity in terms of the learners' needs and potential.

The current educational system in South Africa sees learning as an interactive and cooperative process, during which learners discuss, experiment, research and write, rather than listening to the supposedly omniscient educator standing at the front. Classroom discourse is democratic, in so far as it is constructed mutually by students and the educator. In such discourse, students have equal speaking rights, as well as the right to negotiate the curriculum. Another educator had the following to say about such democratic discourse:

> In this new dispensation, learners need to be treated with respect. And I think it's also part of democracy, the respect that you need. Like previously, the learner had to just listen, grasp and write a test, or whatever. But now, in this type of education, the learner is also involved in the lesson to raise his/her views, come up with ideas, do research which lead to quality education. The learner is involved in all spheres of the lesson. There are discussions where the learner is allowed to speak his mind, there is research, the learner must go outside and do some research in the library, internet or wherever. Learners are sent out to go and interview community leaders. So, the learner can go to the mayor and talk to him/her, so freedom of speech. If these things are linked, these democratic ideals that you are using in the classroom, the learner learns a lot and you can receive that quality education – the learner is being taught holistically. (Mncube & Harber, 2010, pp. 619-620)

The above educator expressed the belief that a curriculum consistent with democracy works well when there is active involvement of learners, during which their views and opinions can be aired through debate, dialogue and discussion. Such an interactive environment allows for the freedom of expression to prevail.

In terms of teaching methods, educators were asked 'which teaching methods educators would you choose to employ in order to democratise your classrooms?'. One educator said:

> In the past learners were considered as empty vessels, which have to listen to the educator filling them with official knowledge. Learners had to do rote learning in preparation for tests and exams. In democratic classrooms learners are active participants who are able to freely raise their opinions, coming up with new ideas. During the teaching–learning encounter, learners are afforded opportunities to air their voices and there is freedom of expression which exists, which is another aspect of democracy. Learners are also provided with opportunities to

do research, for example in their environment, libraries and searching the internet. This is an indication that, in a democracy, quality education does exist. (Mncube & Harber, 2010, pp. 620-621)

Another educator asserted that:

I always make sure that my teaching is learner-centred, developing activities that involve learners, for example, such as experimental investigations. I give learners projects and they come back to report to the class how they went about doing those investigations. If they do projects, I make sure that they get some findings and draw conclusions in their group work. I also give them tasks to complete. All these activities are done in groups and, in the process, they also learn to rate one another, while learning from one another, and appreciate each other's efforts. My role as a teacher does not only have to do with the imparting of knowledge; but, in addition to knowledge acquisition, I make sure that they acquire skills, attitudes and values consistent with what they expect from the community and vice versa. (Mncube & Harber, 2010, p. 621)

Within the new approach to learning in South Africa, teaching should also be learner- centred in the sense that learners use their prior knowledge as building blocks in the assimilation of new knowledge. Lessons should regularly include the daily experiences of the learners. One educator put it as follows:

I always use [the] learners' own environment to clarify the content and this makes learning easy. For example, on their way to school, they see boards [on which is] written 60km/h. I explain to them that the car can only travel at a speed of 60km per hour in this area. Or we can talk about the interest rate. What are the implications of borrowing money? How is interest being calculated on money borrowed? I then show them how it is calculated and advise them to assist their parents. (Mncube & Harber, 2010, p. 621)

However, despite these positive views on learning and teaching, and the reforms to the initial post-apartheid curriculum described above to make it more teacher-friendly, realities in the classroom have been slow to change in many schools. A report on research carried out by the Presidential Education Initiative published in 1999 (Vally, 1999) indicated that OBE is succeeding in the ideological domain, with teachers embracing its main intentions. However, many teachers did not have the conceptual resources to give effect to it in the classrooms. Teachers, particularly in poorly resourced schools, were not in a position to translate the broad outcomes of Curriculum 2005 into appropriate learning programmes, nor to develop their own assessment strategies. The researchers observed significant contradictions between teachers' verbal support of the learner-centred pedagogy of Curriculum 2005 and the actual practices of these same teachers. The following teacher-centred practices were commonly observed:

- Teacher talk and low-level questions dominate lessons;
- Lessons are generally characterised by a lack of structure and the absence of activities which promote higher order skills such as investigation, understanding relationships and curiosity;
- Real world examples are often used but at a very superficial level;
- Little group work or other interaction occurs between pupils; and
- Pupils do little reading or writing. When it exists, it is often of a very rudimentary kind.

Another study of schooling in rural South Africa found that, while 90% of teachers claimed to be using a variety of active teaching methods, the responses from pupils and the observations of the researchers strongly suggested that the majority of teachers continued to use traditional, teacher-centred methods of monologue and rote learning. Classroom activity was dominated by three modes: reading, writing and correcting (Nelson Mandela Foundation, 2005, chap. 5).

Moreover, many teachers in South Africa (as elsewhere) have tended to see school knowledge as factual, safe and uncontested and shied away from values and controversies, even though these are key aspects of life in a democratic society and occur in all curriculum subjects (Carter et al, 2003; Harber & Serf, 2006). This problem is of particular significance in South Africa where HIV and AIDS is also a threat to social well-being, and where teachers are reluctant to tackle sexual issues in the classroom. A teacher's stance on its causes, as well as their response to the pandemic, is very much based on personal values and, therefore is highly controversial (Buthelezi et al, 2007).

One further obstacle to schooling playing a greater role in education for democratic citizenship via the discussion of controversial issues may well be teacher education. Indeed, there is evidence from both teachers and student teachers that suggests teacher education in South Africa does not prepare teachers sufficiently to facilitate the discussion of controversial issues in the classroom This may be because in practice the priorities and internal processes and relationships of teacher education do not facilitate such discursive and explorative methods. (Harber, 2001; Harber & Serf, 2006; Chikoko et al, 2011).

Democratic Structures: school governing bodies

In 1996, the new democratic state published a White Paper on the organisation governance and funding of schools (Republic of South

Africa, 1996b), from which emanated the South African Schools Act No. 84 of 1996 (SASA). The SASA became operative at the beginning of 1997 and mandated that all public state schools in South Africa must have democratically elected school governing bodies (SGBs) composed of teachers, non-teaching staff, parents and learners (the latter in secondary schools). Parents are supposed to be the majority in the SGBs and the chair of the governing body should come from the parent component (Mncube et al, 2011). The SASA mandates that secondary school learners, who are members of the Representative Council for Learners (RCL), should also be part of school governance through participation in school governing bodies. The SASA is regarded as a tool aimed at, inter alia, redressing past exclusions and facilitating the necessary transformation to support the ideals of representation and participation in the schools and the country. By the establishment of the SASA, the state aimed at fostering democratic school governance and thereby introducing a school governance structure that involves all educational stakeholder groups in active and responsible roles in order to promote issues of democracy: tolerance, rational discussion and collective decision-making (Department of Education, 1996, p. 16).

Bush and Heystek (2003) argue that, despite the significant difficulties facing the educational system in South Africa, governing bodies provide a good prospect of enhancing local democracy and improving the quality of education for all learners. In addition, the Ministerial Review Committee (2004, p. 82) regarded the SGBs as a unifying factor in schools and communities.

Crucial to the democratic functioning of schools, including SGBs, is the role of the principal. Naidoo (2012) studied two functioning democratic schools in the Durban area. She found that the principals displayed strikingly similar characteristics, including commitment, openness, integrity, excellent communication and interpersonal skills, being good listeners and having faith in others. The way the principals practiced democracy in the two schools had many similarities:

> These principals practiced the sharing of ideas and sharing of expertise. They fostered a democratic culture that embraced the cultures of collegiality, respect, care and trust, listening, participation, communication, consultation and collaboration ... At both schools participants made reference to collective decision-making, collaboration and voting as democratic processes. From the responses at both schools the structures that make the school democratic included the staff representatives, staff stewards representing the teacher unions, a fully elected Representative Council of Learners, School Governing Body, Senior Management Team, peer mediators and learning (subject) committees. (Naidoo, 2012, pp. 260-261)

However, despite the existence of these democratic principles and practices, Naidoo still found that learners were still insufficiently involved in decision-making in the two schools. Indeed, a number of scholars in South Africa have been critical of the actual practices of SGBs (see, for example, Naidoo, 2005). They have argued that conflicts and dilemmas among the membership of school governing bodies are central to the experience of school governance. Studies of the functioning on the new SGBs (Bush & Heystek, 2003; Ministerial Review Committee, 2004; Mncube, 2005; Brown & Duku, 2008) found that members of governing bodies tended to be male, that principals still played a dominant role in meetings and decision-making processes, and that teachers tended to participate in meetings more than other stakeholders. Parents, the numerically dominant group under the legislation, were hampered in many areas by a skills capacity deficit and communication and transportation problems. Learner participation was only moderate and concentrated on fundraising, learner discipline and sports activities. So, while the structural dimension of democratic governance had been established, power relations, i.e. the dominance of the principal, remained much the same. Moreover, because of existing inequalities in the wider society, by 'devolving functions to the governing body, the State may unintentionally be contributing to a perpetuation of inequalities in the school environment' (Karlsson, 2002, p. 333).

In addition, Brown and Duku, (2008) contend that school governing bodies are fraught with social tension, rejection, domination, and psychological stress which, in turn, leads to the isolation of those parents who are of low socio-economic status as such their participation is compromised. Further research also suggested that low socio-economic status negatively affects how some parents participate in school governing bodies (Ministerial Review Committee, 2004).

A study of four school governing bodies in the province of KwaZulu Natal (Mncube, 2005) further found that, although they exist and operate broadly according to the intention of the SASA which introduced them, there are a number of factors leading to lack of parents' participation, namely: unequal power relations, socio-economic status, lack of confidence and expertise caused by the absence or lack of training, poor communication of information, the rural–urban divide, different cultural expectations of diverse communities, language barriers, poor organisation, and the high turnover rate of governors.

A further study in Gauteng and KwaZulu Natal reinforced the dominant role of principals and teachers and found that:

> many stakeholders, particularly principals and educators, do not necessarily value participation in itself or for advancing democratic participation in school. In their practices, such participation is little more than information sharing or limited consultation. (Grant-Lewis & Naidoo, 2006, p. 422)

Both these studies tend to reinforce the point about the danger of contributing to the social reproduction role referred to by Karlsson above.

In terms of the SASA, learner governors should be full members of the SGBs, but they are often not necessarily afforded a full opportunity to participate in crucial decisions by the adult members of governing bodies, directly or indirectly (Mncube, 2008). Mechanisms to involve learners in the governance of schools have been employed globally as a form of democratising education (Beane & Apple, 1999; Carter et al, 2003; Mncube, 2005; Cox et al, 2010). Some support for more democratic processes in schools in South Africa was noted in the study by Mncube and Harber (2010) where some of the educators interviewed argued that learners should become more involved in decision-making, especially regarding such matters as the code of conduct. One of the educators described the role played by shared decision-making in the adoption of rules pertaining to the classroom:

> The classroom rules are based on the school's disciplinary policy. So we have to decide how we are going to deal with discipline problems in the classroom ... We negotiate on what the classroom rules should be, so that the learners can then take ownership of such rules. (Mncube & Harber, 2010, p. 621)

In response to prompts about what forms of discipline they regarded as appropriate in terms of democratic schooling, many educators suggested using point systems and detentions, as well as the code of conduct for learners. In this regard, one educator suggested the following:

> I think there should be school rules that constitute the code of conduct for learners and these rules should be formulated by both the educators and learners, so that learners know what is expected of them and should also have freedom of expression, being free to say what they like and dislike. Both the educator and learners should mutually agree on the rules, and these rules should be consistent with the code of conduct for learners. It is this code of conduct that would guide the learners if they are still acting rightly or wrongly. Both educators and learners must be responsible in formulating the school rules. This shows democratic ruling within the school, since learners are free to comment and in managing the school/class. And it will be easier, because everyone knows what exactly is required. Further, to learners it will be good or easy to follow the rules they formulated. (Mncube & Harber, 2010, pp. 621-622)

Another educator stressed the importance of classroom rules in the following way:

> One of the structures that you need to put in place is the classroom rules and those rules are incorporated within the school's code of conduct. There is even a disciplinary committee at the school. The classroom rules are based on the school's disciplinary policy. So, we have to decide how we are going to deal with discipline problems in the classroom. At the end of the day, it is not me disciplining them, but we collectively decided on the punishment. We negotiate on what the class rules should be. The learners can then take ownership. We do have a code of conduct at the school. The code of conduct is there to govern the learners, so that they know what is acceptable and what not, and as such to develop the sense of responsibility. The code of conduct was formulated by all the stakeholders of the school namely, the educators, the SGB, as well as the learners. Every quarter the code of conduct in our school is reviewed.
> (Mncube & Harber, 2010, p. 622)

For democratic schooling to take effect, the SASA requires that a code of conduct be implemented at each and every school. Such a code consists of a set of rules that governs the learners' behaviour at the school. Section 8 of the South African Schools Act states that a school governing body of a public school must adopt a code of conduct for the learners after consultation with, and mutual agreement by, all the stakeholders concerned. Such stakeholders consist of the learners at the school, as well as their parents and educators. A code of conduct must aim to establish a disciplined and purposeful school environment, dedicated to the improvement and maintenance of a quality learning process (Republic of South Africa, 1996b). As these quotes suggest, a properly constituted code of conduct for learners should always result in the ownership of the rules involved, with the learners therefore developing a sense of both ownership and responsibility towards the school that they attend.

Finally, this attempt at democratic reform of education in South Africa is in line with an international literature, discussed in chapter 2, that suggests that listening to learners, encouraging their participation and giving them more power and responsibility can enhance school effectiveness and facilitate school improvement, resulting in the delivery of better quality education. Findings in the study by Mncube and Harber (2010), for example, suggest that at least some educators in South Africa do now believe that there is a connection between democratic schooling and quality education. One educator, for example, said:

> Democracy does contribute to the delivery of quality education, because there are people who still belong to the old school of thought who may not understand a lot of issues

pertaining to democracy and transformation, which is required in South Africa today. If the staff or human resources are well equipped, then I think quality education will be delivered to the community and the learners. Motivating educators and learners about the culture of learning and teaching can provide the delivery of quality education, and this can only be possible if educators are enthusiastic about what they are doing, then the culture of learning will come back to the learners. They will see this guy is doing this thing with passion, not just doing textbook teaching. Then quality education will definitely be delivered. (p. 622)

Learners have come to be seen as more active, with a natural desire to learn, making them capable of effective learning and responsible for their own learning. The link between democracy and the delivery of quality education is further expressed in the following statement made by another educator:

I think there is a link between democracy and the delivery of quality education. Outcome-based education, now referred to [as the] National Curriculum Statement, involves learners, parents and educators. This is the new way of looking at our education, rather than looking at the end result. The end result in the past was whether learners passed or failed. Nowadays, the school work is in the industry, so now and again there are collaboration between the educators, learners and parents. If all the stakeholders are involved, there will be an improvement of learners' results. Parents will also know that the school is not only for learners, but that it is a resource centre for them. The parents are fully aware of what is happening in the classroom and the educators are aware of the situation at home. In a democracy, learners are treated with respect. (Mncube & Harber, 2010, p. 622)

Continuing Non-Democratic Features of South African Education

However, despite progress in terms of more democracy in schools since 1994 there continues to be serious problems which contradict a democratic ethos in education. The first is the continuing problem of race. An audit of 90 desegregated schools across all nine provinces published in 1999 showed that racism in schools continued to be pervasive (Vally & Dalamba, 1999). A further study of a community near Cape Town sheds some interesting light into how education continues to reproduce racial separation and antagonism in South Africa. The researcher found that both 'coloured' and 'black' parents and children had negative stereotypes of each other, but that school did little to combat this situation. The national language policy prescribing that children be taught in their mother tongue in the first three grades meant that almost no racial integration took place in those grades. This also affected mixing among teachers with at least one school having a separate common room for each ethnic/linguistic group. Most teachers expressed exasperation at having to commit to adopting an anti-racist pedagogy and effectively turned a blind eye to the racial antagonisms displayed by parents in and out of school. Indeed, most of the churches and cultural and sports groupings that used the schools' facilities also did so on the basis of race (Fataar, 2007). In her study of four schools that had been differently racially categorised under apartheid, Hunt (2007, chap. 7) found that the schools had done little to embrace a new culture actively based on non-discrimination and equality, but that students not from the dominant group had been expected to assimilate into existing practices and discourses.

Motala et al also described the continuation of more subtle, but nevertheless important, manifestations of racism:

> The Education Inclusion and Exclusion in India and South Africa project (INEXSA) has analysed a less overt form of racism. This project investigated processes of integration in 14 schools in the provinces of KwaZulu-Natal, the Eastern Cape and Western Cape (Soudien, 2004), and found that a tendency towards assimilationism was the overriding approach taken by these schools. Assimilationism took three forms: aggressive assimilationism, which is 'brusque [and] characterised by high degrees of intolerance and often violence'; assimilationism by stealth, in schools which have political credentials, such as some former Indian and coloured schools, but which leave racial issues unaddressed; and benign assimilationism, where schools (usually formerly white and English-speaking) presents themselves as multicultural but maintain dominant relationships (Sayed and Soudien, 2003: 104-105). In sum, these schools discriminated against learners who were different from the dominant culture – by race or class – by discouraging their admission, or including them on the assumption that they would be made to fit in with predetermined norms. Using findings from the INEXSA project, Sayed and Soudien (2003) showed that the new exclusionary practices invoked discourses around 'standards', 'language' and school fees. Admission to former white, Indian and coloured schools was controlled at the entry gate as schools attempted to preserve their established ways of doing things and explained their access policies as upholding standards of excellence, or argued that learners' inability to

speak the language of learning and teaching disqualified them
from admission. (2007, pp. 92-93)

However, Vandeyar (2008) struck a slightly more optimistic note arguing
that the data she presented suggested that:

young South Africans are subliminally rejecting racial
categories of old ... A decade of democracy has witnessed
students moving on from overt racial practices as in derogatory
name-calling and stereotyping ... to a situation of improved
inter-cultural attitudes and less negative stereotyping,
prejudice and discrimination in the schools ... Although, as
this study has uncovered, it may be only a few students at
these schools, the potential for intercultural harmony cannot
be underestimated. (p. 296)

Nevertheless, this seems to be despite, rather than because of, schools
because the study also found that the 'attitudes of schools and teachers
have resisted change' (p. 297).

A second problem is that of violence. Indicative of continuing
authoritarian trends is the persistence of violence against learners in
schools. A report by the South African Institute of Race Relations
(SAIRR) (2008) suggested that only 23% of South African pupils said
they felt safe at school. Schools in South Africa have traditionally been
authoritarian institutions stressing obedience, conformity and passivity.
The most tangible manifestation of this authoritarianism was the
widespread use of officially sanctioned violence against children in the
form of corporal punishment (Holdstock, 1990). Corporal punishment is
now illegal in South Africa, though it is still commonly used and still
supported by many parents and students (Morrell, 1999), and, in
KwaZulu Natal, by the then Minister of Education herself, despite the
fact that 'Numerous studies have shown that far from curbing violence,
corporal punishment in fact encourages antisocial aggression, vandalism
and perpetuates the cycle of violence' (Vally, 1999, p. 9).

Hunt (2007), using observation and interviews, found that corporal
punishment was still used in three out of four of her case study schools
in the Cape Town area and that learners were subjected to incidents of
verbal insult and humiliation. Corporal punishment also remains
widespread in rural areas (Nelson Mandela Foundation, 2005, p. 17). In a
recent study of schools in three provinces of South Africa it was noted
that:

Corporal punishment is banned in South Africa, yet such
incidents were observed on numerous occasions. For instance,
during recess at one school in Pietermaritzburg an act of
bullying by a male learner towards a female learner resulted in

> ... six strokes of a stiff plastic tube across the palm of the hand.
> (Hammett & Staeheli, 2011, p. 275)

Sexual violence against girls also remains a particular problem in South African schools.

> Violence within schools and violence against girls is a serious
> problem. Going to and from schools, girls are at risk of
> harassment, beating and rape. Inside schools, relationships
> between male teachers and female learners can find expression
> in everything from the 'sugar daddy' phenomenon to girls
> being demeaned and treated as less than equal in the
> classroom ... Pinning responsibility on teachers for action that
> may be seen as normal by both themselves and children,
> simply by virtue of habit and continual abuse, is a hard task.
> (Nelson Mandela Foundation, 2005, p. 61)

The government appointed Gender Equity Task Team reporting in 1997 stated that the South African education system was 'riddled with gender inequities' and that these included extremely worrying elements of sexual harassment and violence (Wolpe et al, 1997).

This affects primary schools as well as secondary schools. Bhana (2006) argues that a situation where fear and corporal punishment often characterise the classroom creates conditions where violence flourishes so that physical violence is a striking characteristic of young boys' interaction with girls. They use their greater body size and strength to bully, control and get rewards by stealing things – and feel they are entitled to do so. Also evident in the power over girls is verbal and physical harassment relating to sexuality (Bhana, 2006).

In 2001, Human Rights Watch produced a detailed report entitled *Scared at School: sexual violence against girls in South African schools*. This is based on research in KwaZulu Natal, Gauteng and the Western Cape. The report states:

> Based on our interviews with educators, social workers,
> children and parents, the problems of teachers engaging in
> serious sexual misconduct with underage female students is
> widespread. As the testimony offered below demonstrates,
> teachers have raped, sexually assaulted and otherwise sexually
> abused girls. Sometimes reinforcing sexual demands with
> threats of physical violence or corporal punishment, teachers
> have sexually propositioned girls and verbally degraded them
> using highly sexualised language. At times, sexual relations
> between teachers and students did not involve an overt use of
> force or threats of force; rather teachers would abuse their
> authority by offering better grades or money to pressure girls

for sexual favours or 'dating relationships.
(Human Rights Watch, 2001, p. 37)

Perhaps the most startling figure was provided by a Medical Research Council survey carried out in 1998 that found that among those rape victims who specified their relationship to the perpetrator, 37.7% said their schoolteacher or principal had raped them (Human Rights Watch, 2001, p. 42). Section V of the report details many actual cases of sexual abuse carried out by teachers in schools. Section VII of the report describes how when girls reported sexual violence and harassment they encountered a pattern whereby schools failed to respond with any degree of seriousness.

Evidence from the Midlands area of KwaZulu Natal found a culture of silence surrounding gender violence in schools, despite this becoming a norm in 'black' urban and rural schools. Most teachers who violate girls get away with it because victims do not report it as they are afraid of being blamed or victimised by parents and other teachers which, as the authors state, highlights an unhealthy over-respect for the teachers, and this perpetuates the myth that the person who was raped must have asked for it. In addition, parents do not report sexual harassment because they fear that the girl will be asked to leave school. Parents may even feel that monetary payment from the perpetrator is far more useful than lengthy trials and enquiries. In some cases the payment can be as little as 20 rand (less than £2.00) and parents are prepared to accept this (Mshengu & the Midlands Women's Group, 2003).

In total, 27 complaints of sexual misconduct against teachers were received by the South African Council of Educators between January and October 2008, and in some cases the teacher–pupil relationships took place with the consent of the children's parents based on some kind of financial agreement. The Chief Executive Officer of the Council said:

It has been very disturbing that there have been cases where students have been minors. Children as young as nine have been found to be involved with teachers. There have also been cases of impregnation. Council finds that completely intolerable. While girl learners are abused by other members of society, we definitely have jurisdiction over teachers. The age of learners, their consent, parental consent or their location in a different school will not mitigate the culpability of a teacher in this regard. (Mail & Guardian Online, December 8, 2008)

In 2006, the Minister of Education, Naledi Pandor, simply stated outright that schools were 'not safe' for girls (cited in Motala et al, 2007, p. 93).

Overall, from a study of four different secondary schools in Cape Town, each with a different racial categorisation under apartheid, Hunt concludes that:

Students had unequal access to substantive rights within and between the four schools, as well as different possibilities to voice ideas and take part in democratic practices. Only one school (serving mainly middle class communities) had safe and encouraging spaces for students to engage in citizenship practices ... Having access to a 'rights agenda' gave many students a language to express a citizen identity, but without the agency or safe spaces to take this further, for many it remained a rhetoric of citizenship as opposed to a practice ... What was apparent in the case study schools was how little had changed in the post-apartheid period and the differences that were there in the past continued. (2011, p. 56)

Contradictions and Tensions in
Post-apartheid Education and Development

So, schools in post-apartheid South Africa, as elsewhere, have two faces. On the one hand they are capable of helping individuals gain knowledge and develop skills and values which can be of great benefit to both the individual and the wider society in terms of both 'modernity' and democracy. On the other hand they do not necessarily present a coherent and effective model of 'modern' professional and moral behaviour, they reinforce authoritarian attitudes and, worse of all, reproduce and actively perpetrate violence. Why have some schools in South Africa been slow and reluctant to change in a democratic direction despite the new political and policy dispensation? There are certainly local, contextual explanations, as well as the more general explanations for the persistence of authoritarian schools put forward elsewhere in this book. Jansen (2001), for example, accuses the South African government of 'political symbolism' in terms of its educational reform. He argues that in the light of the known severe resource, personnel and training constraints there was never any real expectations that the ambitious reforms would seriously alter education in South Africa for everybody, but it was important to be seen to be doing something. To this Harley and Wedekind (2004) added the notion of 'policy meliorism', that is the belief that the mere vision of a policy is enough to ameliorate the actual conditions, i.e. that 'the good intentions expressed by education reforms have more influence on the policy agenda than school and social realities themselves' (Spreen & Vally, 2010, p. 437).

Indeed, the democratic policy reforms were introduced into a context of continuing serious poverty and inequality which made it likely that access to power, decision-making and experiences of democratic citizenship within education would also remain unequal. Despite a relatively strong performance in terms of economic growth since 1994, South Africa still has one of the most unequal societies in the world, with between 45% and 55% of the population categorised as poor, and between 20% and 25% as in extreme poverty, and there are spatial, racial and gender dimensions to this poverty (McGrath & Akooje, 2007, pp. 422-423). At the same time that efforts have been made to redistribute resources from the rich to the poor in South Africa, there has also been an acceptance that some of the funding burden will have to be borne by users of education in the form of fees as part of the government's adoption of the more neo-liberal Growth, Employment and Redistribution policy (GEAR) in 1996. The South African Schools Act permitted the governing bodies of all state schools to levy fees after a majority vote at a meeting of parents and most now do so. This can be interpreted either as a pragmatic recognition that the state did not have sufficient resources to provide a sufficiently good quality education for all, or as further evidence of acceptance of the global influence of the World Bank's agenda of shifting the balance of funding for education from the public to the private sphere. It was certainly the case that in a situation where resources were to be redistributed the government accepted the advice of international consultants that there was a danger of a flight of middle class parents from the state to the private sector if traditionally advantaged schools were not allowed to raise further resources. This would result in the state sector losing the financial, managerial and persuasive capacities of the better educated and financially advantaged segment of the population (Department of Education,1996, p. 34).

Whatever the explanation, the result has been to perpetuate or even exacerbate inequality rather than to reduce it. Schools serving well-off communities can charge high fees to maintain excellent facilities and employ more teachers, while schools in poorer communities will not be able to do so. Admission on the grounds of race may now be illegal but high fees may well have the same net effect. In their detailed study of two provinces tellingly entitled *Elusive Equity*, Fiske and Ladd (2004, pp. 233-234) conclude that South Africa has made progress on equal *treatment* in terms of allocation of state resources, but the country has been less successful in terms of equal educational *opportunity* because of the very unequal access to good quality schooling, and not successful at all in terms of educational *adequacy* in that repetition and drop-out rates among black students remain high and matriculation pass rates low with little evidence of improvement. This is a similar conclusion to that reached by Spreen and Vally (2006, pp. 354-357) who also point out that many children go to school hungry and that 27% of schools have no running water, 43% have no electricity, 80% have no library and 78% have no computers. A study of rural schools in South Africa graphically brings home the way poverty both prevents access to education and success within it (Nelson Mandela Foundation, 2005).

Another major obstacle to the successful implementation of democratic policies is the existing nature of teacher identity. For example, a commitment to teaching as a profession may not form a strong part of all teachers' personal identity. The National Teacher Education Audit (Hofmeyr & Hall, 1996) stressed that many students in teacher education colleges did not have a genuine desire to teach, and similarly in a study of teacher voice, which included interviews from a sample of 68 South African teachers, more than half attributed purely instrumental reasons related to salary, status, the desire to urbanise, and the attainment of qualifications to their choice of teaching as a career. For these teachers, 'the teacher was a person whom socio-economic circumstances had conspired to choose' (Jessop & Penny, 1998, p. 396).

The same study also found that there was considerable nostalgia for an imagined golden age in which children respected elders and certainty prevailed. For some South African teachers, nostalgia for the old order was coupled with suspicion of the new and radical democratic values accompanying the end of apartheid. In her study of democratic educational reform in South Africa, Schweisfurth (2002b, p. 75) noted that teachers faced a number of competing imperatives:

- A previously clear ideological curriculum versus an unclear replacement (OBE);
- Resource needs of a new curriculum versus resource constraints;
- A need for political education within the curriculum versus disinterest or suspicion about politics;
- Curriculum more individualised versus a more common curriculum; and
- Personal development of individual students versus overall standards of achievement.

She argues that although teachers supported the reforms in spirit, their implementation was problematised by dilemmas stemming from such competing imperatives. As a result teachers adopted a number of different responses:

> One was to deny – rightly or wrongly the impact of the reforms; another was to interpret them in order to accommodate pre-existing perceptions and capacities. Frustration and demoralisation prevailed occasionally. Where the reforms were perceived to be imposed from above, forms of strategic compliance appeared, governed by external demands of accountability. Sometimes the irreconcilable imperatives co-existed, creating strange hybrid practices, sometime with built-in contradictions, incorporating persistent continuities with new approaches. (2002b, pp. 75-76)

Another study concluded that:

teachers are caught in anxieties of transition, feeling trapped
in the 'old' and wanting to work in the 'new' ways. They also
lack the professional autonomy and competence to fulfil what
is officially expected of them ... South African teachers do not
currently see themselves as owning the transformation of
education in South Africa but as subjects of it. They also do
not see themselves as formulators of policies but implementers
of them, which are handed down to them from on top ...
teacher education in South Africa would need to prioritise the
sense of professionalism and autonomy of teachers as well as
their role to inform and formulate policies as much as their
own rights as human beings within a democracy are
emphasised. Failure to achieve these aims in teacher
development is likely to result in acute feelings of
disempowerment and demoralisation of the teaching corps,
albeit now ironically within a democratic educational
dispensation. (Carrim, 2003, p. 319)

The study of four schools in the Cape Town area by Hunt (2007) found
that there were difficulties for some teachers in reconciling the
contradictions of the collapse of apartheid (a good thing) with the
breakdown of traditional values (a bad thing). This desire for certainty
and fixed rules sits awkwardly with one of the key desired outcomes of
the new curriculum – the development of creative and critical thinking.
Most recently in a study of schools in three different provinces, the
authors still conclude that:

Many educators are suspicious of the transition to more
democratic schooling, having been trained within traditional
authoritarian pedagogics and power relations; many of these
educators see the new pedagogical approach as undermining
their status, power and respect. (Hammett & Staeheli, 2011,
p. 276)

Given the context of existing teacher identity, it was even more
unfortunate that the reforms in South Africa were imposed in a top-down
manner. Spreen and Vally (2010 argue that South Africa could have
learned much from Paulo Freire and the educational reforms in Sao
Paulo, Brazil:

Unlike the top-down imposition of policy in South Africa, in
Sao Paulo teachers played a critical role in curriculum reform.
Brazilian educational reforms also involved the active
participation of the community at large and the contributions
of social movements; they respected the dynamics in each
school; they used the Freirean methodology of action-
reflection in the curriculum; and they used a model of

continuing teacher training, with a critical analysis of the curriculum in practice. By contrast, in South Africa, the mass democratic movement was largely marginalized from the education policy and school reform process. As a result, in envisioning a new educational system, South Africa's own rich traditions of alternative education, even under the apartheid period, were neglected. (2010, p. 434)

Conclusion

So schooling in South Africa, as elsewhere, is contradictory – there is both good news and bad news. On the one hand, schooling has the potential to contribute positively to economic, social and political development, including more democratic citizens and sometimes, as we have seen, it can achieve this potential. On the other hand, it can reproduce social inequality and negative attitudes, fail to provide an efficient model of modern organisation and actively perpetrate authoritarianism and violence. These tensions persist in South Africa despite an educational policy framework that is overtly and consistently democratic. The struggle in South Africa, as elsewhere, is to ensure that schools provide genuine opportunities within a safe, peaceful and democratic environment for learners. These tensions in education and democracy have consistently surfaced throughout this book and now we need to ask the fundamental question of whether or not it is actually possible to change education in a more democratic direction on a more consistent and widespread basis.

CHAPTER 6

Democratic Educational Change?

'It is a great triumph of compulsory government monopoly of
mass schooling that among even the best of my fellow
teachers, and among even the best of my students parents,
only a small number can imagine a different way to do things'
(John Taylor Gatto, cited in Meighan, 1994, pp. 3, 6)

In chapter 1, we noted that every year the United Nations Development
Programme produces a book called the *Human Development Report*
which ranks all the countries of the world according to what they term
the 'Human Development Index', based on life expectancy at birth, the
adult literacy rate, wealth per capita, and the combined enrolment rates
for primary, secondary and tertiary levels of formal education. Thus it is
assumed that enrolment in formal education is inherently beneficial for
development. Yet a key problem with this and many discussions of
education, whether it is school effectiveness, educational leadership or
educational change, is that too much of the status quo of formal
education is taken for granted and not enough attention is paid to the
question of basic goals – Effectiveness at what?; Leadership for what?;
Change towards what?; At a fundamental level, what are we trying to
achieve? As has been argued elsewhere (Harber & Davies, 1997, 2003),
too often educational discussions have a technical and descriptive feel to
them as though such debates exist in a moral vacuum, and there is
insufficient acknowledgement of the role of values and ideology in
education. Effectiveness is not just a question of congruence between
goals, processes and outcomes – the key question is: what are the goals
that we are trying to achieve in the first place?

All educational practices have to be understood and only have
meaning within their ultimate philosophical and ideological
frameworks. Even generally agreed on educational objectives
such literacy and numeracy are not fundamental goals as it has
to be asked, literacy for what? Numeracy for what? How do we
want people to use these skills? Even phrases like 'more
flexibility', more creativity', 'more imagination', 'more
independence' or 'more sense of enquiry', are meaningless

unless given an ideological context. Even happiness, a
commodity in short supply in many formal education systems,
is not context free. Let us take the theoretical example of a
terrorist training camp. You could have a terrorist training
regime which aimed to produce flexible, creative, imaginative
and independent terrorists and did so. They may well also be
very literate and numerate. And on top of that they may be
happy and enjoy their training. Within its own goals it would
have to be regarded as effective. But are the *goals themselves*
effective? Are terrorists and terror a good thing to produce?
(Harber, 2004, p. 15)

In this book we have tried to be clear about the importance of democratic
institutions and democratic citizens as key political goals for education
and development everywhere, but increasingly in developing countries.
We have seen in chapter 3, and to an extent in chapter 5 on South Africa,
that schooling can be changed in a democratic direction in a complete
way, in substantial ways, and in various minor, but significant ways. Yet
such examples still represent the minority of cases as democratic change
in schools requires transformational change away from the currently
dominant authoritarian model. However, as Farrell (2007) argues in his
review of the practice of alternative forms of education in developing
countries:

These programs demonstrate that child-centred, active
pedagogy, with heavy involvement of parents and the
community in the learning of young people works – it can be
done, and where it is done generally produces remarkable
learning gains among even the poorest and most
disadvantaged children ... It is also important that these
change programs do not simply alter one feature of the
standard established school (for example, adding more
textbooks or improving teacher training of the standard sort, or
altering this or that bit of the standard curriculum), or provide
extra money to the school. Rather, they represent a thorough
reorganisation and fundamental re-visioning of the standard
model of schooling such that the learning program for the
youngsters, although occurring in, or based in, a building
called a school, is far different from what we have come to
expect to be happening in a school, and far more effective than
what we have typically seen in even very good schools even
for young people from well-off families. (Farrell, 2007, p. 219)

Yet the traditional model of schooling persists, is dominant, and is taken
for granted. Hawkins, in discussing what he terms 'The Intractable
Dominant Educational Paradigm', recounts a research project in Ethiopia
where he was regularly reminded by Ethiopians that they were one of the

only African nations never to be colonised by the West, and that therefore, they did not suffer from many of the post-colonial legacies found in other African and developing countries. Yet visits to schools and colleges revealed little that was truly Ethiopian – indeed, they were like schools anywhere in the world, only poorer: 'When pressed as to the rationale of models from the West (or global north), the answer almost invariably was 'so we can develop like them' (Hawkins, 2007, p. 137).

Hawkins argues that the features of this dominant paradigm which exists almost everywhere despite the political nature of the regime are that:

> – An authoritarian relationship often lies at the core of the teacher–learner interaction;
> – Teachers are generally insecure because of a lack of training and poor remuneration;
> – Teaching methods do not generally benefit from knowledge of cognitive psychology and child development;
> – Teachers generally discourage discussion and questioning, and adhere to textbooks;
> – A principal function of schooling is to select entrants to the next educational level;
> – The selection is through a highly competitive examination system which requires the reproduction of rote learning rather than critical thought;
> – The main activities of the formal school system are directed towards preparing pupils for these examinations; and
> – Students and parents are preoccupied with certificate-status rather than with the essence of what is taught. (pp. 150-151)

The problem is that this model of schooling has come, almost universally, to be regarded as the only possibility, the only model of a 'real' school:

> the whole thing was mindless, that we do what we do because we've always done it ... we are so stuck in what has become the conventional way of schooling that we don't think twice about it. (Theodore Sizer on the American education system, cited in Farrell, 2008, p. 203)

Yet we have questioned whether such a model of schooling can truly contribute to democratic political development. In practice, in developing countries, it often does not even contribute to the development of the knowledge, skills and attitudes necessary for the effective functioning of the basically authoritarian, but nevertheless necessary, bureaucratic social structures and institutions upon which to further build and develop a successful and sustainable democratic state.

The literature on educational change (for example, Fullan, 2007) makes it clear that significant shifts in the practices of schools and teachers are rarely achieved and they cannot simply be mandated from above. Pedagogical and organisational practices are stubborn and resistant to change both at the cultural level (Alexander, 2000) and at the level of individual teachers (Schweisfurth, 2002b). So, can schools in developing countries therefore be changed in a democratic direction on a widespread and substantial scale? Some think not. Le Fanu (forthcoming), discussing the related topic of social inclusion in schools in developing countries, notes that if schools were to adopt what he calls, UNESCO's policy 'global inclusionism' of all children in terms of equality of access and treatment, then this would essentially require schools becoming much more democratic and reflective. He thinks this level of change to education systems is very unlikely. He draws on evidence from sub-Saharan Africa and Papua New Guinea to argue that such education systems simply lack the physical resources and skills capacity to actually implement such change. Also, key stakeholders are unwilling to implement such change because they fundamentally accept what he terms a 'transmissive epistemology' which assumes that:

> learners are predominantly passive, homogenous and
> absorptive; that learning is therefore essentially an imitative,
> repetitive and decontextualised process; that knowledge tends
> to be fixed, invariant and context-transcendant; and teaching
> should take the form of the top-down transmission of a pre-
> established body of knowledge and skills – a process
> characterised by teacher explanation, description and
> demonstration. This epistemology tends to permeate education
> systems at all levels, and, according to some analyses, is
> possessed by students as well as teachers, leading to student
> resistance to attempts by teachers to encourage them to take
> more responsibility for their own learning.
> (Le Fanu, forthcoming)

Moreover, a recent review of five books on education and violent conflict in a wide range of developing countries that also examined the potential post-conflict opportunities for schools to contribute to democratic peace building and reconciliation found little, if any, evidence of education actually playing such a role and concluded that:

> based on their contents it would be hard to be optimistic about
> the realistic possibilities of transforming the authoritarian and
> (as documented in these books) often violent nature of schools
> in a more peace-building direction as a result of the experience
> of violent conflict. The traditional model of schooling still
> seems too firmly entrenched in the minds – and perhaps

vested interests – of key actors locally and internationally.
(Harber, forthcoming)

The net result is that, although as we discussed in chapter 3, there are more nuanced relationships in schools in developing countries than suggested by a straightforward democratic versus authoritarian binary – and indeed there are working examples of democratic schools and aspects of schools – there will be no quick fix for education systems as a whole to transform them in a democratic direction.

Indeed, one of the authors of the present study is on record as being pessimistic about the possibilities of large scale or significant change in formal education globally:

> The problems with schooling seem so deep and intractable
> that sometimes it is difficult to be optimistic about the future.
> Indeed, little of a fundamental nature has changed in the last
> fifty years and in some ways matters now actually appear to be
> worse ... traditional, compulsory bureaucratic models of
> schooling as education are an entrenched, powerful and
> hegemonic orthodoxy in the minds of governments, parents
> and many within education itself. Current models of schooling
> are consistently portrayed in a taken-for-granted, common
> sense manner as the *only* way to organise education in the
> media, by governments, by international institutions, by many
> national and international non-governmental organisations
> and by most academics. They are seen as a given good and
> even serious crises can't dent official faith in the traditional
> school as an inherently and solely beneficial institution.
> (Harber, 2009, p. 140)

A study of human rights education provided via an NGO in the state of Tamil Nadu, India (Bajaj, 2011) based on observation and interviews, provides an interesting case study of both the potential of education for democratic change and the serious obstacles facing it. One of the key aims of the human rights education course is 'The enabling of all persons to participate effectively in a free and democratic society governed by the rule of law'. We describe the research here in some detail as an illustration of the potential for both changing education and education facilitating social change, but also of the difficulties such changes can and will face.

The context where the human rights education programme operates is government schools where predominantly low-income pupils attend. These schools tend to be highly examination-driven and in them corporal punishment is still common, there is serious caste-discrimination by teachers against Dalit children, and there is a shortage of separate toilets for girls which causes them to drop out of school when they reach puberty. There are also corrupt practices such as the

163

extraction of money from pupils by teachers and head teachers, the siphoning off of government-allotted funds intended for students' midday meals and/or uniforms by teachers and heads, and the sexual abuse of children without report or sanction. Given these issues in Indian schools, the Institute of Human Rights Education developed a three-year course which is now used in 3500 schools across India, many of which are in Tamil Nadu. The course is aimed at a combination of information, values and behavioural changes and active responses. Implementation of the course involves in-service training of teachers to teach human rights education (HRE). Pupils were interviewed about the impact of the course on human rights on them and responses fell into four categories: (1) intervening in situations of abuse; (2) reporting or threatening to report abuse; (3) spreading awareness of human rights; and (4) attitudinal or behavioural shifts at home or in school that were more aligned with human rights. Examples of each were:

1. Trying to convince a peer involved in full-time remunerated work to return to school or visiting a family in the neighbourhood to convince them not to kill a female baby – female infanticide is quite a common practice in the communities where the study took place. Another example was trying to stop the practice of early marriage of their female classmates as it impeded their right to education.
2. Reporting was usually to a head teacher, village leader, or the police. Again this tended to concern child labour, marriage under the age of 18, and female infanticide, all of which are illegal.
3. This involved sharing human rights education books or learning with parents, siblings, neighbours and friends.
4. Here pupils mentioned renegotiating norms related to gender, such as a boy noting that he cleaned his plate after eating rather than leaving it to his sister. However, girls faced more difficulty in actually asserting their own rights in the home. Another example was interacting with pupils of different backgrounds more readily than before the course, even if it meant disapproval by other members of the family or neighbours.

The author notes that the majority of responses from pupils fell into the first category and that 'This suggests that students, through human rights education, are imbibed with a sense of agency to intervene and confront violations, and that such intervention might produce positive changes' (Bajaj, 2011, p. 76).

However, there was resistance and failure to change, as well as the risk of backlash. In a school where pupils complained about the poor quality of the food provided based on a human right to decent food, the head simply beat the children who complained, and threatened to expel them. One human rights teacher was concerned about the fact that Dalit pupils were not turning up regularly and found that other teachers were using the pupils as unpaid domestic servants during the school day when their parents thought they were at school. While the head teacher stopped this practice, the teacher noted the anger of her colleagues in response to her actions. Bajaj notes that a 'Similar backlash was felt by HRE teachers who attempted to intervene to stop corporal punishment or other abusive/unlawful practices, suggesting the difficulty in eradicating school-level abuses without support from higher authorities' (2011, p. 77). One 13 year old girl who tried to tell a drunken neighbour not to beat his wife and daughter ended up getting slapped as well.

Bajaj argues that the successes of the course was down to three factors: written official government support and endorsement; teachers buying in through good quality training programmes provided over sufficient time, in pleasant settings, by noted educationalists in a participatory format; the legitimacy of printed information about human rights in low-income communities in which knowledge printed in a book was automatically afforded legitimacy and authority. Bajaj concludes that:

> At the level of the school and community, for the programme to be a 'transformative force', teachers and headmasters were needed who were willing to comply with officials and the NGO to carry out the programme. When rigid hierarchies or entrenched corruption dampened the motivation for teachers and headmasters to take on a new programme or to be open to students' demands about their rights, the programme seemed to remain at the level of 'time pass'. Ingredients that contributed to a more transformative role for the HRE programme included: close contact between the school teachers, and the NGO; frequent visits by NGO staff and participation in regional programmes; teachers' interest in nurturing student activism and teachers' willingness to act in situations of inequality or abuse in schools, students' homes and the broader community ... Ultimately engaging with educational efforts towards democratic citizenship and human rights for marginalized youth provides information about the possibility and promise of schooling to impact, in some way, broader processes of social change. (2011, pp. 78-79)

As this case study shows, just because something is very difficult and slow to change does not mean that nothing should or could be done, and perhaps there are even some grounds for a restricted optimism. What, then, is realistically possible and achievable and should be a firm goal for education in the context of developing countries? First, it is important to have the ultimate or eventual goal of democratic education clearly and authoritatively stated in policy documents and the implications thought through at the policy level to provide a legitimising framework – even if not necessarily achievable in the short-term on a large scale. South Africa provides a good example of this official commitment. Second, before or at the same time as attempting to change towards more positive, democratic forms of education, it is equally important to stop doing harm via education. Before any sort of major or minor educational change in a democratic direction it is, at the very least, vital to stop the direct forms of harm and violence inflicted on young people via schooling that have been described in chapter 4. Elsewhere (Harber, 2009, p. 142), the gradual reduction of corporal punishment in schools globally has been described and, similarly, it is to be hoped and expected that increasing international awareness and debates about sexual harassment and abuse in schools will, probably slowly, but eventually, stop this practice in schools. Third, reducing the instances of practices such as these would also help with a reduction of un-professionalism and the gradual development of a minimum level of restricted professionalism, as discussed in chapter 3, i.e. where a majority, or at least a critical mass, of teachers and other educational professionals actually turn up and on time, teach and assess competently and impartially, and behave in a generally professional manner. This would help to contribute to the development of individuals, institutions, societies and polities 'suffused with bureaucratic rationality' that Inkeles (1969a, p. 1122) saw as essentially modern and the social foundation onto which democratic behaviours and institutions can be built. Fourth, continuing (and continuing writing about and publicising) the types of work of individuals and organisations involved in more democratic forms of education as described and discussed in chapter 3 of this book, even though at the moment it remains minority practice.

To end on a more hopeful or optimistic note, from the review of literature carried out in this book, there is evidence that schooling can be changed in a democratic direction in a complete way, in substantial ways, and in various minor, but significant ways in developing countries. There was sufficient evidence of democratic practice from developing countries in Africa, Latin America, Asia, and the Middle East to confirm that it can be, and is, done where the will, determination, and skills are there. However, perhaps the most important and promising places to start or continue making an effort are those with some wider influence in the educational system. Other than policy-makers themselves, this would include head teachers, teacher educators and inspectors. We have included concrete examples of the potential democratic influence of these in the book and, in particular, the promising role of action research and critical reflection in changing educational practice. These key actors interact with teachers, student teachers and (directly and indirectly) with pupils on a daily basis. Helpfully, there is also no shortage of published material on the theory and practice of democratic education to guide professional development.

It is important to continue the struggle for, as John Dewey wrote:

The only form of society which facilitates the continued evolution of the human species is a democratic form of society, and furthermore, the development of such a democratic society is dependent to a large degree on the democratisation of schools and schooling. (Cited in Meighan, 1994, p. 86)

References

Abello, M. (1997) Are the Seeds of Violence Sown in Schools, *Prospects*, XXVII, 447-465.

Ackers, J. & Hardman, F. (2001) Classroom Interaction in Kenyan Primary Schools, *Compare*, 31(2), 245-261.

Adeyemi, M. (2002) An Investigation into the Status of the Teaching and Learning of the Concept of Democracy at the Junior School Level in Botswana, *Educational Studies*, 28(4), 385-401.

Advisory Group on Citizenship (1998) *Education for Citizenship and the Teaching of Democracy in Schools* (The Crick Report). London: Qualifications and Curriculum Authority.

Aedo-Richmond, R. (2002) Dynamics of Improvement and Reform in Chilean Education, in R. Griffin (Ed) *Education in Transition*. Oxford: Symposium Books.

Agemoglu, D., Johnson, S., Robinson, J. & Yared, P. (2005) From Education to Democracy?, *American Economic Review*, 95(2), 44-49.

Aguirre, C. (2011) *Something Fierce*. London: Douglas & McIntyre.

Agyemang, B. (2007) Education for Democratic Citizenship: the role of teacher education in Ghana. MPhil thesis, University of Birmingham.

Agyemang, B. (2011) Towards School Improvement and Democratic Education: an exploration of the views of pupils and teacher trainees in Ghana. Research for PhD thesis, University of Birmingham, in progress.

Ahmad, I. (2008) The Anatomy of an Islamic Model: citizenship education in Pakistan, in D.L. Grossman (Ed) *Citizenship Education in Asia and the Pacific*. Dordrecht: Springer.

Aikman, S. (2010) Grasping Rare Moments for Change: children's participation in conflict contexts, in S. Cox, A. Robinson-Pant, C. Dyer & M. Schweisfurth (Eds) *Children As Decision Makers in Education*. London: Continuum.

Akyeampong, K. (2003) *Teacher Training in Ghana – Does it Count?* London: Department for International Development.

Al Aswany, A. (2011) Police Alone Can't Keep the Rulers in Power. Egypt's Battle is On, *The Guardian*, 28 January.

Albrow, M. (1970) *Bureaucracy*. London: Macmillan.

Alexander, R. (2000) *Culture and Pedagogy: international comparisons in primary education*. Oxford: Blackwell.

Alexander, T. (2001) *The Citizenship School*. London: Campaign for Learning/UNICEF.

Almond, G. (1970) *Political Development: essays in heuristic theory.* Boston: Little Brown.

Altbach, P. & Kelly, G. (1978) *Education and Colonialism.* London: Longman.

Altinyelken, H.K. (2010) Pedagogical Renewal in Sub-Saharan Africa: the case of Uganda, *Comparative Education*, 46(2), 151-171.

Amable, B. (2004) *The Diversity of Modern Capitalism.* Oxford: Oxford University Press.

Amnesty International (2008) *Safe Schools: every girl's right.* London: Amnesty International Publications.

Angula, N. & Grant Lewis, S. (1997) Promoting Democratic Processes in Educational Decision-making: reflections from Namibia's first 5 years, *International Journal of Educational Development*, 17(3), 233-250.

Apple, M. (1993) *Official Knowledge: democratic education in a conservative age.* New York: Routledge.

Aristotle (1962) *The Politics.* Harmondsworth: Penguin.

Asimeng-Boahene, L. (2007) Creating Strategies to Deal with Problems of Teaching Controversial Issues in Social Studies Education in African Schools, *Intercultural Education*, 18(3), 231-242.

Avalos, B. (2000) Policies for Teacher Education in Developing Countries, *International Journal of Educational Research*, 33(5), 457-474.

Azevedo, M. (1980) A Century of Colonial Education in Mozambique, in A.T. Mugomba & M. Nyaggah (Eds) *Independence without Freedom.* Santa Barbara: ABC-Clio.

Bajaj, M. (2011) From 'Time Pass' to Transformative Force: school-based human rights education in Tamil Nadu, India, *International Journal of Educational Development*, 32(1), 72-80.

Balarin, M. & Benavides, M. (2010) Curriculum Reform and the Displacement of Knowledge in Peruvian Rural Secondary Schools: exploring the unintended local consequences of global education policies, *Compare* 40(3), 311-325.

Bancroft, S. (2006) As Row over Caste Quoya Rages, India's Real Scandal is Ignored, *Times Educational Supplement*, June 2.

Barnes, B. (1982) Education for Socialism in Mozambique, *Comparative Education Review*, 26(3), 406-419.

Barrett, A. (2005) Teacher Accountability in Context: Tanzanian primary school teachers' perceptions of local community and education administration, *Compare*, 35(1), 43-61.

Barrett, A. (2007) Beyond the Polarisation of Pedagogy: models of classroom practice in Tanzanian primary schools, *Comparative Education*, 43(2), 273-294.

Bartholemew, J. (1976) Schooling Teachers: the myth of the liberal college, in G. Whitty & M.F.D. Young (Eds) *Explorations in the Politics of School Knowledge.* Driffield: Nafferton Books.

Bates, R. (2007) Developing Capabilities and the Management of Trust, in M. Walker & E. Unterhalter (Eds) *Amartya Sen's Capability Approach and Social Justice in Education*. Basingstoke: Palgrave Macmillan.

Beane, J. & Apple, M. (1999) *Democratic Schools: lessons from the chalkface*. Buckingham: Open University Press.

Beetham, J. & Boyle, K. (1995) *Introducing Democracy: 80 questions and answers*. London: Polity Press/UNESCO.

Behal, S. (2002a) Rebellion in Delhi over Biased History Texts, *Times Educational Supplement*, October 18.

Behal, S. (2002b) Caste Cruelty Makes School a Nightmare, *Times Educational Supplement*, April 26.

Benavot, A. (1996) Education and Political Democratisation: cross-national and longtitudinal findings, *Comparative Education Review*, 40(4), 377-403.

Bernal, E.C. (1997) Colombia: country and schools in conflict, in S. Tawil *Final Report and Case Studies on the Workshop on Educational Destruction and Reconstruction in Disrupted Societies*. Geneva: International Bureau of Education and the University of Geneva.

Berrebi, C. (2003) Evidence about the Link between Education, Poverty and Terrorism among Palestinians. http://www.irs.princeton.edu/pubs/pdfs/477.pdf

Bhana, D. (2006) Doing Power; confronting violent masculinities in primary schools, in F. Leach & C. Mitchell (Eds) *Combating Gender Violence in and around Schools*. Stoke-on-Trent: Trentham Books.

Bhattarai, T. (2010) Children's Clubs and Corporal Punishment: reflections from Nepal, in S. Cox, A. Robinson-Pant, C. Dyer & M. Schweisfurth (Eds) *Children as Decision Makers in Education*. London: Continuum.

Binder, H., Pye, L., Coleman, J.S., LaPalombara, J. & Weiner, M. (1971) *Crises and Sequences in Political Development*. Princeton: Princeton University Press.

Bloch, G. (2009) *The Toxic Mix*. Cape Town: Tafelberg.

Bourne, R., Gungara, J., Dev, A., Ratsoma, M., Rukanda, M., Smith, A., et al (1998) *School-Based Understanding of Human Rights in Four Countries; a Commonwealth study*. London: Department for International Development.

Boyle, P. (1999) *Class Formation and Civil Society: the politics of education in Africa*. Aldershot: Ashgate.

Brannelly, L., Lewis, L. & Ndaruhutse, S. (2011) *Higher Education and the Formation of Developmental Elites*. Reading: CfBT Developmental Leadership Programme.

Bratton, M., Mattes, R. & Gyimah-Boadi, E. (2005) *Public Opinion, Democracy and Market Reform in Africa*. Cambridge: Cambridge University Press.

Bray, M. & Lee, W. (2001) *Education and Political Transition: themes and experiences in East Asia*. Hong Kong: Comparative Education Research Centre, University of Hong Kong.

Brown, B. & Duku, N. (2008) Negotiated Identities: dynamics in parents' participation in school governance in rural Eastern Cape schools and implication for school leadership, *South African Journal of Education*, 28, 431-450.

Brown, G. (2007) Making Ethnic Citizens: the politics and practice of education in Malaysia, *International Journal of Educational Development*, 27(3), 318-330.

Bush, K. & Saltarelli, D. (Eds) (2000) *The Two Faces of Education in Ethnic Conflict*. Florence: UNICEF.

Bush, T. & Heystek, J. (2003) School Governance in the New South Africa, *Compare*, 33(2), 127-138.

Buthelezi, T., Mitchell, C., Moletsane, R., De Lange, N., Taylor, M. & Stuart, J. (2007) Youth Voices about Sex and AIDS; implications for life skills education through the 'Learning Together' project in KwaZulu Natal, South Africa, *International Journal of Inclusive Education*, 11(4), 445-459.

Caddell, M. (2006) Private Schools as Battlefields: contested visions of learning and livelihood in Nepal, *Compare,* 36(4), 463-480.

Carnie, F. (2003) *Alternative Approaches to Education*. London: RoutledgeFalmer.

Carothers, T. (1999) *Aiding Democracy Abroad: the learning curve*. Washington: Brookings Institution Press.

Carr, W. & Hartnett, A. (1996) *Education and the Struggle for Democracy*. Buckingham: Open University Press.

Carrim, N. (2003) Teacher Identity: tensions between roles, in K. Lewin, M. Samuel & Y. Sayed (Eds) *Changing Patterns of Teacher Education in South Africa*. Sandown: Heinemann.

Carroll, R. (2002) The Eton of Africa, *The Guardian*, November 25.

Carter, C., Harber, C. & Serf, J. (2003) *Towards Ubuntu: critical teacher education for democratic citizenship in England and South Africa*. Birmingham: Teachers in Development Education.

Castello-Climent, A. (2008) On the Distribution of Education and Democracy, *Journal of Development Economics*, 87(2) 179-190.

Chabal, P. & Daloz, J-P. (1999) *Africa Works: disorder as political instrument*. Oxford: James Currey.

Chabbott, C. & Ramirez, F. (2000) Development and Education, in M.T. Hallinan (Ed) *Handbook of the Sociology of Education*. New York: Kluwer.

Chikoko, V., Gilmour, J., Harber, C. & Serf, J. (2011) Teaching Controversial Issues in England and South Africa, *Journal of Education for Teaching*, 37(1), 5-21.

Chisholm, L. & Leyendecker, R. (2008) Curriculum Reform in Post 1990s Sub-Saharan Africa, *International Journal of Educational Development*, 28(2), 195-205.

Chiwela, G.M. (2010) Participatory School Governance: children in decision-making in the Zambian context, in S. Cox, A. Robinson-Pant, C. Dyer & M. Schweisfurth (Eds) *Children As Decision Makers in Education*. London: Continuum.

Christie, P (1998) Schools as (Dis) organisations: the breakdown of the culture of learning and teaching in South African schools, *Cambridge Journal of Education,* 28(3), 283-300.

Clarke, M. & Otaky, D. (2006) Reflection 'on' and 'in' Teacher Education in the United Arab Emirates, *International Journal of Educational Development,* 26(1), 111-122.

Clarke, P. (2003) Culture and Classroom Reform: the case of the District Primary Education Project, India, *Comparative Education,* 39(1), 27-44.

Colclough, C., King, K. & McGrath, S. (Eds) (2010) The New Politics of Aid to Education. Special issue, *International Journal of Educational Development,* 30(5).

Coleman, J. (1965) *Education and Political Development.* Princeton: University of Princeton Press.

Conway, M. & Damico, S. (1993) Facing up to Multiculturalism: means as ends in democratic education. Paper presented at the International Conference on Education for Democracy in a Multicultural Society, June 12-14, in Jerusalem, Israel.

Cox, S., Dyer, C., Robinson-Pant, A. & Schweisfurth, M. (Eds) (2010) *Children as Decision Makers.* London: Continuum.

Dadey, A. & Harber, C. (1991) *Training and Professional Support for Headship in Africa.* London: Commonwealth Secretariat.

Davies, L. (1993) Teachers as Implementers or Subversives, *International Journal of Educational Development,* 8(4), 293-304.

Davies, L. (1995) International Indicators of Democratic Schools, in C. Harber (Ed) *Developing Democratic Education.* Ticknall: Education Now.

Davies, L. (1999) Comparing Definitions of Democracy in Education, *Compare,* 29(2), 127-140.

Davies, L. (2008) *Educating against Extremism.* Stoke-on-Trent: Trentham Books.

Davies, L. (2011) Learning for State-building: capacity development, education and fragility, *Comparative Education,* 47(2), 157-180.

Davies, L., Harber, C. & Schweisfurth, M. (2002) *Democracy through Teacher Education.* Birmingham: CIER/CfBT.

Davies, L., Harber, C. & Schweisfurth, M. (2005) *Democratic Professional Development.* Birmingham: CIER/CfBT.

Davies, L., Harber, C., Schweisfurth, M., Yamashita, H., Cobbe, S. & Williams, C. (2008) *Risk Reduction for Vulnerable Groups in Education in Emergencies in South Asia.* Nepal: UNICEF.

Davies, L. & Kirkpatrick, G. (2000) *The EURIDEM Project: a review of pupil democracy in Europe.* London: Children's Rights Alliance.

Day Ashley, L. & Cadell, M. (Eds) (2006) The Private Education Sector: towards a reconceptualisation. Special issue, *Compare,* 36(4).

Dawson, R., Prewitt, K. & Dawson, K. (1977) *Political Socialisation.* Boston: Little, Brown.

Dean, B. (2005) Citizenship Education in Pakistani Schools: problems and possibilities, *International Journal of Citizenship and Teacher Education*, 1(2), 35-55.

Dean, B. (2006) Creating a Critical Mass: the Visiting Teacher Programme, in I. Farah & B. Jaworski (Eds) *Partnerships in Educational Development*. Oxford: Symposium Books.

De Baessa, Y., Chesterfield, R. & Ramos, T. (2002) Active Learning and Democratic Behaviour in Guatemalan Rural Primary Schools, *Compare*, 32(2), 205-218.

De Grauwe, A. (2001) *School Supervision in Four African Countries*. Paris: UNESCO.

Department of Education (1995) *White Paper on Education and Training*. Pretoria: Government Printers.

Department of Education (1996) *South African Schools Bill*. Pretoria: Government Printers.

Department of Education (2001a) *Draft Revised National Curriculum Statement*. Pretoria: Government Printers.

Department of Education (2001b) *Manifesto on Values, Education and Democracy*. Pretoria: Government Printers.

Department of Education (2011) *Revised National Curriculum Statement*. Pretoria: Government Printers.

Diamond, L. (1993) *Political Culture and Democracy in Developing Countries*. Boulder: Lynne Reiner.

Diamond, L. (1999) *Developing Democracy: towards consolidation*. Baltimore: Johns Hopkins University Press.

Dimmock, C. (1995) Building Democracy in the School Setting: the principal's role, in J. Chapman, I. Froumin & D. Aspin (Eds) *Creating and Managing the Democratic School*. London: Falmer Press.

Divala, J. (2007) Malawi's Approach to Democracy: implications for the teaching of democratic citizenship, *Citizenship Teaching and Learning*, 1(1), 32-44.

Dore, R. (1976) *The Diploma Disease*. London: Allen & Unwin.

Dull, L. (2006) *Disciplined Development: teachers and reform in Ghana*. Oxford: Lexington Books.

Ehman, L. (1980) The American High School in the Political Socialisation Process, *Review of Educational Research*, 50, 99-119.

Enslin, P. & Horsthemke, K. (2004) Can *Ubuntu* Provide a Model for Citizenship Education in Africa?, *Comparative Education*, 40(4), 545-558.

Entwistle, H. (1971) *Political Education in a Democracy*. London: Routledge & Kegan Paul.

Ersson, S. & Lane, J-E. (1996) Democracy and Development: a statistical exploration, in A. Leftwich (Ed) *Democracy and Development*. Cambridge: Polity Press.

Evans, G. & Rose, P. (2007) Support for Democracy in Malawi: does schooling matter?, *World Development*, 35(5), 904-919.

Fagerlind, I. & Saha, L. (1989) *Education and National Development: a comparative perspective*. Oxford: Pergamon.

Farrell, J. (2007) Education in the Years to Come: what we can learn from alternative education, in M. Mason, P. Hershock & J. Hawkins (Eds) *Changing Education: leadership, innovation and development in a globalizing Asia Pacific*. Hong Kong: Comparative Education Research Centre.

Fataar, A. (2007) Educational Renovation in a South African Township on the Move: a social-spatial analysis, *International Journal of Educational Development*, 27(6), 599-612.

Fearnley-Sander, M. & Yulaelawati, E. (2008) Citizenship Discourse in the Context of Decentralisation; the case of Indonesia, in D.L. Grossman, W.O. Lee & K. Kennedy (Eds) *Citizenship Curriculum in Asia and the Pacific*. Hong Kong: Comparative Education Research Centre.

Feinstein, S. & Mwahombela, L. (2010) Corporal Punishment in Tanzania's Schools, *International Review of Education*, 56(4), 399-410.

Fife, W. (1997) The Importance of Fieldwork: anthropology and education in Papua New Guinea, in M. Crossley & G. Vulliamy (Eds) *Qualitative Educational Research in Developing Countries*. New York: Garland.

Fiske, E. & Ladd, H. (2004) *Elusive Equity: education reform in post-apartheid South Africa*. Cape Town: HSRC Press.

Freire, P. (1972) *Pedagogy of the Oppressed*. London: Sheed & Ward.

Fullan, M. (2007) *The New Meaning of Educational Change*. London: Routledge.

Fuller, B. (1991) *Growing Up Modern*. London: Routledge.

Gambian Department of State for Education (1998) *Gambia Education Policy*. Banjul: Government Printer.

Gandin, L.A. & Apple, M. (2003) Beyond Neo-liberalism in Education: the citizen school and the struggle for democracy in Porto Alegre, Brazil, in S. Ball, G.E. Fischman & S. Gvirtz (Eds) *Crisis and Hope: the educational hopscotch of Latin America*. London: RoutledgeFalmer.

Ghana Ministry of Education, Youth and Sports (2003) *National Action Plan 2003-2015*. Accra: Ghana Ministry of Education, Youth and Sports.

Glaeser, E., Ponzetto, G. & Shleifer, A. (2007) Why Does Democracy Need Education?, *Journal of Economic Growth*, 12, 77-99.

Gramsci, A. (1977) *Selections from the Prison Notebooks of Antonio Gramsci*, trans. and ed. Q. Hoare & G. Nowell Smith. London: Lawrence & Wishart.

Grant-Lewis, S. & Naidoo, J. (2006) School Governance and the Pursuit of Democratic Participation: lessons from South Africa, *International Journal of Educational Development*, 26(4), 415-427.

Green, A. (1990) *Education and State Formation*. London: Macmillan.

Gribble, D. (1998) *Real Education: varieties of freedom*. Bristol: Libertarian Education.

Gyimah-Boadi, E. (Ed) (2004) *Democratic Reform in Africa*. London: Lynne Rienner.

Hallak, J. & Poisson, M. (2006) *Corrupt Schools, Corrupt Universities: what can be done?* Paris: IIEP.

Hammad, W. (2010) Teachers' Perceptions of School Culture as a Barrier to Shared Decision-Making in Egypt's Secondary Schools, *Compare*, 40(1), 97-110.

Hammett, D. & Staeheli, L. (2011) Respect and Responsibility: teaching citizenship in South African high schools, *International Journal of Educational Development*, 31(3), 269-276.

Harber, C. (1989) *Politics in African Education*. London: Macmillan.

Harber, C. (1993) Democratic Management and School Effectiveness in Africa: learning from Tanzania, *Compare*, 23(3), 289-300.

Harber, C. (1997) *Education, Democracy and Political Development in Africa*. Brighton: Sussex Academic Press.

Harber, C. (1998) Desegregation, Racial Conflict and Education for Democracy in the New South Africa, *International Review of Education*, 44(4), 569-582.

Harber, C. (2001) *State of Transition: post-apartheid educational reform in South Africa*. Oxford: Symposium.

Harber, C. (2002) Education, Democracy and Poverty Reduction in Africa, *Comparative Education*, 38(3), 267-276.

Harber, C. (2004) *Schooling as Violence: how schools harm pupils and societies*. London: RoutledgeFalmer.

Harber, C. (2006) Democracy, Development and Education: working with the Gambian Inspectorate, *International Journal of Educational Development*, 26(6), 618-630.

Harber, C. (2008) Perpetrating Disaffection: schooling as an international problem, *Educational Studies*, 34(5), 457-468.

Harber, C. (2009) *Toxic Schooling: how schools became worse*. Nottingham: Educational Heretics Press.

Harber, C. (2010) Long Time Coming: children as only occasional decision-makers in schools, in S. Cox, A. Robinson-Pant, C. Dyer & M. Schweisfurth (Eds) *Children As Decision Makers in Education*. London: Continuum.

Harber, C. (forthcoming) Education in and after Violent Conflict: stability and the status quo or transformation and peace?, *International Journal of Educational Development*.

Harber, C. & Davies, L. (1997) *School Management and School Effectiveness in Developing Countries*. London: Cassell.

Harber, C. & Davies, L. (2003) Effective Leadership for War and Peace, in M. Brundrett, N. Burton & R. Smith (Eds) *Leadership in Education*. London: Sage.

Harber, C. & Muthukrishna, N. (2000) School Effectiveness and School Improvement in Context: the case of South Africa, *School Effectiveness and Improvement*, 11(4), 421-434.

Harber, C. & Serf, J. (2006) Teacher Education for a Democratic Society in England and South Africa, *Teaching and Teacher Education*, 22(8), 986-997.

Harber, C. & Stephens, D. (2009) *From Shouters to Supporters: the Quality Education Project*. Oslo: Save the Children.

Harding, L. (2002) A Vision of Hell in Indian City Gorging on Violence, *The Guardian*, March 2.

Hardman, F., Abd-Kadir, J., Agg, C., Migwi, J., Ndambuku, J. & Smith, F. (2009) Changing Pedagogical Practice in Kenyan Primary Schools: the impact of school-based training, *Comparative Education*, 45(1), 65-86.

Hardman, F., Abd-Kadir, J. & Smith, F. (2008) Pedagogical Renewal: improving the quality of classroom interaction in Nigerian primary schools, *International Journal of Educational Development*, 28(1), 55-69.

Harley, K. & Wedekind, V. (2004) Political Change, Curriculum Change and Social Formation, 1990 to 2002, in L. Chisholm (Ed) *Changing Class – Education and Social Change in Post-Apartheid South Africa*. Cape Town: HSRC Press.

Hawes, H. (1979) *Curriculum and Reality in African Primary Schools*. Harlow: Longman.

Hawkins, J. (2007) The Intractable Dominant Educational Paradigm, in M. Mason, P. Hershock & J. Hawkins (Eds) *Changing Education: leadership, innovation and development in a globalizing Asia Pacific*. Hong Kong: Comparative Education Research Centre.

Hedges, J. (2002) Becoming a Teacher in Ghana: a qualitative study of newly qualified teachers in Central Region, Ghana. Unpublished PhD thesis, University of Sussex.

Helliwell, J.F. (1994) Empirical Linkages between Democracy and Economic Growth, *British Journal of Political Science*, 24, 225-248.

Hepburn, M. (1984) Democratic Schooling: five perspectives from research, *International Journal of Political Education*, 6, 245-262.

Herrera, L. & Torres, C.A. (Eds) (2006) *Cultures of Arab Schooling*. New York: State University of New York Press.

Higgott, R. (1983) *Political Development Theory*. London: Croom Helm.

Hofmeyr, J. & Hall, G. (1996) The National Teacher Education Audit, *Perspectives in Education*, 17(1), 135-140.

Hofstede, G. (1991) *Culture and Organisations: software of the mind*. London: McGraw-Hill.

Holdstock. T. (1990) Violence in Schools: discipline, in B. McKendrick & W. Hoffman (Eds) *People and Violence in South Africa*. Oxford: Oxford University Press.

Human Rights Watch (1999) *Broken People: caste violence against India's 'Untouchables'*. New York: Human Rights Watch.

Human Rights Watch (2001) *Scared at School: sexual violence against girls in South African schools*. New York: Human Rights Watch.

Humphreys, S. (2006) Corporal Punishment as Gendered Practice, in F. Leach & C. Mitchell (Eds) *Combating Gender Violence in and around Schools*. Stoke-on-Trent: Trentham Books.

Hunt, F. (2007) Schooling Citizens: a study of policy in practice in South Africa. PhD thesis, University of Sussex.

Hunt, F. (2011) Schooling Citizens: policy in practice in South Africa, *Compare*, 41(1), 43-58.

Huntingdon, S. (1991) *The Third Wave: democratisation in the late twentieth century*. Norman: University of Oklahoma Press.

Inkeles, A. (1961) National Character and Modern Political Systems, in F.L.K. Hsu (Ed?) *Psychological Anthropology*. Homewood: Dorsey Press.

Inkeles, A. (1969a) Participant Citizenship in Six Developing Countries, *American Political Science Review*, 43, 1122-1133.

Inkeles, A. (1969b) Making Men Modern, *American Journal of Sociology*, 75, 208-225.

Inkeles, A. & Smith, D. (1974) *Becoming Modern*. London: Heinemann.

Jabr, D. (2009) Growing Education in Difficult Environments Promoting Problem Solving: a case from Palestine, *Compare*, 39(6), 723-736.

Jansen. J. (2001) Explaining Non-Change in Education Reform after Apartheid: political symbolism and the problem of policy implementation, in J. Jansen & Y. Sayed (Eds) *Implementing Education Policies: the South African experience*. Cape Town: University of Cape Town Press.

Jaros, D. (1973) *Socialization to Politics*. London: Thomas Nelson.

Jennings, Z. (2001) Teacher Education in Selected Countries of the Commonwealth Caribbean: the ideal of policy versus the reality of practice, *Comparative Education*, 37(1), 107-134.

Jessop, T. & Penny, A. (1998) A Study of Teacher Voice and Vision in the Narratives of Rural South African and Gambian Primary School Teachers, *International Journal of Educational Development*, 18(5), 393-404.

John, P. & Osborn, A. (1992) The Influence of Ethos on Pupils' Citizenship Attitudes, *Educational Review*, 44(2).

Karlsson, J. (2002) The Role of Democratic Governing Bodies in South African Schools, *Comparative Education*, 38(3), 327-336.

Kelly, A.V. (1995) *Education and Democracy: principles and practices*. London: Chapman.

Kendall, N. (2008) 'Vulnerability' in AIDS-affected States: rethinking child rights, educational institutions, and the development of paradigms, *International Journal of Educational Development*, 28(4), 365-383.

Kendall, N. (2009) International Development Education, in R. Cowen & M. Kazamias (Eds) *International Handbook of Comparative Education*. Amsterdam: Springer.

Kennedy, K. & Chi-kin Lee, J. (2008) *The Changing Role of Schools in Asian Societies*. Abingdon: Routledge.

Khamis, A. & Jawed, S. (2006) Teacher Education and School Improvement: a case study from Pakistan, in I. Farah & B. Jaworski (Eds) *Partnerships in Educational Development*. Oxford: Symposium Books.

Khan, F. (2006) Who Participates in School Councils and How?, *Prospects*, 36(1), 97-119.

Kigotho, W. (2006) Brutal Beatings End Use of Cane, *Times Educational Supplement*, September 1.

Kingdom, E. (1976) Political Education, *Research in Education*, 16, 1-12.

Kitaev, I. (2007) Education for All and Private Education in Developing and Transitional Countries, in P. Srivastava & G. Walford (Eds) *Private Schooling in Less Economically Developed Countries*. Oxford: Symposium Books.

Knight, T. (2001) Longitudinal Development of Educational Theory: democracy and the classroom, *Journal of Education Policy*, 16(3), 249-263.

Koosmile, A. & Suping, S. (2011) Pre-service Teachers' Attempts at Debating Contemporary Issues in Science Education: a case study from Botswana, *International Journal of Educational Development*, 31(5), 458-464.

Krueger, A. & Maleckova, J. (2003) Education, Poverty and Terrorism: is there a causal connection?, *Journal of Economic Perspectives*, 4, 119-144.

Kunje, D., Lewin, K. & Stuart, J. (2003) *Primary Teacher Education in Malawi: insights into practice and policy*. London: Department for International Development.

Law, K. (2007) Globalisation, City Development and Citizenship Education in China's Shanghai, *International Journal of Educational Development*, 27(1), 18-38.

Le Fanu, G. (forthcoming) Reconceptualising Inclusive Education in International Development, in A. Barrett & L. Tikkly (Eds) *Education Quality and Social Justice in the South: challenges for policy*. London: Routledge.

Lefoka, J. & Sebatane, E. (2003) *Initial Primary Teacher Education in Lesotho*. London: Department for International Development.

Leftwich, A. (Ed) (1996) *Democracy and Development*. Cambridge: Polity Press.

Leftwich, A. (1998) Forms of the Democratic Developmental State, in M. Robinson & G. White (Eds) *The Democratic Developmental State: political and institutional design*. Oxford: Oxford University Press.

Levinson, B. (2004) Hopes and Challenges for the New Civic Education in Mexico: towards a democratic citizen without adjectives, *International Journal of Educational Development*, 24(3), 269-282.

Lewin, K. & Stuart, J. (2003) *Researching Teacher Education: new perspectives on practice, performance and policy*. London: Department for International Development.

Lewis, R. (1999) Teachers' Support for Inclusive Forms of Classroom Management, *International Journal of Inclusive Education*, 3(3), 269-285.

Liebenberg, H. (2011) What are the Curriculum and Assessment Policy Statements? Department of Education. http://www.education.gov.za (accessed May 11, 2012).

Lipset, S.M. (1959) Some Social Requisites of Democracy: economic development and political development, *American Political Science Review*, 53, 69-105.

London, N. (2002) Curriculum Convergence: an ethno-historical investigation into schooling in Trinidad and Tobago, *Comparative Education*, 38(1), 53-72.

Loomba, A. (1998) *Colonialism/Postcolonialism*. London: Routledge.

Lwehabura, J. (1993) School Effectiveness in Tanzania. PhD thesis, University of Birmingham.

Lynch, J. (1992) *Education for Citizenship in a Multicultural Society*. London: Cassell.

Martin, C. (1994) Let the Young Birds Fly: schooling, work and emancipation in rural west Mexico, *Compare*, 24(3), 259-276.

Massialas, B. & Jarrar, S. (1991) *Arab Education in Transition: a source book*. New York: Garland.

McCowan, T. (2006) Educating Citizens for Participatory Democracy: a case study of local government education policy in Pelotas, Brazil, *International Journal of Educational Development*, 26(5), 456-470.

McCowan, T. (2010a) Prefigurative Approaches to Participatory Schooling Experiences in Brazil, in S. Cox, A. Robinson-Pant, C. Dyer & M. Schweisfurth (Eds) *Children as Decision Makers in Education*. London: Continuum.

McCowan, T. (2010b) School Democratisation in Prefigurative Form: two Brazilian experiences, *Education, Citizenship and Social Justice*, 51, 21-41.

McGrath, S. (2010) The Role of Education in Development: an educationalist's response to some recent work in development economics, *Comparative Education*, 46(2), 237-243.

McGrath, S. & Akoojee, S. (2007) Education and Skills for Development in South Africa: reflections on the accelerated and shared growth initiative for South Africa, *International Journal of Educational Development*, 27(4), 421-434.

McGreal, C. (2000) Crash Course in Chaos Shocks the Minister, *The Guardian*, February 1.

McMahon, W. (1999) *Education and Development: measuring the social benefits*. Oxford: Oxford University Press.

Mehran, G. (2003) Khatami, Political Reform and Education in Iran, *Comparative Education*, 39(3), 311-329.

Mehrotra, S. & Panchamukhi, P.R. (2006) Private Provision of Elementary Education in India: findings from a survey in eight states, *Compare*, 36(4), 421-442.

Mehrotra, S. & Panchamukhi, P.R. (2007) Universalising Elementary Education in India: is the private sector the answer?, in P. Srivastava & G. Walford (Eds) *Private Schooling in Less Economically Developed Countries*. Oxford: Symposium Books.

Meighan, R. (1994) *The Freethinkers' Guide to the Educational Universe*. Nottingham: Educational Heretics Press.

Meighan, R. & Harber, C. (2007) *A Sociology of Educating*. London: Continuum.

Meyer-Bisch, P. (1995) *Culture of Democracy: a challenge for schools*. Paris: UNESCO.

Ministerial Review Committee (2004) *Review of School Governance in South African Public Schools: Report of the Ministerial Review Committee on School Governance*. Pretoria: Government Press.

Mkhatshwa, S. (1997) Education in South Africa. Speech Delivered at the Culture of Learning, Teaching and Service Campaign Consultative Conference, August 22-24, in Pretoria.

Mncube, V. (2005) School Governance in the Democratisation of Education in South Africa: the interplay between policy and practice. PhD thesis, University of Birmingham.

Mncube, V. (2008) Democratisation of Education in South Africa: issues of social justice and the voice of learners, *South African Journal of Education*, 28(1), 77-90.

Mncube, V. & Harber, C. (2010) Chronicling Educator Practices and Experiences in the Context of Democratic Schooling and Quality Education, *International Journal of Educational Development*, 30(6), 614-624.

Mncube, V.S., Harber, C. & Du Plessis, P. (2011) Effective School Governing Bodies: parental involvement, training and issues of school effectiveness in two provinces of South Africa, *Acta Academica*, 43(3), 210-242.

Molteno, M., Ogadhoh, K., Cain, E. & Crumpton, B. (2000) *Towards Responsive Schools: supporting better schooling for disadvantaged children*. London: Department for International Development/Save the Children.

Montefiore, S. (2007) Stalin in Love, *The Sunday Times*, May 6.

Morrell, R. (1999) Beating Corporal Punishment: race, masculinity and educational discipline in the schools of Durban, South Africa. Paper presented at the Voices in Gender and Education Conference, March 12, in Warwick.

Motala, S., Dieltiens, V., Carrim, N., Kgobe, P., Moyo, G. & Rembe, S. (2007) *Educational Access in South Africa: country analytic review. Project Report*. Brighton: Consortium for Research on Educational Access, Transitions and Equity (CREATE).

Moumouni, A. (1968) *Education in Africa*. London: Andre Deutsch.

Mshengu, S. & the Midlands Women's Group (2003) Ngiyahhala – I am Crying, *Children First*, 7(49), 18-21.

Nagata, Y. (2007) *Alternative Education: global perspectives relevant to the Asia-Pacific Region*. Amsterdam: Springer.

Nagel, T. (1992) *Quality between Tradition and Modernity: patterns of communication and cognition in teacher education in Zimbabwe*. Oslo: University of Oslo Pedagogisk Forskningsintitutt.

Naidoo, P. (2005) *Educational Decentralisation and School Governance in South Africa*. Paris: Institute for Educational Planning.

Naidoo, R. (2012) Experiences and Practices of School Principles in Creating, Leading and Governing Democratic Schools. PhD thesis, University of KwaZulu Natal.

Namibia Ministry of Education (1993) *A Report on the Training of Trainers.* Windhoek: Namibia Ministry of Education.

Nazir, M. (2010) Democracy and Education in Pakistan, *Educational Review,* 62(3), 329-342.

Nelson Mandela Foundation (2005) *Emerging Voices.* Cape Town: HSRC Press.

Nyerere, J. (1967) *Education for Self-Reliance.* Dar Es Salaam: Government Printer.

O'Brien, D. (1972) Modernisation, Order and The Erosion of the Democratic Ideal: American political science 1960-70, *Journal of Development Studies,* 8, 351-378.

Oplatka, I. (2003) The Principalship in Developing Countries: context, characteristics and reality, *Comparative Education,* 40(3), 427-448.

Oryema, D. (2007) Decentralisation Policy and Education Provision in Uganda. PhD thesis, University of Birmingham.

Osher, D., Kelly, D., Tolani-Brown, N., Shors, L. & Chen, C-S. (2009) *UNICEF Child Friendly Schools Programming: Global Evaluation Final Report.* Washington, DC: American Institutes for Research.

O'Sullivan, M. (2004) The Reconceptualisation of Learner-Centred Approaches: a Namibian case study, *International Journal of Educational Development,* 24(6) 585-602.

Oxenham, J. (Ed) (1984) *Education versus Qualifications.* London: George Allen & Unwin.

Palme, M. (1997) Teaching Hieroglyphs with Authority, in M. John (Ed) *A Charge against Society: the child's right to protection.* London: Jessica Kingsley.

Parkes, J. (2009) Perspectives on Children and Violence, in R. Cowen & A. Kazamias (Eds) *International Handbook of Comparative Education.* Dordrecht: Springer.

Pearl, A. & Knight, T. (1999) *The Democratic Classroom: theory to inform practice.* Cresswell, NJ: Hampton Press.

Pinheiro, P. (2006) *World Report on Violence against Children.* Geneva: United Nations.

PLAN (2008) *The Global Campaign to End Violence in Schools.* Woking: PLAN.

Prophet, R. & Rowell, P. (1990) Curriculum in Action: the 'practical' dimension in Botswana classrooms, *International Journal of Educational Development,* 10(1), 17-26.

Pryor, J., Ampiah, J., Kutor, N. & Boadu, K. (2005) Student Councils in Ghana and the Formation of the Liberal Democratic Citizen, in K. Mutua & C. Sunal (Eds) *Forefronts of Research.* Vol. 2 of *Research on Education in Africa, the Caribbean and the Middle East.* Greenwich CT: Information Age.

Przeworski, A., Alvarez, M., Cheibub, J.A. & Limongi, F. (2000) *Democracy and Development: political institutions and well-being in the world 1950-1990.* Cambridge: Cambridge University Press.

Ramachandran, V. (2009) Democratic Inequalities: the dilemma of elementary education in India, in R. Cowen & A. Kazamias (Eds) *International Handbook of Comparative Education*. Dordrecht: Springer.

Rameckers, J. (2002) Effective Monitoring of the Quality of Education, in *Secondary Education in Africa: strategies for renewal*. Washington, DC: World Bank.

Ratnavadivel, N. (1999) Teacher Education: interface between practices and policies – the Malaysian experience 1979-1997, *Teaching and Teacher Education*, 15(2), 193-213.

Republic of South Africa (1996a) *The Constitution*. Pretoria: Government Printer.

Republic of South Africa (1996b) *The South African Schools Act*. Pretoria: Government Printer.

Retamal, G. & Aedo-Richmond, R. (Eds) (1998) *Education as a Humanitarian Response*. London: Cassell.

Richardson, P. (2004) Possible Influences of Arabic-Islamic Culture on the Reflective Practices Proposed for an Education Degree at the Higher Colleges of Technology in the United Arab Emirates, *International Journal of Educational Development*, 24(4), 429-436.

Riggs, F. (1964) *Administration in Developing Countries: The theory of prismatic society*. Boston: Houghton Mifflin.

Rojas, C. (1994) The Escuela Nueva School Programme in Colombia, in P. Dalin (Ed) *How Schools Improve*. London: Cassell.

Rose, P. & Adelabu, M. (2007) Private Sector Contributions to Education for All in Nigeria, in P. Srivastava & G. Walford (Eds) *Private Schooling in Less Economically Developed Countries*. Oxford: Symposium Books.

Rousmaniere, K., Dehli, K. & de Conink-Smith, N. (1997) *Discipline, Moral Regulation and Schooling*. New York: Garland.

Rust, V. (2000) Education Policy Studies and Comparative Education, in R. Alexander, M. Osborn & D. Phillips (Eds) *Learning from Comparing*, vol. 2. Oxford: Symposium Books.

Rutter, M., Maughn, B., Mortimore, P. & Ouston, J. (1979) *Fifteen Thousand Hours; secondary schools and their effects on children*. 2nd edn 1994. London: Paul Chapman.

St John, R.B. (2005) Democracy in Cambodia – one decade, *Contemporary Southeast Asia*, 27(3), 406-428.

Saito, E., Tsukui, A. & Tanaka, Y. (2008) Problems of Primary School-Based In-Service Training in Vietnam: a case study of Bac Giang Province, *International Journal of Educational Development*, 28(1), 89-103.

Sandbrook, R. (1976) The Crisis in Political Development Theory, *Journal of Development Studies*, 12, 165-185.

Save the Children (2006) Save the Children: Mongolia to protect over 650,000 children. http://www.politics.co.uk/press-releases/domestic-policy,children/child-abuse/save-ch

Sayed, Y. & Soudien, C. (2003) (Re) Training Education Exclusion and Inclusion Discourses: links and possibilities, in R. Subrananian, Y. Sayed,

S. Balagopalan & C. Soudien (Eds) *Education Inclusion and Exclusion: Indian and South African perspectives. IDS Bulletin*, 34(1), 9-19. Lewes: University of Sussex.

Sayed, Y., Subrahmanian, R., Soudien, C., Carrim, N., Balgopalan, S., Nekhwevha, F., et al (2007) *Education and Exclusion: policy and implementation in South Africa and India*. London: Department for International Development.

Scholtz, Z., Braund, M., Hodges, M., Koopman, R. & Lubben, F. (2008) South African Teachers' Ability to Argue: the emergence of inclusive argumentation, *International Journal of Educational Development*, 28(1), 21-34.

Schweisfurth, M. (2002a) Democracy and Teacher Education: negotiating practice in The Gambia, *Comparative Education*, 38(3), 303-314.

Schweisfurth, M. (2002b) *Teachers, Democratisation and Educational Reform in Russia and South Africa*. Oxford: Symposium Books.

Schweisfurth, M. (2011) Learner-centred Education in Developing Country Contexts: from solution to problem?, *International Journal of Educational Development*, 31(5), 425-432.

Searle, C. (1981) *We're Building the New School!* London: Zed Books.

Seierstad, A. (2004) *The Bookseller of Kabul*. London: Virago.

Sen, A. (1999) *Development as Freedom*. Oxford: Oxford University Press.

Serpell, R. (1993) *The Significance of Schooling: life journeys in an African society*. Cambridge: Cambridge University Press.

Shamim, F. & Halai, A. (2006) Developing Professional Development Teachers, in I. Farah & B. Jaworski (Eds) *Partnerships in Educational Development*. Oxford: Symposium Books.

Shipman, M. (1971) *Education and Modernisation*. London: Faber.

Sigauke, A. (2012) Young People, Citizenship and Citizenship Education in Zimbabwe, *International Journal of Educational Development*, 32(2), 214-223.

Smith, B.C. (2009) *Understanding Third World Politics: theories of political change and development*. Basingstoke: Palgrave Macmillan.

Soudien, C. (2004) Constituting Class: an analysis of 'integration' in South African Schools, in L. Chisholm (Ed) *Changing Class: education and social change in post-apartheid South Africa*. Cape Town: HSRC Press.

Soudien, C. (2007) The 'A' Factor: coming to terms with the question of legacy in South African education, *International Journal of Educational Development*, 27(2), 182-193.

South African Institute of Race Relations (SAIRR) (2008) South African Schools Most Dangerous in the World. http: //www.saiir.org.za/press (accessed March 1, 2010).

Spreen, C. & Vally, S. (2006) Education Rights, Education Policies and Inequality in South Africa, *International Journal of Educational Development*, 26(4), 352-362.

Spreen, C. & Vally, S. (2010) Prospects and Pitfalls; a review of post-apartheid education policy research and analysis in South Africa, *Comparative Education*, 46(4), 429-448.

Sriprakash, A. (2010) Child-centred Education and the Promise of Democratic Learning, *International Journal of Educational Development*, 30(3), 297-304.

Srivastava, P. & Walford, G. (2007) *Private Schooling in Less Economically Developed Countries*. Oxford: Symposium Books.

Stacey, B. (1978) *Political Socialisation in Western Society*. London: Edward Arnold.

Stephens, D. (2007) *Culture and Education in Development*. Oxford: Symposium Books.

Stephens, D. (2009) *Qualitative Research in International Settings*. London: RoutledgeFalmer.

Suarez, D.F. (2008) Rewriting Citizenship? Civic Education in Costa Rica and Argentina, *Comparative Education*, 44(4), 485-503.

Tabulawa, R. (1995) Culture and Classroom Practice: a socio-cultural analysis of geography classrooms in Botswana secondary schools and implications for pedagogical change. PhD thesis, University of Birmingham.

Tabulawa, R. (2003) International Aid Agencies: learner-centred pedagogy and political democratisation: a critique, *Comparative Education*, 39(1), 7-26.

Tafa, E. (2002) Corporal Punishment: the brutal face of Botswana's authoritarian schools, *Educational Review*, 54(1), 17-26.

Tan, C. (2008) Two Views of Education: Promoting civic and moral values in Cambodia schools, *International Journal of Educational Development*, 28(5), 560-570.

Tedesco, J. (1994) Knowledge versus Values, *Educational Innovation*, 78(1), 1-12.

Toffler, A. (1970) *Future Shock*. London: Bodley Head.

Toh, S. & Floresca-Cawagas, V. (2003) Globalization and the Philippines Education System, in K. Mok & A. Welch (Eds) *Globalization and Educational Restructuring in the Asia Pacific Region*. London: Palgrave Macmillan.

Tooley, J. (2009) *The Beautiful Tree*. Washington, DC: The Cato Institute.

Torres, R. (1992) Alternatives in Formal Education: Colombia's Escuela Nueva Programme, *Prospects*, 22(4), 510-520.

Torres, C.A. (1998) *Democracy, Education and Multiculturalism: dilemmas of citizenship in a global world*. Lanham: Rowman & Littlefield.

Trafford, B. (2003) *School Councils, School Democracy and School Improvement*. Leicester: SHA.

Tran, M. (2009) African Prize Judges Fail to Find Governance Winner, *The Guardian*, October 20.

Trippett, L., with Banez-Ockelford, J., Mamaliga, D., Saksena, P. & Vigil, L. (2010) EveryChild: NGO experiences with children as decision-makers in Peru, India and Moldova, in S. Cox, A. Robinson-Pant, C. Dyer & M. Schweisfurth (Eds) *Children as Decision Makers in Education*. London: Continuum.

Tubaundule, G. (1999) Promoting Active Participation in the Education Theory and Practice Classroom, in K. Zeichner & L. Dahlstom (Eds) (1999) *Democratic Teacher Education Reform in Africa: the case of Namibia.* Boulder: Westview Press.

UNDP (1997) *Human Development Report.* Oxford: Oxford University Press.

UNDP (2010) *Human Development Report.* Basingstoke: Palgrave Macmillan.

UNDP (2011) *Human Development Report.* Basingstoke: Palgrave Macmillan.

UNESCO (2005) *The Quality Imperative.* Paris: UNESCO EFA Global Monitoring Report.

UNESCO (2011) *The Hidden Crisis: armed conflict and education.* Paris: UNESCO EFA Global Monitoring Report.

United Nations Convention on the Rights of the Child (1989) New York: United Nations.

Vally, S. (1999) Teachers in South Africa: between fiscal austerity and getting learning right, *Quarterly Review of Education and Training in South Africa,* 6(2), 14-16.

Vally, S. & Dalamba, Y (1999) *Racism, Racial Integration and Desegregation in South African Public Secondary Schools.* Johannesburg: South African Human Rights Commission.

Van Der Steen, N. (2011) School Improvement in Tanzania: school culture and the management of change. PhD thesis, Institute of Education, University of London.

Van Der Werf, G., Creemers, B., De Jong, R. & Klaver, E. (2000) Evaluation of School Improvement through an Educational Effectiveness Model; the case of Indonesia's PEQIP Project, *Comparative Education Review,* 44(3), 329-355.

Vandeyar, S. (2008) Shifting Selves: the emergence of new identities in South African schools, *International Journal of Educational Development,* 28(3), 286-299.

Vavrus, F. (2009) The Cultural Politics of Constructivist Pedagogies: teacher education reform in the United Republic of Tanzania, *International Journal of Educational Development,* 29(3), 303-311.

Vulliamy, G. (1998) Teacher Development in Primary Schools: some other lessons from Taiwan, *Teacher Development,* 2(1), 81-86.

Walker, M. & Unterhalter, E. (2007) *Amartya Sen's Capability Approach and Social Justice in Education.* Basingstoke: Palgrave Macmillan.

Watkins, K. (1999) *Education Now: break the cycle of poverty.* Oxford: Oxfam.

Watson, K. (1982) Education and Colonialism in Peninsular Malaysia, in K. Watson (Ed.) *Education in the Third World.* Beckenham: Croom Helm.

Welgemoed, A. (1998) Democratising a School in South Africa, in C. Harber (Ed) *Voices for Democracy: a North-South dialogue on education for sustainable democracy.* Nottingham: Education Now in association with the British Council.

WHO (World Health Organisation) (2002) *World Report on Violence and Health.* Geneva: WHO.

Wibowo, R. (2005) Do Adults Listen to Children's Voices? EdD thesis, University of Birmingham.

Wolpe, A-M., Quinlan, O. & Martinez, L. (1997) *Gender Equity in Education: Report of the Gender Equity Task Team.* Pretoria: Government Press.

Woods, P. (2005) *Democratic Leadership in Education.* London: Paul Chapman.

Zeichner, K. & Dahlstrom, L. (Eds) (1999) *Democratic Teacher Education Reform in Africa: the case of Namibia.* Boulder: Westview Press.

Notes on the Authors

Clive Harber is Emeritus Professor of International Education at the University of Birmingham, United Kingdom, and Honorary Professor at the University of South Africa in Pretoria. From 1995-1999, he was Head of the School of Education at the then University of Natal, now KwaZulu Natal, and from 2003-2006, he was Head of the School of Education at the University of Birmingham. He has a long-standing interest in education and politics, and particularly education and democracy, in developing countries and has carried out research and published widely on these themes. He has been an editor of the *International Journal of Educational Development* since the early 1980s and was Chair of the British Association for International and Comparative Education between 2004 and 2006.

Vusi Mncube is Associate Professor of Educational Leadership and Management in the College of Education at the University of South Africa (UNISA). His main academic and research interests concern education for and in democracy. He has carried out research and published on various aspects of school governing bodies in South Africa in relation to education for a more democratic society. He has recently been leading a research team on violence in schools. He is a member of the editorial board of the Southern African Society of Educators (SASE) and is an active member of BAICE, SASE, and the Education Association of South Africa (EASA).